A NOCTURNAL HISTORY OF ARCHITECTURE Edited by Javier Fernández Contreras, Vera Sacchetti and Roberto Zancan (HEAD – Genève, HES-SO) ISSUE 2

A NOCTURNAL HISTORY OF ARCHITECTURE

INTRODUCTION
A Nocturnal History of Architecture
Javier Fernández Contreras, Vera Sacchetti, and Roberto Zancan

For centuries, architectural theory, discourse, and agency have been based on daylight and solar paradigms. References to the night in Vitruvius' *De architectura* (30-15 BC), widely considered the founding text of Western architectural theory, are residual, and they are similarly scarce in the most influential Renaissance treatises, such as Leon Battista Alberti's *De re aedificatoria* (1452) and Andrea Palladio's *I quattro libri dell'architettura* (1570). Likewise, seminal writings on modern architecture rarely refer to nighttime environments, which can be evaluated both textually and photographically. In this sense, Philip Johnson and Henry-Russell Hitchcock's *The International Style* (1932), the book resulting from the MoMA exhibition that introduced modernism to America, illustrates a clear preference for daytime pictures, (1) noting that "the photographs and the plans were for the most part provided by the architects themselves (2)." This diurnal rationale is further discernible in the books that would establish the intellectual ethos of architectural modernity, such as Nikolaus Pevsner's *Pioneers of the Modern Movement* (1936) and Sigfried Giedion's *Space, Time and Architecture* (1941), where less than 5% of the architectural images are purely nocturnal, understanding the term in the circadian sense of the absence of daylight—accompanying texts only help but to emphasize this nocturnal omission. Likewise, the canonical architecture history books published in the last sixty years, such as Leonardo Benevolo's *Storia dell'architettura moderna* (1960) and Kenneth Frampton's *Modern Architecture: A Critical History* (1980), have institutionalized the diurnal episteme in architectural media.

1 Only five out of 83 photographs depict spaces that are partially or fully artificially lit: Alvar Aalto's Turun Sanomat building, Uno Åhren's Flamman Soundfilm Theater, Marcel Breuer's Berlin apartment, Mies van der Rohe's apartment study in New York, and Jan Ruhtenberg's apartment living room in Berlin. See Henry-Russell Hitchcock and Philip Johnson, *The International Style* (New York—London: W. W. Norton & Company, 1932/1995).   2   Hitchcock and Johnson, *The International Style*, 9.

In the second half of the 20th century, authors such as Reyner Banham, Robert Venturi & Denise Scott Brown, and Rem Koolhaas went some way to correct the invisibility of the night in architectural theory with influential books such as *The Architecture of the Well-Tempered Environment* (1969), *Learning from Las Vegas* (1972), and *Delirious New York* (1978), which partially examine the role of technology and night in the construction of modern domesticity and leisure culture in Western architecture. From apartments to offices, casinos to nightclubs, movie theaters to theme parks, these texts render the night visible in architectural representation by addressing the technologies, networks and forms of design deployed in nocturnal spaces and their associated communities. In the 1980s, audiovisual and written research about "night as a heterotopia" was extensive, illustrated in in-depth investigations by dystopian cinema, such as the films *Escape from New York* (1981) or *Blade Runner* (1982), which explore the condition of the qualities of darkness, indefiniteness, and the uncanny aura of architecture in the absence of sunlight. Night is somehow seen as an "other" (hetero) space: disturbing, intense, incompatible, contradictory, and transforming the regular condition of the human habitat. In recent decades, significant contributions include John A. Jakle's book *City Lights* (2001), Dietrich Neumann's *Architecture of the Night* (2003), Edward Dimendberg's *Film Noir and the Spaces of Modernity* (2004), and Jonathan Crary's *24/7: Late Capitalism and the Ends of Sleep* (2013). In the latter, Crary explores how sleep, through its very existence and progressive reduction in recent decades, has become the last remaining bastion of resistance to the increasing monetization of human activity in market economies. In the same line, Netflix CEO Reed Hastings openly declared in 2017 that "We are competing with sleep, on the margin, it's a very large pool of time (3)," envisioning human biology as the biggest challenger to his company's market.

These references typify the extent to which the identity of contemporary human beings and their domestic, professional and cultural spaces are inseparable from the night. Nevertheless, as of today, influential contemporary architecture magazines such as *El Croquis, Apartamento,* or *A+U*, still feature more than 90% daytime photography. Accompanying essays rarely refer to night spaces, not to mention nighttime activities or related behaviors. Of all the architecture biennials celebrated worldwide since the Venice Architecture Biennale was inaugurated in 1980, none has been entirely dedicated to the night. And yet, night has been the most important laboratory of architectural experimentation since the invention of electricity in the 19th century, prompting an endless intensification of human activity that has forever transformed the means of material, cultural and space production. From the dominance of daytime photography in publications to the absence of dedicated nocturnal events, architectural media has, albeit with a few exceptions, uncritically inherited the pre-modern diurnal episteme that preceded the invention of artificial light. Ultimately, is architectural representation diurnal by default? (4)

For us at the Department of Interior Architecture at HEAD–Genève, this question became an important source of fascination. It was this fascination that prompted the

---

3 Aatif Sulleyman, "Netflix's biggest competition is sleep, says CEO Reed HastingMS," *The Independent,* April 19, 2017. 4 The historical introduction in the first paragraphs of this essay is part of the research project *Scènes de Nuit* and was first presented in the publication: *Scènes de Nuit. Night and Architecture,* ed. Javier F. Contreras, Youri Kravtchenko and Manon Portera (Geneva: HEAD— Publishing / Madrid: Ediciones Asimétricas, 2021).

Scènes de Nuit project, originally a bachelor-level studio at the Department, from which an exhibition and series of events at the Forum des Architectures (f'ar) in Lausanne, developed in May 2019. Curated by Javier Fernández Contreras and Youri Kravtchenko with the assistance of Manon Portera, five different types of nocturnal spaces were created by BA students—the nightclub, the restaurant, the corner shop, the city and the cinema—and the exhibition was open for five evenings only. Each night explored one of the programs, with a varied agenda of performative exhibitions, international conferences, debates and projections, proposing a mutable scenography that could change according to the night-types to be discussed, explored, and enacted. The edition and later publication of this material in the form of a catalog (5) motivated us to continue our exploration of night and architecture, progressively questioning the forms of representation and media that have constructed the diurnal episteme of the discipline. In this line, in February 2020, the Department of Interior Architecture organized a workshop on nocturnal photography with the director of *El Croquis*, Richard Levene, interrogating the recurrent absence of this kind of imagery in the magazine. For two weeks, students engaged in night photography around Geneva to produce an unofficial, nocturnal version of the journal edited together with Levene, *El Croquis Night,* with provoking results. (6)

In 2020, *Scènes de Nuit* (www.scenesdenuit.ch) was launched as an official research project funded by the HES-SO, University of Applied Sciences and Arts of Western Switzerland. The Department associated a team to the project that included Javier Fernández Contreras,

5   See Contreras, Kravtchenko and Portera, *Scènes de Nuit. Night and Architecture.*   6   Javier F. Contreras, "El Croquis Night: Excursus into Nocturnal Obliteration in Architectural Media," *Interiority* 4, nº 2 (2021): 181-190.

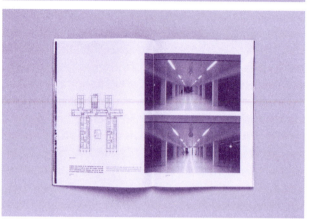

A NOCTURNAL HISTORY OF ARCHITECTURE
Javier Fernández Contreras, Vera Sacchetti, and Roberto Zancan

7 Scientific Committee: Javier F. Contreras, Roberto Zancan, Vera Sacchetti, and Youri Kravtchenko. Lectures by: Efrosyni Boutsikas, Murielle Hladik, Maarten Delbeke, Lucía J. Oyarzun, Carlotta Darò, Yan Rocher, Alexandra Sumorok, Léa-Catherine Szacka, Hilary Orange, and Nick Dunn.

Youri Kravtchenko, Manon Portera, Roberto Zancan, and Vera Sacchetti, and several different activities were organized around the theme. From lectures to workshops and from individual thesis projects to large-scale installations in international architecture events, the Department's research has extensively contested the omission of nocturnal perspectives in architectural media, generating fruitful results such as this book.

The origin of this publication lies in the international symposium "Nocturnal History of Architecture", which took place at HEAD–Genève on 6–7 December 2021. (7) The symposium advanced the hypothesis that a nocturnal history of architecture is yet to be made and proposed a first attempt at this effort. While the Department of Interior Architecture organizes an annual research symposium, the 2021 edition marked the first time the entire event was structured around a research theme that originated within it. The symposium proposed a survey on the interconnections between architecture and night, with an expanded network of contributors whose practice lies beyond the disciplines of design and architecture, encompassing philosophy, urbanism, anthropology, media studies and history, among others. On the one hand, this allowed for an expanded understanding of the importance of a nocturnal perspective; on the other hand, it showcased the centrality of space production and space design when thinking about the theme of night.

The two days of the event were enriched by the investigation of different historical contexts, geographies, and media, from Classical Greece to modern Europe and from ancient Japan to the spaces of MTV. The contributions looked beyond the traditional Western centers of historiography, bringing to the fore other cultural outlooks or even hidden and traditionally ignored realities. Additionally, the presentations sought to probe the ambiguous dimension of nocturnal ideas, delving into spaces and narratives of transgression and alternative spatial dimensions. Finally, the ambition to complete a broader historiography of the architectural night took us to the 76th annual international conference of the Society of Architectural Historians, held in Montreal on 12-16 April 2023. Entitled "Night Scenes: For a Nocturnal History of Architecture", (8) our panel welcomed presentations problematizing the relationship between night, space and agency in contexts as diverse as the Byzantine architecture of the 10th century, the Brazil of the 19th century, the rural areas of Switzerland and the nightclubs of Italy in the first and second half of 20th century.

This first attempt at a Nocturnal History of Architecture you are now perusing takes us back to ancient times and ends in our contemporary moment. Organized chronologically, it starts with a philosophical introduction to the epistemology of darkness in the history of the built environment by Sébastien Grosset. Taking us to Greece, Efrosyni Boutsikas focuses on the nocturnal power of ancient Greek architecture, with an emphasis on religious spaces. Similarly, Maria Shevelkina explores the subterranean night as a productive space in sacred Byzantine architecture. Murielle Hladik immerses us in a study of the presence of the moon as an essential element in Japanese aesthetics and architecture. Back in Europe, in the baroque period of 17th century Rome, Maarten Delbeke chases darkness and night as the performance of metaphor. Across the Atlantic, Amy Chazkel questions the conditions of urban slavery and sleep in 19th-Century Brazil, whereas Lucía Jalón Oyarzun casts light on the Underground Railroad and its connections with clandestinity and night-faring practices in the United States and Canada. In the 20th century, Carlotta Darò and Yann Rocher take a closer look at the typology of atmospheric cinemas and how they have contributed to the artificialization of the sky. Looking at communist Poland, Aleksandra Sumorok analyzes artificial light in the interiors of Socialist Realism, observing the careful determination of the emotions they should provoke. On a contrasting position, Chase Galis reflects upon the resistance to electrification in certain rural areas of Switzerland, whereas Catharine Rossi studies the technological innovations in the nightclub architecture of Italian designers in the second half of the 20th century. Back in the United States, Léa-Catherine Szacka investigates the birth of MTV and how it brought clubbing to the basements of American suburbia. Back in Europe, within the industrial coal-mining landscapes of the German Ruhr area, Hilary Orange explores the night vision of the IBA Emscher Park, and Nick Dunn envisions in contemporary Manchester the creation of nocturnal spaces that are convivial, inclusive, and sustainable. Finally, Youri Kravtchenko contributes a postscript on the design studio *Scènes de Nuit* that he has led at HEAD–Genève since 2018, working on practice-based research with students in Interior Architecture to test these hypotheses in nocturnal projects and exhibitions that have been presented in different venues and events like the Designers Saturdays

8 Scientific Committee: Javier F. Contreras, Roberto Zancan. Lectures by: Maria Shevelkina, Amy Chazkel, Chase Galis, and Catharine Rossi.

2018 in Langenthal, the Design Parade 2019 in Toulon, or indeed Alcova / Milan Design Week 2021 with the iconic *Milk Bar* project co-curated by India Mahdavi.

Welcome to the *Nocturnal History of Architecture*, an epic journey through more than 2000 years of entanglements between night and space design across different continents and geographies. From its own perspective, this book proposes a beginning, an endeavor to be continued by other scholars, designers, and colleagues. The absences of the nocturnal spaces of Africa, China or Oceania are just a few examples that illustrate the vast scope of both the task to be completed and the opportunity that lies ahead. From the elusive darkness of Greek temples to the constantly illuminated American suburbia, and from ornate Italian baroque interiors to derelict West German coal-mining landscapes, what emerges from this volume are scenes and fragments that tell the stories of multiple semantic, physical nights of which much remains to be told. Its authors are aware that absences are more numerous than presences and that many topics have not been dealt with within the limits of time and space allowed here. By analyzing and studying "night scenes", this book hopes to show how the night has historically been a central laboratory for the development of new forms of thinking, architecture and, ultimately, of living.

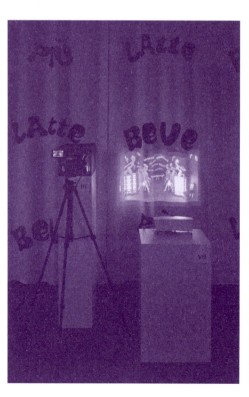 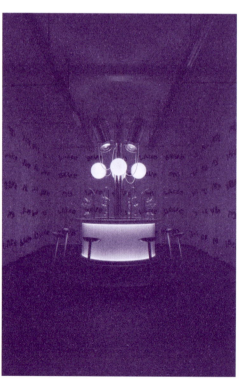

OBSCURE ORIGINS
Sketch for a History of Habitat Under the Shadow of Architecture
Sébastien Grosset

Architecture is All About Light…

In *Empire et décor*, the philosopher Pierre Caye provides a surprising summary of the history of Western architecture as that of the gradual illumination of building interiors by daylight.
Taking as his starting point the Vitruvian notion of *arrangement* (9) and, more precisely, the lines in Book VI of *De Architectura* devoted to the art and manner of bringing outside light into a building, (10) he recounts the evolution of a humanist form of architecture that gradually replaces the magic of the hearth with the brightness of daylight, eventually reaching the full transparency of glass architecture, which Caye paradoxically describes as a way of "reinstalling opacity in transparency":
> Vitruvian architecture and its art of arrangement strive to provide natural light, equally distributed throughout the building, to dispel the darkness that contributes to the manifestation of the fireplace. Openings, doors and windows, pierce the length of the primitive hut and liberate the building from its chthonian zones and its troglodytic destiny. The building sheds its mystery. The glow of the fireplace is replaced by the light that the arrangement captures, differentiates and distributes. (11)

Since the rest of the story does not fit within the scope of a book devoted to *architecture and the question of technology in the humanist and classical age*, (12) it is recounted in a footnote:
> Until, having reached the end of its logic, architecture achieves the transparency of the Crystal Palace. Here, architecture is reversed: it is no longer a question of

9 "Arrangement is the disposition in their just and proper places of all the parts of the building, and the pleasing effect of the same, keeping in view its appropriate character. It is divisible into three heads, which, considered together, constitute design: these, by the Greeks, are named Ιδέαι: they are called ichnography, orthography, and scenography." Vitruvius, *De Architectura*, I, 2,2.   10 Vitruvius, *De Architectura*, VI, 6, 6–7.   11 Pierre Caye, *Empire et décor: l'architecture et la question de la technique à l'âge humaniste et classique* (Paris: Librairie Philosophique J. Vrin, 1999), 18.   12 This is the subtitle of his book.

[13] Caye, *Empire et décor*, 18. [14] He shows, for example, how Palladio, when he had to redo the façade of the *Chiesa San Franseco della Vigna* in Venice, did not change the proportions, even though they had been chosen for their commensurability with those of the cosmic harmonic of the Pythagoreans: since all measurements were arbitrary anyway, it was not necessary to change them to challenge the analogies of Neoplatonism. On the other hand, Palladio blocked the *oculus* of the façade, which was intended to be the visible symbol of a relationship between heaven and the church. The architectural confrontation between humanism and Neoplatonism thus played out on the terrain of light (Caye, *Empire et décor*, 16). [15] "What the good itself is in the intelligible realm, in relation to understanding and intelligible things, the sun is in the visible realm, in relation to sight and visible things… You know that, when we turn our eyes to things whose colours are no longer illuminated by the light of day but by night lights, the eyes are dimmed and seem nearly blind, as if clear vision were no longer in them… Yet whenever one turns them on things illuminated by the sun, they see clearly, and vision appears in those very same eyes." Plato, *The Republic*, VI, 508 B–509 A. [16] Caye, *Empire et décor*, 15. [17] Vitruvius, *De Architectura*, II, 1, 1. [18] Le Corbusier, *Toward an Architecture*, trans. John Goodman (Los Angeles: Getty Research Institute, 2007), 16. These lines were first published in the October 1920 issue of *L'Esprit nouveau*.

conquering light over the darkness of the primitive hut but rather of reinstalling opacity in transparency. The modern movement is born. (13)

In his book, Caye contrasts the rationalism of Andrea Palladio's humanistic architecture with a form of Neoplatonic idealism that sees the correctness of architectural proportions as the manifestation of the ideal numerical relationships that govern the cosmos. (14) Yet, the narrative he unfolds takes up the Platonic analogy between good and daylight. (15)

And indeed, Plato's idealism and the classical rationalism of the 16th century have in common that they prioritize ideas over matter. The difference, as Caye himself says, is the origin of the idea:

> It all depends on the nature we attribute to architectural measure and proportion. Is the architectural number an imitation of Nature or a method of the mind? Does *symmetria* or the system of architectural measures reflect the discrete and general mathematical harmony that structures nature and accounts for the necessary and regulated ballet of the supra-lunar world, or is it merely the fruit of the ratiocinating mind that uses mathematics to make its procedures more certain and to execute the building in perfect conformity with its mental project? (16)

Here, I would like to suggest that if architecture likes to frame itself as a story of light (from the discovery of fire evoked by Vitruvius at the beginning of the second book of his treatise (17) to its definition as "a learned game, correct and magnificent, of forms assembled in the light" (18) by Le Corbusier), it is because it is a fundamentally idealistic discipline, whatever the aesthetic and doctrinal translations of this idealism may have been throughout its history.

Indeed, it seems to me that idealism is consubstantial with the poiesis of the *project*, that methodical art of bringing the idea to life in matter, from the sketch to the plan, from the plan to the model, from the model to the estimate and from the estimate to the construction site. (19)

Architecture is, therefore, not so much idealistic because its representatives adhere to some Platonic or Neoplatonic doctrine but because its creative principle is based entirely on the manifestation of an idea in matter. And it is in order to correspond to this principle that it so often defines itself as the art of light, taking up, consciously or not, the Platonic analogy. This multi-voiced narrative is a chimera, since it would require the collage of many texts—at times contradictory—to faithfully render it. I propose to summarize it here by starting a little earlier than Caye does and ending just after. According to what I will henceforth call *architecture's autobiography of light*, humans are to begin with, like Filarete's *Adam in Vitruvius*, forced to place their hands above their heads to protect themselves from the weather:

> There is no doubt that the art of building was invented by man. We do not know who the first man was to build houses and dwellings, but we can assume that Adam, driven out of Paradise, could only put his hands over his head to protect himself from the first rain, and just as one must eat to live, so one must have a dwelling to protect oneself from the elements. (20)

[19] This structure of production may well be idealistic, but it also has very concrete effects on the division of labour: the measured design of the architects is also an enterprise that dominates the building site, an enterprise that goes hand in hand with the idealization of the poiesis of construction. The architect turns the empiricism of the craftsperson on its head and thereby takes control of the construction process. Pierre Caye points out this fact, but without emphasising the class antagonism it implies: "By marking his building sketches, the architect not only improves and simplifies construction and its forms, but above all displaces the worker's gesture from its tradition and tears the form from its constructive necessity: the number becomes efficiency" (Caye, *Empire et décor*, 16). [20] Quoted in Georg Germann, *Vitruve et le vitruvianisme: introduction à l'histoire de la théorie architecturale*, trans. Michèle Zaugg and Jacques Gubler (Lausanne: Presses polytechniques et universitaires romandes, 1991), 70.

To continue the story with some coherence, let us pass the floor to Vitruvius, for whom primitive humans began by domesticating fire, before inventing first language and then, thanks to the exchange of ideas that this allowed, architecture in the rudimentary form of the primitive hut:

> In addition, since men were of a nature that inclined towards imitation and learning, every day they showed each other the achievements of their building, bragging about their discoveries; and thus, with their native talents sharpened by rivalry, the structures improved day by day as a result of better decisions. First, they covered the walls with mud after they had set up forked props connected by twigs. Others, drying mud clods of earth, constructed walls, binding them together with timber and covering them with leaves and reeds to keep off the rain and heat. Then when they had discovered that the roofs were not able to endure the rains during the wintry storms, they made gables and drew off the rain water on sloped roofs covered with clay. (21)

As you can see, the first walls were opaque. But they carried within them the principle of their future perforation: the *project*. Indeed, the Vitruvian hut is made of several walls—probably four. A single wall is already a separation, not yet a shelter. Now, if humans were looking for protection from the elements and built a hut made of several walls (rather than a circular hut as is the case in other stories), (22) it is because they had a *project* that they carried out step by step: *separating* first, using the two sides of a wall, then *enclosing* with the two (23) or three others, and finally *protecting* with the roof.

In the idealistic autobiography, it should be noted, the *separation* between the outside and the inside thus precedes their existence. The first wall states the opposition between the *in-side* and the *out-side* even before forming an inside and an outside. The rest of the story (I will not have time here to detail all its episodes) is the one Pierre Caye evokes: the twofold, complementary art of *dividing* the interior (which is nothing other than the further development of the seminal gesture of separation) and *diffusing* the light from outside everywhere, to the point of achieving the glass architecture of the 20th century. We could go one step further by evoking the postmodernist shift from transparency to reflection that Fredrik Jameson analyzes in John Portman's *Westin Bonaventure*, whose "glass skin repels the city outside". (24) By adding this shift of glass into mirror, we likely have the main stages of the great diurnal narrative of Western architecture.

... But it Produces Only Shadows

To this autobiography of light, I would like to oppose another story that does not claim to be more scientifically true, but which would allow us to do justice to the shadowy side of architecture, kept hidden by the idealistic narrative. The aim here is to offer an alternative narrative and not to re-establish any factual truth. In order to make the allegorical nature of my story clear, I will take as my starting point two photographs that their author explicitly designates as *metaphors*, since they are two of the many photographs that Ettore Sottsass gathered together in his eponymous series.

---

21 Vitruvius, *De Architectura*, II, 1, 3. 22 See, for example, Eugène Emmanuel Viollet-Le-Duc, *Histoire de l'habitation humaine depuis les temps préhistoriques jusqu'à nos jours* (Paris: J. Hetzel, 1875; Paris: Hachette, BnF, Gallica, 2012), 6, accessed November 30, 2022, http://gallica.bnf.fr/ark:/12148/bpt6k6258576d. 23 The hypothesis of a triangular hut is rarely mentioned but remains theoretically possible. 24 Fredric Jameson, *Postmodernism, or, the Cultural Logic of Late Capitalism* (Durham, NC: Duke University Press, 1991), 88.

These two images each show the same basic installation consisting of a chair and a makeshift wall casting its shadow on the ground. In the first image, entitled *vuoi sederti al sole…* (do you want to sit in the sun…), the chair is outside the shade. In the second, *…o voi sederti a l'ombra* (…or do you want to sit in the shade?), it is inside the shade. (25) That is all.

And yet, one suspects, it is a lot, because this wall that sits between the sun and the chair does not require any other. It is not *one* of the walls of the hut, but the *only* wall.

With this installation, Sottsass reminds us that, although architecture may constantly speak of light, in reality it has only ever produced shade. He also places architects and architectural historians at a crossroads: "vuoi racontare il sole… o vuoi racontare l'ombra?"—do you want to further the bright, idealistic story of the gradual piercing of the walls of the primitive hut? Or do you want to tell the story of a form of architecture that neither creates nor seeks light, but has in fact never stopped *opposing* it?

This opposition is the fundamental, principial shadow side of architecture upon whose denial the autobiography of light is built, but a trace of which we nevertheless find—paradoxically—in the passage of *De Architectura* devoted to the distribution of light, the very one upon which Caye relies to tell his bright tale:

> We must take care that all buildings are well lighted, but this is obviously an easier matter with those which are on country estates, because there can be no neighbour's wall to interfere, whereas in town high party walls or limited space obstruct the light and make them dark. Hence, we must apply the following test in this matter. On the side from which the light should be obtained let a line be stretched from the top of the wall that seems to obstruct the light to the point at which it ought to be introduced, and if a considerable space of open sky can be seen when one looks up above that line, there will be no obstruction to the light in that situation. But if there are timbers in the way, or lintels, or upper storeys, then, make the opening higher up and introduce the light in this way (26). And as a general rule, we must arrange so as to leave places for windows on all sides on which a clear view of the sky can be had, for this will make our buildings light. (27)

The delicate art of framing in windows to let light in, Vitruvius tells us, lies entirely in this struggle against the "timbers, lintels or upper stories" that *"interfere (officient)"*, just as Sottsass's wall interferes between the sun and the ground to cast its shadow. In striving to conquer light, architecture is thus at odds not with its environment, then, but with itself (its own timbers, lintels and storeys).

The verb *officere* used here by Vitruvius, which can be translated as "to obstruct, hinder, interpose" or, more precisely, "to hide the sun", (28) is a compound of *ob* (against, toward) and *facere*, to do. It is, therefore, a verb of action. It is not simply a matter of the timber, the lintel or the upper storey just being there, in the way of the light, but

---

25 Ettore Sottsass, *Ettore Sottsass: Metaphors*, ed. Barbara Radice and Milco Carboni, trans. Béatrice Arnal (Milan: Skira; Paris: Seuil, 2002), 86–87.
26 "Sin autem *officient* trabes seu lumina aut contigationes de superioribus partibus aperitur et ita inmittatur."   27 Vitruvius, *De Architectura*, VI, 6, 6-7.   28 Félix Gaffiot, *Le grand Gaffiot : dictionnaire latin-français* (Paris: Hachette, 2008), s. v. „officio".

of actively standing in the way, of *obstructing* it. To stand between is not a quality or a state of architecture, it is its *office*, its *officium*; in other words, its "function". (29) We owe it to lexical rigour to specify that the verb *officere* (to interpose, to hide the sun) and the noun *officium* (the function, the office), despite their morphological proximity, do not have quite the same origin, since *officium* is a contraction of *opus facere*, "to do work". It is, therefore, (I readily admit) by forcing the Latin language slightly that I propose here a definition of architecture as the *office of the shade*.

The word "office" can be understood both in the local sense (the place itself) and in the sense of a service (the good offices) that architecture renders to us by allowing us, if we wish, to "sit in the shade".

In order to tell the story of architecture as office of the shade, we cannot, of course, start from the piercing of the walls of the primitive hut, as Caye does. However, we can take seriously his observation that these openings "liberate the building from its chthonian zones and its troglodytic destiny".

According to this remark, the reason why window openings are so important is, I believe, because the dark side of buildings harkens to an obscure and subterranean origin to which architecture always threatens to return. Light must be brought in at all costs to erase the mark of an infamous origin, i.e., the cave, which is a disgrace for a lineage of architects who, they say, "began by *setting up* forked props". (30) If the story begins underground, the origin is the cavity, not the erection. One can then guess what other repressed sentiments accompany the denial of the shadow…

Speaking of the "troglodytic destiny" of the hut, Caye points out that the autobiography of light still takes the cave into account, but as a threat rather than an origin: the cave is the dark age of architecture, prior to the origin itself and whose return must be warded off, because it would correspond to savage regression. Indeed, Vitruvius ranks caves among the habitats that the first humans had in common with beasts:

Men of old were born like the wild beasts, in woods, caves, and groves. (31)

But this return of the repressed troglodyte, as we shall see, will still take place when the bright exteriority has changed into a hostile environment. In the meantime, if the autobiography of light cannot completely overlook the cave, it strives to push it out of its realm: the family tree begins on earth. With the trunk. Its subterranean roots must remain invisible because the cave as origin makes architecture doubt itself. In more ways than one.

Fireplace Tricks

Since this is above all a question of light, let us begin, following Caye, with the problem of the fireplace. In the hut, its duplicity is limited to appearing more sparkling than it really is:

The hearth where the fire glows and the gloom that makes it brighter are like so many obstacles to the deployment of [the] arrangement. (32)

29 Gaffiot, s. v. „officium". 30 Vitruvius, *De Architectura*, II, 1, 3. 31 Vitruvius, *De Architectura*, II, 1, 1. 32 Caye, *Empire et décor*, 18.

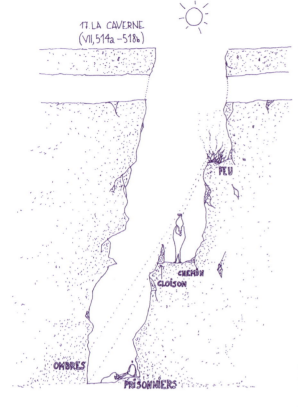

The lie is venial. But in the cave, the fire goes so far as to make shadows dance on the walls, giving the illusion of life to inanimate objects. In this respect, it is noteworthy that Plato, in his famous allegory, is careful to differentiate between daylight and the light of the fire in front of which the figures in his shadow theater are brandished:

Imagine human beings living in an underground, cave-like dwelling, with an entrance a long way up, which is both open to the light and as wide as the cave itself. They have been there since childhood, fixed in the same place, with their necks and legs fettered, able to see only in front of them, because their bonds prevent them from turning their heads around. Light is provided by a fire burning far above and behind them. Also behind them, but on higher ground, there is a path stretching between them and the fire. Imagine that along this path a low wall has been built, like the screen in front of puppeteers above which they show puppets. (33)

As a drawing by architect Daniel Zamarbide illustrates, the fixed light of the outside (and of truth) is explicitly distinguished from the changing light of the fire and the lying shadows.

The famous allegory of the cave thus also reminds us that we did not need to wait for gas or electricity to produce artificial light. And in Plato's cinematic dwelling, the artificiality is twofold: fire is fabricated to produce simulacra. (34) Daylight brings the truth of the outside world through the window of the hut, while the light of the fireplace projects phantasmagoria against the walls of the cave.

Obscured Origin

Even if there were no fireplace, the cave would already be a challenge to the idealistic narrative, insofar as, regardless of the shadows that dance in it, its subterranean walls were not built.

Under the sun, as we have seen, the first act is to erect a wall. Everything begins with the construction of a separation between the inside and the outside. In a cave, however, there is nothing to build and nothing to separate. The inside is given to us, and in order to make it an inside, it must be *arranged*.

In other words, in the hidden story, everything begins with *interior architecture*: the aim is no longer to construct a building whose interior is then arranged, but to arrange an interior that has never been built.

This precedence of interior architecture over architecture is much more than a wound to the latter's pride: it goes so far as to open up the distressing prospect of the *absent origin*. Indeed, one can only arrange what is *already there*. This is the very opposite of

33 Plato, *The Republic*, VII, 512 A. 34 Besides, around the fire, keeping watch, the aim is not only to warm up but also to tell stories.

the idealistic logic of the project. Arranging is secondary. But if the origin is the cave, then the first architectural act is this secondary act. There is no beginning.
This is probably also what the night lacks: it has no origin. Day comes from the sun, but what makes night? Its absence. So at the origin, there is absence. The absence of the sun, of the project, of construction. Everything begins with a negation.

Sun and Death

It is only once we have emerged from the earth that we begin to build. Not to *invent* the distinction between the inside and the outside, but to *find it again* and to find with it the natural shelter that a cave provides against rain and wind, as well as against the heat. Caves stay cool.
In accounts of the origins of architecture, the hut is often presented as a shelter against bad weather. For Filarete, for example, rain plays an essential role in the birth of the art of building. However, the *Codex Magliabechiano* adds a very interesting detail to my story:

> Adam, having made a shelter with his hands, thinks about how to protect himself from the rain, but also from the heat of the sun. (35)

You have to protect yourself from the sun too. Because it burns and because it dazzles. "Neither the sun nor death can be looked at steadily", (36) says the famous maxim number 26 of La Rochefoucauld.
In the autobiography of light, the sun and death are in opposition, as darkness is usually associated with the grave. (37) The idealistic narrative seems to forget that the sun not only shines but also heats and even burns. It is no coincidence that Sottsass's photographs were taken in "the stone deserts south-east of the Ebro": (38) the shadow cast on the ground by its rudimentary architecture, which stands in the way of the sun, is the recreation of a bearable microclimatic space. It is already an interior. As simple as possible since it has only two dimensions. (39)
This minimal living space, this first interior to come to the surface, can also be read as a *metaphor*, as Sottsass invites us to do: that of a discipline, an art, interior architecture, which has long developed humbly *in the shadow of architecture*.
But perhaps it is time to pay more attention to the art of interior design at a time when the architecture of light, that which rises shamelessly under the sun, no longer protects against solar warming but rather contributes to it.
I take one example (among, alas, many others) from recent reporting on global warming in a French cultural weekly:

> Phoenix is an "urban heat island": temperatures in the city are higher than in the surrounding countryside. This is due to pollution, but also to the dark, impermeable surfaces that cover the streets and buildings. It's hard to believe, but it's cooler in the desert than in its palm-lined avenues—a difference of up to 5 degrees at times! (40)

By forgetting its solar interposition function, architecture has come to produce places that could claim the status of "circle of hell": urban heat islands in the middle of the desert!

---

35 Quoted by Germann, *Vitruve et le vitruvianisme*, 70.   36 F. de la Rochefoucauld, *Réflexions ou sentences et maximes morales*, 2nd ed., ed. J. Lafond (Paris: Gallimard, 2021), 48.   37 "Humanist and classical architecture took leave of this symbolic and mystical conception of the building as both hearth and tomb and broke with the model of the 'primitive hut' which expressed it" (Caye, *Empire et décor*, 18).   38 Sottsass, *Ettore Sottsass: Metaphors*, 9.   39 Indeed, on a line, there can still only be 'between'—in Latin: *inter*. The line is *between* the two points that limit it. It can be crossed, but not entered. The surface, on the other hand, which several lines delimit, is already *more than between*—in Latin: *interior*. This is why you can place a chair in the shade if that is where you want to sit.   40 Romain Jeanticou, "Sous le feu du réchauffement," *Télérama*, no. 3747, November 3, 2021.

Peter Sloterdijk says that islands "form climatic enclaves in the general air conditions", (41) but what of an island that differentiates itself from its surrounding environment through heightened hostility? Perhaps this is an effect of the denial of the dark origin: it is only by forgetting that its function is not so much to delimit new zones as to find the ancient dimness of the cave that architecture comes to such deadly aberrations. Yet, according to some geographers, troglodytism is a verified response to climatic hostility:

> These excavation dwellings seem to depend primarily on soil types. However, if we study their distribution, we see that they are also related to climatic facts. They seem to have been maintained mainly in arid and hot climates, where vegetation was scarce and woods almost absent, but also in regions with sudden variations in temperature, where they provide protection from excess heat and light as well as from violent winds and extreme cold. (42)

Judging by what Pierre Deffontaines writes in *L'Homme et sa maison*, it is not the nature of the soil but that of the climate that shall take us back to caves. The new environmental hostility calls for the return of the repressed cave. But this return can take unexpected forms.

Enclaves

Denise Scott Brown, Sven Izenour and Robert Venturi give an example of this kind of reappearance when they show that the pairing of patio and gambling room characteristic of Las Vegas casinos functions as a double alternative to the climatic hostility of the outside—the patio is an enclave of coolness, the gambling room an enchanted cavern where artificial light triumphs:

> The gambling room is always very dark; the patio, always very bright. But both are enclosed: the former has no windows, and the latter is open only to the sky. The combination of darkness and enclosure of the gambling room and its subspaces makes for privacy, protection, concentration, and control. The intricate maze under the low ceiling never connects with outside light or outside space. This disorients the occupant in space and time. One loses track of where one is and when it is. Time is limitless, because the light of noon and midnight are exactly the same. Space is limitless, because artificial light obscures rather than defines its boundaries. Light is not used to define space. Walls and ceilings do not serve as reflective surfaces for light but are made absorbent and dark. Space is enclosed but limitless, because its edges are dark. Light sources, chandeliers, and the glowing, jukebox-like gambling machines themselves are independent of walls and ceilings. The lighting is antiarchitectural. Illuminated baldacchini, more than in all Rome, hover over tables in the limitless shadowy restaurant at the Sahara Hotel.
> The artificially lit, air-conditioned interiors complement the glare and heat of the agoraphobic, auto-scaled desert. But the interior of the motel patio behind the casino is literally the oasis in a hostile environment. (43)

---

41 Peter Sloterdijk, *Foams, Plural Spherology (Spheres III)*, trans. Wieland Hoban (South Pasadena: Semiotext(e), 2016), 291. 42 Pierre Deffontaines, *L'homme et sa maison*, ed. Germain Viatte (Marseille: Parenthèses, 2021), 58. 43 Robert Venturi, Denise Scott Brown and Steven Izenour, *Learning from Las Vegas* (Cambridge, Mass: MIT Press, 2001), 49.

As climatic enclaves in the middle of the Nevada desert, the casinos of Las Vegas combine the protection of shade with the simulacrum of artificial lighting. As an oasis, they are the opposite of the surrounding aridity, but their "antiarchitectural" light also "complements" the sunlight outside.

In this seminal act of postmodernism, *Learning from Las Vegas*, the cave returns to the circle of built architecture. In vigorous opposition to the transparency of modern idealism, it returns in all its majesty, with its radical obscurity and insular climate that opposes its surroundings, but also with the artificiality of its lighting and all the simulacra of the Platonic cave.

Phantasmagoria

This tight link between the habitable shade and the triumph of the simulacrum does raise questions: should we conclude that, at a time when sunlight makes the outside so inhospitable, the interior space only gains its habitability through simulacra that make the world bearable? The question of the Platonic analogy of truth and light is posed afresh: if the sun is both the origin of architectural light and the shining symbol of truth, does the fact that we have to take refuge in new caves to escape it burning us mean that truth is no longer habitable?

At any rate, this is what Walter Benjamin already seems to be suggesting when he describes the interior as a space of phantasmagoria:

> The private individual, who in the office has to deal with reality, needs the domestic interior to sustain him in his illusions. This necessity is all the more pressing since he has no intention of allowing his commercial considerations to impinge on social ones. In the formation of his private environment, both are kept out. From this arise the phantasmagorias of the interior—which, for the private man, represents the universe. In the interior, he brings together the fair away and the long ago. His living room is a box in the theater of the world. (44)

Judging by *The Arcades Project*, the hostility of the outside does not begin in Phoenix in the 21st century or even in Las Vegas in the 20th, but in Paris in the 19th. Benjamin reminds us that, even before degrading the climate, capitalist expansion had already made social exteriority uninhabitable, even for the bourgeois businessman forced to reinvent a domestic shadow theater in order to avert his eyes from the consequences of his economic activity.

The common merit of *Learning from Las Vegas* and *The Arcades Project* is that they explain the reasons that call for the emergence of a dark history of architecture today: due to the violence of the division of labour after the industrial revolution and the effects of the capitalist economy on urban development (and, beyond that, on the climate itself), the rationality of the outside world has gradually ceased to be habitable. The light of the outside world has become unbearable both symbolically (45) and physically since the cars that run through the desert and the buildings that architecture erects there have warmed the atmosphere to the point of turning the shade into what we might call (with a slight twist of the meaning that economists give to this expression) a "safe haven".

44 Walter Benjamin, *The Arcades Project* (Cambridge, Harward University Press, 1999), 8.   45 Benjamin's private individual can only stare at capitalist *realities* during office hours if he knows he can curl up at home in the fantasies of his interior.

According to this hypothesis, the shade would be both the last habitable climatic enclave and the kingdom of simulacra. We would only be able to live within its borders, not only because the sun had become deadly, but also because the truth would no longer be bearable.

This is, as you can see, a pessimistic hypothesis, and I would like to try to write a happier ending to our dark story by suggesting that, contrary to what the autobiography of light proclaims, it is not light but shadow that opens up a path to the world of ideas.

The Habitable Truth

We know how highly idealism, from Plato to Le Corbusier, holds geometry. The author of *Toward and Architecture* writes, for example:
> Cubes, cones, spheres, cylinders or pyramids are the great primary forms which light reveals to advantage; the image of these is distinct and tangible within us without ambiguity. (46)

Even if the list of his favourite solids differs somewhat from that in *Timaeus*, (47) Le Corbusier is like Plato in his search for essential figures. For Plato, their perfection is the guarantee of the intimate organization of matter. But of course we cannot experience this immediately. For Le Corbusier, on the other hand, they retain their purity on an architectural scale, and the sign of their proximity to the ideal world is the ease with which they receive light.

These few lines show to what extent, as Paul Turner writes, "Le Corbusier's attitude towards architecture was fundamentally idealistic". (48) Yet, between the lines, we can guess that this idealism has its limits: the interplay of these solids may be "correct, magnificent and learned", but, in the end, the light under which they are assembled remains the empirical and changing light of the everyday sun and not the eternal, immobile glow of ideas. Moreover, it is only to the "image" of these solids that we have access, because in architecture, geometry *cannot* be ideal. In this sense, architectural idealism is perhaps always *thwarted idealism*. As Peter Eisenman lamented when he was searching for a *conceptual form of architecture* that could compete with the art of the same name:
> The fundamental difference between art and architecture is that the idea of architecture demands the idea of an object presence, while the idea of art does not. (49)

Whatever its conceptual pretensions, architecture is destined to become an *object*, and a *useful object* at that.

Now, in the *Republic*, Socrates sees geometry as a preparation for the study of ideal truth only on condition that it ceases to be taught as a practical science but concentrates on its figures, its elements, its theorems, i.e. on its *ideal truths,* whose applications in the sensible world will necessarily be altered by the imperfections of the latter. As Socrates puts it, it is only in this way that:
> Geometry will draw the soul towards truth, and create the spirit of philosophy, and raise up that which is now unhappily allowed to fall down. (50)

46 Le Corbusier, *Toward an Architecture*, 16.   47 Plato, *Timaeus*, 53c to 57b.   48 Paul Venable Turner, *The Education of Le Corbusier*, trans. Pauline Choay (Paris: Macula, 1987), 6.   49 Peter Eisenman, *Peter Eisenman: écrits 1963-1984*, trans. Gauthier Herrmann (Paris: Éditions Form[e]s, 2017), 112.   50 Plato, *The Republic*, VII 527b.

In order for geometry to provide access to the truth, a movement of reversal from the bottom to the top is required, which is the same movement that the prisoners of the cave must make once they are liberated:

> At first, when any of them is liberated and compelled suddenly to stand up and turn his neck round and walk and look towards the light, he will suffer sharp pains; the glare will distress him, and he will be unable to see the realities of which in his former state he had seen the shadows. (51)

We can see how painful the movement is and how uncertain the result is, precisely because "Neither the sun nor death can be looked at steadily".

But shade? Yes. The shade does not dazzle.

Rather surprisingly, it is Proclus, one of Plato's most faithful disciples, who, in a sentence of his very learned *Commentary on the First Book of Euclid's Elements*, casually opens the way to shade:

> And we can get a visual perception of the line if we look at the middle division separating lighted from shaded areas, whether on the moon or on the earth. For the part that lies between them is unextended in breadth, but it has length, since it is stretched out all along the light and the shadow. (52)

In the phenomenal world in which we live the depth of matter can only be left aside by an ideal *epoché*. Only architects and idealist artists in search of the *spiritual in art* (53) believe that drawing is made of *points and lines on the plane*. (54) In reality, it is always ink or graphite that is involved, with its thickness and weight, however slight. Even flat screens are deep. With the exception of solids that we can touch, Euclid's elements do not belong to physics. And this is why Plato says that geometry *draws the soul towards truth*. In the physical world that we continually experience, there is no point, no line, not even a surface... except for the shade.

This is Proclus's great and unstoppable discovery: *shade is the only real surface of the sensible world*. And its boundary with light is the only real line we know. (55)

Sottsass may not like it, but shade is the only thing that is *not* a metaphor. It does not go *beyond* itself; you do not have to turn away from it to face the dazzling idea of which it would only be a simulacrum dancing on a wall. No, the shade must be *entered*. Simply sit in the shade. Settle into its hospitable climate.

Because if shade has no depth, it does have its climate. The dark surface that stretches out at the foot of the makeshift wall erected by Sottsass may well be flat, its effects on the physical world are no less concrete: very quickly the temperature drops, and if you took the trouble to leave it for a long time, you would gradually see the interior of its perimeter change into an ecosystem. Just think of undergrowth.

Inside the Truth

When La Rochefoucauld writes that "neither the sun nor death can be looked at steadily", he does not mean that courage in the face of death does not exist; he only points to "the impossibility we have of (...) looking it in the face". (56) One can face the sun and

---

51 Plato, *The Republic,* VII, 515c. 52 Proclus Lycius, *A Commentary on the First Book of Euclid's Elements*, trans. Paul Ver Eecke (Bruges: Desclée de Brouwer, 1948), 91. 53 Wassily Kandinsky, *Concerning the Spiritual in Art—and Painting in Particular*, ed. Philippe Sers, trans. Nicole Debrand and Bernadette Du Crest (Paris: Gallimard, 1989). 54 Wassily Kandinsky, *Point and Line to Plane: Contribution to the Analysis of the Pictorial Elements*, trans. Suzanne Leppien and Jean Leppien (Paris: Gallimard, 2006). 55 Light projection (which made cinema possible) is nothing more than the inversion of shadow; that is why it is destined for dark rooms. 56 As Jean Lafond writes in his edition of the maxims (La Rochefoucauld, *Réflexions ou sentences et maximes morales*, no. 7., 288).

death with courage, but this confrontation is doomed to failure if it takes the form of a face-off. It must be done differently.

In La Rochefoucauld, the comparison is between the sun and death. Here we have added truth to draw an analogical triangle: sunlight is both a metaphor for truth and, in Phoenix for example, the actual source of death.

It is easy to understand why we should not look the sun in the face as the bearer of death, less obvious as a metaphor for truth. Should we say with Plato that truth is too dazzling to be stared at by those whose philosophical mind has not yet been developed by geometry?

I would tend to think that if the sun and the truth cannot be stared at, it is because staring implies a distinction between the viewer and the viewed, between the subject and the object, whereas truth is probably more of an environment in essence: to access it, you have to participate in it. Truth must be lived in.

Certainly we get a *sense* of the line when we *cast our eyes* at the shadow, but we only *experience* the surface when we enter it. By interposing itself in front of daylight, architecture relieves us of a face-to-face encounter with light that would only lead us to disengaged knowledge. The contemplation of objects by a subject who does not participate in them is a game that is certainly learned, perhaps correct, often magnificent, but always external.

This interposition, as we have seen, is not simply negative. Firstly, because it is an act and not a mere presence. Secondly, because the consequences of this act are not so much to keep the light away as to bring the darkness from the depths to the surface of the world. And it is indeed the surface that is at stake: *the shade is a superficial cave*—a cave that has adapted to life above. Paradoxically, what the shade inherits from the depths of the cave is that it has no depth. The shade is flat, but it is *really* flat. It is not the sign or idea of the surface; it is a real and hospitable surface. You can *really* sit in the shade, it is not an idea or a metaphor, but a habitable truth.

The function of architecture is, therefore, to *provide* for the return of a habitable truth from the depths of the cave. And this habitable truth is interior architecture.

THROUGH THE GATES OF DARKNESS
Discovering the Nocturnal Power of Ancient Greek Religious Architecture
Efrosyni Boutsikas

This paper tackles two problems. First, the recognition that modern experience of darkness in the over-illuminated West is vastly different to experiencing darkness before the invention of electricity. Second, that our understanding of ancient spaces and landscapes is inevitably conditioned by diurnal visits to these spaces. [57] In contrast to modern perception of these spaces in daylight, many ancient monuments were constructed to be used with equal frequency at night. For most of us, understanding how these spaces appear in real darkness requires employing our imagination, which can be challenging; we no longer experience such conditions or spaces in our day-to-day lives. Today, our experience of night is dramatically different to 200 years ago, not to mention 2,500 years ago, the time we concern ourselves with here. Thus our comprehension of the night-sky or what a dark open space feels like, is limited. We only know "artificial darkness ... fogged with electric light". In this setting, the night sky appears as "a smudged and meaningless background". [58]

57 See, e. g., John A. Jakle and George F. Thompson, *City Lights: Illuminating the American Night* (Baltimore: Johns Hopkins University Press, 2001), viii. 58 David E. Nye, *When the Lights Went Out: A History of Blackouts in America* (Cambridge, Massachussets: MIT Press, 2010), 9.

A NOCTURNAL HISTORY OF ARCHITECTURE

These concepts are important, as this paper explores the intended sensory experience of dark religious spaces and ancient Greek monumental architecture built to be used under dark conditions. The only artificial visual aids present in this setting were in antiquity flaming torches and oil lamps. To appreciate some of the points of this paper, it is essential to detach ourselves from modern concepts of dark and light environments and bear in mind that in antiquity the only means of achieving artificial brightness was through a different means: fire.
The power of fire was recognized from an early stage of human development. Not simply because ancient cultures were aware that humans were the only species able to create, harness, and use fire, but because the power of fire was unsurpassed. The ancient Greeks recognized this incredible force, which allowed the consumption of cooked food, the production of weapons, even the destruction of entire landscapes and cities. But most importantly, fire was the force which made them able to reverse the natural course of night and day by creating light after sunset, when the chariot of Helios, the sun god, had disappeared in the west, and allowed them to reverse the effects of the seasons by being able to keep warm when the gods decreed that it should be winter. In a world where everything was assigned divine will, it was empowering to be able to reverse conditions that were determined by divinity. It is not a surprise then that in Greek mythology, fire was a gift to mankind from the Titan god Prometheus, who was punished for eternity for this action. Until then, only gods made use of fire. Perhaps it is because of this belief

that fire was so closely associated with magic and divination and extensively used in religious festivals in ancient Greece. We learn of massive bonfires, altars being stacked with piles of wood and set on fire, living animals being thrown into the flames of great fires, nocturnal torch processions, and torch races, ritual dances with fire, etc. (59) In this religious context, the movement of the flames was perceived as a sign of divine presence. (60) The ability of fire to connect the human and divine realms is witnessed further in *empyromancy*, the art of divination by observing the movement and shape of flames in order to foretell the future. Thus in ancient Greece, fire does not simply illuminate, destroy, or create. It is further perceived as the medium of communication between gods and humans.

Fire has a further, cognitive importance. It makes our relationship with darkness more intimate. Fire-lit spaces are not washed in bright light. The flickering light of flaming torches and lamps creates a mystic atmosphere through the heavy shadows it throws and the limited distance it extends to. The ancient Greeks were well-aware of this power of fire and used it extensively to control religious experience and the senses during religious performances. Such examples are particularly evident in mystery cults and divination. At the Oracle of the Dead in Acheron for instance, upon entering the oracular structure, the consulter would not see sunlight for several days. After observing a strict diet, performing purification and sacrificial rituals, the enquirer was led into an inner chamber, where

59 Martin P. Nilsson, "Fire festivals of ancient Greece," *The Journal of Hellenic Studies* 43, no. 2 (1923): 144–8. 60 Walter Burkert, *Greek Religion. Archaic and Classical* (Cambridge, Mass: Harvard University Press, 1985), 60–64. 61 Wiebke Friese, "Facing the dead: Landscape and Ritual of Ancient Greek Death Oracles," *Time and Mind* 3, no. 1 (March 2010): 33.

he anticipated to meet the dead. (61) The only light the enquirer would see during this time was that of flaming torches and lamps. During the stage of revelation in the Eleusinian Mysteries, we are told that the mystic words and sacred object would be revealed to the initiates at night, inside the Telesterion during consecutive alternations of darkness and bright light.

In ancient Greek religious experience, the polarity of light and darkness was very common. We will explore some examples of this. The importance of this polarity derives from the cosmogonic significance of darkness, which permeated the two most significant events in human existence: birth and death. These two major existential transitions bore direct light/darkness connotations (62) because they were characterized by symbolic and physical darkness: birth brought people from darkness to light; at the moment of death, they moved back into eternal darkness.

The moments of this transition (when darkness becomes light or night turns to day) seem to have been key in ancient Greek cognition. We have day and night rituals in ancient Greece with sunrise heralding either the time of commencement or the end of a number of rituals. One example of ancient Greek dawn rites, which commenced with the appearance of the first rays of the rising sun, is the Argive rite performed at the altar of Helios. (63) Here the sacrifice of a ram took place at night, then, after crossing the river Inachos, a further sacrifice was offered to Helios at his altar at dawn. (64) The time of day or night a ritual commenced was part of its careful staging and performance.

62 See, e.g., Homer, *Iliad*, 16.187–188; 19.103–104, 118–119. 63 Pausanias, *Description of Greece*, 2.18.3. 64 Walter Burkert, *Homo Necans. The Anthropology of Ancient Greek Sacrificial Ritual and Myth* (Berkley and Los Angeles: University of California Press, 1983), 107.

In ancient Greece, religious rituals were framed by monumental architecture. Monumental architecture in modern and ancient societies the world over talks about inspiration, power, wealth, impact, political investment, and artistic achievement. It would not be wrong then for us to perceive of monumental architecture as the mirror a society stands in front of, day in, day out. It reveals the reflection a society has chosen to represent itself. In the context of ancient Greek monumental architecture, the mirror negotiates also deeper societal cultural and spiritual elements. It functions as a stimulus for deeper cognitive processes that express cosmovision and the comprehension of divinity. The time of day or night these structures were experienced and came to life is fundamental to this process. This experience is significantly supplemented by the oral tradition which accompanies sight and guides the mind to the desired state. The combination of these elements makes the cognitive impact and discourse with architecture a more complex process.

It is certain that the volume and direction of natural light was highly controlled in religious architecture. Ancient Greek temple construction directed the admission of sunlight (direct or indirect) through the size and positioning of doors, windows, and roof openings, thus satisfying specific needs for illumination or darkness. This practice attests to the importance of darkness, shadow, and light effects in Greek religion, which ultimately intended maximum visual impact when viewing the cult image and temple's interior. Variations in *cella* depth and width, as well as in the size and number of openings, indicate that different trends were followed. Seventh century BCE temples, for example, were long and narrow and thus darker, compared to those constructed in the second century BCE. Later temples seem to also have a greater amount of natural light admitted through larger window and door openings. (65) In addition, a vast number of lamps unearthed in the interior of temples and in the open space of Greek sanctuaries demonstrates the extensive use of fire to illuminate these spaces at night. (66) The discovery of lamps inside temple *cellas* complements the testimony of written sources on the use of artificial light inside temples such as the Sanctuary of Demeter Malophoros at Selinous or the Temple of Artemis at Ephesus. In conjunction with the varied orientations of temples (which did not always simply face the east), it is evident that general overarching conclusions on the amount of light received inside Greek temples are not particularly meaningful. (67)

Instead, ancient Greek monumental architecture needs to be examined case by case. We start our exploration of 'dark architecture' in ancient Greece with a brief discussion on the use of darkness in the greatest religious festival of Classical Athens, the Panathenaia. It is beyond the aims of this study to fully explore the importance of the night in this open-air ritual. Instead, the example serves as a starting point to thinking further of the intended significance of nocturnal open-air festivals framed by monumental architecture, with direct references to mythology and cosmology. We will subsequently survey the interior architectural features of specific religious structures, as we

65 Christina Williamson, "Light in Dark Places: changes in the application of natural light in sacred Greek architecture," *Pharos* 1 (1993). 66 Eva Parisinou, *The Light of the Gods: The Role of Light in Archaic and Classical Greek Cult* (London: Duckworth, 2000), 14–7, 136–161. 67 Efrosyni Boutsikas, *The Cosmos in Ancient Greek Religious Experience: Sacred Space, Memory, and Cognition* (Cambridge and New York: Cambridge University Press, 2020), 31–70.

unravel the importance of darkness in ancient oracular consultation. This type of cult exemplifies the way darkness was employed for an impactful experience, which assisted in comprehending the world via senses other than vision. Through this practice, oracular consultation succeeded in enhancing religious belief.

The main celebrations of the most important festival of Classical Athens, the Panathenaia, commenced at night in early/mid-August with an impressive torch race, which carried a flame from the Academy in the city, to the Great Altar of Athena on the Acropolis. The altar had been piled with logs, which were set on fire by the torch race victor. This was then followed by an all-night celebration of women dancing and singing on the Acropolis (*the Pannychis*). The festival commemorated the birth of the city's patron deity, Athena, and her decisive role in the cosmological Battle of the Giants. It was however, by no means the only occasion of nocturnal rituals held on the Acropolis. Ancient sources tell us of other times in the year when worshippers climbed the steep hill after dark for religious performances, asserting the presence of visitors on the Acropolis at night. (68) The time in the year chosen for the nocturnal activities of the Panathenaia, coincided with the most significant moments in the annual movement of the constellation of Draco, which was clearly visible from the Acropolis. (69) The timing of the festival on the last few days of the waning moon, or on a moonless night, assured consistently dark nights with particularly low moon luminosity during the Panathenaic celebrations. This would have increased the visibility of Draco in the Athenian

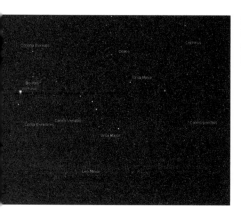

68   See, e.g., Euripides, *Heraclidae*, 782–783; Aristophanes, *Frogs*, 371.
69   Efrosyni Boutsikas, *The Cosmos in Ancient Greek Religious Experience: Sacred Space, Memory, and Cognition* (Cambridge and New York: Cambridge University Press, 2020), 119–125.

night sky during the moments the participants were present on the Acropolis, while a reference in Euripides, verifies that Draco was associated with cosmic time by the fifth century BCE. (70)

Most importantly, Draco was connected in mythology both with the festival and Athena. The myth of the Battle of the Giants marks the time of Athena's birth, as we are told that she launches into the battle as soon as she is born. Ancient sources tell us that the sun-god Helios paused time as soon as Athena appeared out of Zeus's head, so that she could take her armour from her shoulders and that Zeus could rejoice in her birth. (71) Then, time resumed, as did the battle between the Olympians and the Giants, during which Athena snatched a giant snake from the Giants and tossed it into the sky, thus forming the constellation of Draco. Time is of significance during the episode, and, as has been discussed elsewhere, cosmic time is also depicted in the scene of Athena's birth on the Parthenon's façade. (72)

When gazing at the Parthenon's east pediment, which narrates the scene of Athena's birth, the festival participants were reminded of the cosmological significance of these mythological events. At the center, Zeus and Athena are surrounded by the other gods. Yet the importance of this scene is not at the center but rather on the two corners of the pediment. In the south-eastern corner, Helios, the sun god in his chariot, rises above the waters of the Ocean. In the opposite corner, Selene (the moon) in her chariot, has almost sunk below the base of the pediment,

70   *Pirithous, Frag.* 594; Efrosyni Boutsikas, *The Cosmos in Ancient Greek Religious Experience: Sacred Space, Memory, and Cognition* (Cambridge and New York: Cambridge University Press, 2020), 150.
71   *Homeric Hymn to Athena*, 13–18.   72   Efrosyni Boutsikas, *The Cosmos in Ancient Greek Religious Experience: Sacred Space, Memory, and Cognition* (Cambridge and New York: Cambridge University Press, 2020), 150–152.

which functions as a virtual horizon. The heads of her horses with their open mouths and protruding nostrils gasp for one last breath before they disappear completely into the space below. It is the moment when night turns into day. The composition creates a balanced center of an eternally rotating cosmos, as the two contrasting heavenly siblings gravitate to either corner.

As a structure, the Parthenon frames the space of nocturnal and diurnal open-air ritual performance.

Cognitive and Physical Darkness in Ancient Greek Oracles

The most impactful examples of the importance of darkness in Greek architecture come from divinatory sanctuaries. The various methods of ancient Greek divination and the multiplicity of processes resulted in a variety of architectural forms and temple features. Very often, divination required dreams or visions (healing visions in certain cases) to be experienced, for instance in healing sanctuaries (Asklepeios, Amphiaraos) or the oracles of the dead (and dead heroes, e.g. Trophonios). (73) Healing sanctuaries such as that of Asklepeios in Epidaurus required visitors to reside in the sanctuaries for several days prior to being treated and to receive a specific diet appropriate to their condition. When fully prepared, visitors were led to specific rooms, where they waited for the god to appear to them

73 Homer, *Odyssey*, 11.207; Lucian, *Philopseudes*, 27; Euripides, *Phoenissae*, 1539–45; Pausanias, *Description of Greece*, 1.34.5, 9.39.11; Raymond J. Clark, "Trophonios: The Manner of His Revelation," *Transactions and Proceedings of the American Philological Association* 99 (1968): 64–65.

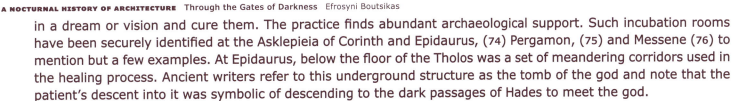

in a dream or vision and cure them. The practice finds abundant archaeological support. Such incubation rooms have been securely identified at the Asklepieia of Corinth and Epidaurus, (74) Pergamon, (75) and Messene (76) to mention but a few examples. At Epidaurus, below the floor of the Tholos was a set of meandering corridors used in the healing process. Ancient writers refer to this underground structure as the tomb of the god and note that the patient's descent into it was symbolic of descending to the dark passages of Hades to meet the god.

To test the enquirer's faith, anticipation of a god in darkness could would often involve sensory deprivation intended to detach the enquirer from the human world and induce a unique, unexpected state of mind. An extreme example was the oracle of Trophonios, where enquirers had to descend and crawl into a narrow underground chamber at night and wait for hours or days to see or hear an apparition. Even ancient authors described this as a near-death experience, and it was achieved with the help of architecture. (77)

Very informative in this respect are oracles of the dead (divination through communication with the dead). Ancient descriptions of such oracles state that they resembled the dark, gloomy landscape of the Underworld. A dark setting characterized the Oracle of the Dead in Avernus near Cumae in Campania, located in a volcanic landscape close to the sea, within "a wild wood of black and impenetrable trees", causing the area to be inhabited by ghosts. (78) The necromanteion at Heraclea Pontica on the south coast of the Black Sea had an entrance to a cave leading down

74 Carl Roebuck, *Corinth. Results of Excavations Conducted by the American School of Classical Studies at Athens, vol. XIV, the Asklepieion and Lerna* (Princeton: The American School of Classical Studies at Athens, 1951), 24, 42, 45, 46, 55, 57. 75 Oskar Ziegenaus and Gioia de Luca, *Das Asklepieion 1. Teil. Der südliche Temenosbezirk in hellenistischer und frühromischer Zeit*, Altertümer von Pergamon XI 1 (Berlin: De Gruyter, 1968), 29–31, 39–47, 111–5, 125–34.
76 Nino Luraghi, *The Ancient Messenians: Constructions of Ethnicity and Memory* (Cambridge: Cambridge University Press, 2008), 279, 280.
77 Pausanias, *Description of Greece*, 9.39.9–11; Plutarch, *Moralia*, 590a–592e; Aristophanes, *Clouds*, pp. 506–508; Pierre Bonnechere, "Mantique, transe et phénomènes psychiques à Lébadée: entre rationnel et irrationnel en Grèce et dans la pensée moderne," *Kernos* 15 (January 2002): 182; Raymond J. Clark, "Trophonios: The Manner of His Revelation," *Transactions and Proceedings of the American Philological Association* 99 (1968): 64f; Yulia Ustinova, *Caves and the Ancient Greek Mind: Descending Underground in the Search for Ultimate Truth* (Oxford: Oxford University Press, 2009), 91f.
78 Strabo, *Geography*, 5.4.5.

to an underground chamber through a stairway (79) and that at Tainaron had a temple constructed in the shape of a cave, (80) located in a dry and rocky landscape with commanding views of the sea, that gave the visitor the impression of arriving at the end of the land.

Necromantic consultations required several days of preparation and the obligatory seclusion of oracle seekers in dark, windowless chambers, where they also slept while seeking contact with the dead. (81) A Greek magical papyrus recording a magic spell capable of conquering death bears witness to a similar procedure in the Idaean Dactyls involving an initiation during which the oracle seeker descended to an underground *megaron* and witnessed visions. (82)

It seems that the privilege of attaining secret knowledge could only be achieved in darkness and architecture was used to facilitate this contact. Unfortunately, only very few examples of oracles of the dead have been securely identified by archaeologists. Most date to later periods and their architecture does not survive well enough to allow an in-depth study of this practice. From ancient accounts we know, however, that contact with the divine and especially with the dead required a massive cognitive and sensorial leap, which was achieved through strict fasting and immersion into extremely dark, sensory-deprived conditions. This made the architectural form of these oracles key to the success of the practice.

79 Quintus Smyrnaeus, *Postomerica*, 6.469–91; Pomponius Mela, 2.51. 80 Pausanias, *Description of Greece,* 3.25.4. 81 Euripides, *Phoenissae*, 1539–45). 82 PGM LXX.13–16; see also Hans D. Betz, "Fragments from a catabasis ritual in a Greek magical papyrus," *History of Religions* 19, no. 4 (May 1980): 288, 292f.

This psychological and physical preparation of consulters is witnessed in several other types of oracles. In these, emotional manipulation was somehow lighter in comparison to that of necromantic consultations, but here too darkness played a seminal role. The most notable of such examples are oracles associated with Apollo. In two of his oracles on the west coast of Turkey, at Didyma and Claros, we observe very interesting methods of creating light/dark conditions. This was achieved through spatial movement within the religious structure, as the consultant progressed through labyrinthine passages and narrow, sloping, dark corridors. The aim was clear: separation from the surrounding world through a dark passage or chamber, the path being lit with torches or lamps.

At Claros on the west coast of Turkey, we find one of the most famous oracles of Apollo. The fourth-century BCE Doric temple was constructed on the remains of an earlier open-air structure which included a hypaethral courtyard and a well. Written sources predating the existing temple mention that the seat of the oracle was in a cave and the source of its inspiration was the water of the well. By the time the temple was constructed over it, the cave and well were inside the temple's crypt and underground. This is an intriguing structure; the internal courtyard sinks three meters below the temple's floor.

With the construction of the temple above the earlier structures, the game of perception started. The temple's ground floor has the plan of a standard *peripteral* temple. But oracular consultation took place exclusively in the lower,

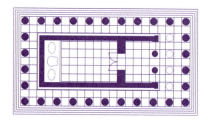
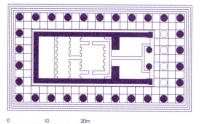

underground level of the crypt, which stretched below the entire temple *cella* and *pronaos.* The crypt comprised of two rooms: the Hall of the Consulters, accessed first, probably used as a waiting room for oracle seekers, and the Hall of the Oracle, thought to have been the room where the god's mouthpiece pronounced the prophecies.

Oracular consultation at Claros took place only after dark. The consulter entered the temple's front gallery on the ground floor. From there they descended to the crypt. Access points in the form of six steps located near the front of or inside the temple's *pronaos* led underground to the crypt and corridors. This way, during nocturnal consultations, oracle seekers with the right to enter the crypt could do so without requiring access to the temple's interior. From the front gallery, two symmetrical staircases led to corridors dressed in black marble. The extremely narrow width of these corridors could not fit two people across. One corridor was used for entering the crypt and the other for exiting. This set-up was continued in the first room of the crypt, which had two doors: one would have been used to enter and the other to exit the space. The architecture of the narrow, black marble corridors was evidently aimed at enhancing a sense of mysticism and emotional intensity.

To further intensify this dark, solitary process, the corridors had a meandric layout, requiring the visitor to change direction seven times before arriving at the Hall of the Consulters. (83) The intended cognitive impact on the descending and disorientated consulters was one of sensory deprivation and a formidable, but alerted, state of mind.

83 Efrosyni Boutsikas, *The Cosmos in Ancient Greek Religious Experience: Sacred Space, Memory, and Cognition* (Cambridge and New York: Cambridge University Press, 2020), 96.

There was no natural way of illuminating or ventilating the crypt. The consultation was carried out in a windowless underground cell, under the light of torches or lamps. In addition, an installation attached to the marble blocks of the arches which formed a type of barrel vault did indeed make the crypt appear like a cave. (84) The features were barely visible under torchlight and the low height of the crypt's barrel vault ceiling. This construction gave Claros oracle seekers the impression of being in an underground cave environment. It seems this mental state was a requirement for communicating with the god.

Recent cognitive research on crucial factors determining human perception of dark spaces has much to offer for our understanding of this experience. The 'predictive processing' model, in particular, informs us about the workings of the human brain in light-deprived and low sensory conditions. For example, a cognitive experiment aimed to monitor reactions of agents using a virtual reality model as a proxy for real-life religious experience demonstrates that in low light conditions, in contexts of low sensory reliability and when the agent expects it, the human brain commonly imagines encounters with the supernatural, even when there is no actual presence. (85) This false detection has been interpreted as giving rise to or strengthening religious beliefs, (86) while the experiment affirms the cognitive power of combining contact with the divine with low sensory conditions. At Claros, from the moment the oracle seeker commenced their descent through the windings of the narrow passages, their senses were intensively

84 Efrosyni Boutsikas, *The Cosmos in Ancient Greek Religious Experience: Sacred Space, Memory, and Cognition* (Cambridge and New York: Cambridge University Press, 2020), 98–100. 85 Mark Andersen et al., "Agency Detection in Predictive Minds: A Virtual Reality Study," *Religion, Brain and Behavior* 9, no. 1 (January 2019). 86 Justin L. Barrett, *Why Would Anyone Believe in God?* (Walnut Creek, CA: Altamira Press, 2004); Justin L. Barrett and Jonathan A. Lanman, "The Science of Religious Beliefs," *Religion* 38, no. 2 (February 2011).

engaged. The liminality of the dark space prepared their transition into an altered state of mind. This alteration of consciousness induced by a disorientation caused by the descent and the architectural form of the underground structures, was fundamental to the consultation and a precondition for contact with the divine sphere. The flickering flame of the torches or lamps enhanced and complemented this cognitive experience. The intention was a sensory encounter, cognitively linking oracular consultation with an underground, light-deprived experience.

The human body-brain-mind engages with its surroundings using orientations, lines of sight, and spatial movement, in order to construct an understanding and interpretation of the cosmic structure and of our place within it. The consultation procedure and the temple structure at Claros confirm that ancient Greek religious practice was aware of, and successfully employed, these cognitive processes for several centuries.

At the other celebrated oracle of Apollo, that of Didyma, 100km south of Claros along the west coast of Turkey, we observe another example of an impressive structure that played with perception. The unique architecture of a temple from the later Hellenistic period envelops the remains of an earlier sanctuary. The vast structure was meant to make a strong visual and spatial mark of the presence of the god in the landscape, but was, in fact, hollow. Externally, the temple resembled a *dipteros* on a seven-stepped platform. It had a ten-column-wide façade. The visitor climbed the high steps only to find out that the main monumental entrance was blocked by a wall, barring access to the temple's interior from the *pronaos*. This was unexpected! Above the wall, a wide opening or window allowed the visitor to get a glimpse of the inaccessible interior.

The way in was unexpectedly through two particularly narrow, dark, sloping barrel-vaulted passageways flanking the *pronaos*. Each passageway was over twenty-one meters long and just over one meter wide. Each led laterally from either side of the *pronaos* to the lower level, grassy floor of the temple's unroofed interior. So instead of entering the temple in the conventional way, the visitor passed through the almost claustrophobic vaulted passages before arriving at the temple's ancient core: a sacred open-air grove embellished with a small *prostyle* temple. The Didymaean vaulted corridors, wide enough only for one person at a time, are in direct contrast with the enormous size of the temple. They play with human perception of scale. Visitors encountered an unusual, god-sized threshold, shrouded in darkness by the heavy shadows cast by the forest of the gigantic columns of the *pronaos* and *prostyle*. The clever Hellenistic 'hollow' design allowed the temple's architects to create an imposing approach with an enormous visual and psychological impact of what was essentially an unroofed cell. The structure allowed direct contact with the sky and so maintained the older natural spring amidst trees that had long been considered the sacred source of the oracle's power. At the same time, the construction left intact the ancient structure. This interior composition was open to the elements while being completely cut off from the outside world thanks to walls rising as high as twenty-two meters. (87)

87 Herbert W. Parke, *The Oracles of Apollo in Asia Minor* (London: Croom Helm, 1985), 51.

Unfortunately, we do not know whether consultations took place at night or during the day, but the way the temple is built shows a clear intention to play with the visitor's sense of scale and trick anticipation through the fake gigantic doorway, the dark vaulted passageways and the open space of the interior. Contrary to expectation, the interior was a living space, ever-changing through its contact with the elements and natural light, creating reflections and shadows during the course of the day and the seasons, as the sun moved around it.

Experience of architecture is reliant on time, motion and sensory perception and at Didyma, the impressive deception of scales and the alternations of light/darkness through multiple transitions prepared oracle seekers psychologically for contact with Apollo. At the same time, as at Claros, these passages create a mental distance between human and divine spaces. Both structures offered a sense of seclusion and transition.

Discussion

Material reality cannot be divorced from experience for the same reasons that the formulation of concepts should not be separated from sensorimotor regions of the brain. (88) The presence of darkness has an indisputable impact on the emotional reactivity of ritual participants, whether performances take place in open-air spaces or indoors.

> 88 Vittorio Gallese, "Embodied Simulation: from neurons to phenomenal experience," *Phenomenology and the Cognitive Sciences* 4 (March 2005); George Lakoff and Mark Johnson, *Philosophy in the Flesh: The Embodied Mind and its Challenge to Western Thought* (New York: Basic Books, 1999); Holley Moyes et al., "Darkness and the Imagination: The Role of Environment in the Development of Spiritual Beliefs," in *The Oxford Handbook of Light in Archaeology,* ed. Costas Papadopoulos and Holley Moyes (Oxford: Oxford University Press, 2021), 93.

Such cognitive processes are congruent to studies of the human sensorium in dark landscapes, which observe that the human body compensates for the absence of vision by altering the way it receives information: it relaxes, opens, and extends its attention outward into the world by engaging the other senses more intensely. (89)

In the religious sphere, darkness shapes experience both in modern and ancient cultures. Aside from the visual spectacles created by the use of fire in nocturnal activities (e.g. torch races, processions, dances with fire), darkness functions as the backdrop that allows revelations to inspire awe, focal points to stand out, and spectacles to be appreciated. The examples we discussed here demonstrate how critical the absence of light can be in certain contexts. Specifically designed 'dark architecture' was, and still is, employed as a means of achieving the desired intimacy with divinity. In such mechanisms, awareness of the supernatural is achieved through darkness, shadows, and spatial movement.

Ultimately, in ancient Greek monumental architecture, the importance of darkness is twofold. First, experience of these structures during open-air festivals at nighttime meant that the surrounding landscape was shrouded in darkness. This setting provided the backdrop against which the constellations and artificial light could be appreciated. In this context, darkness created the ideal conditions for the commemoration of star myths. As we discussed, star myths were brought to life through the carefully timed open-air rituals occurring during key moments of the appearance of associated constellations. These orchestrated occurrences seemingly facilitated a dialog between the

> 89 John Tallmadge, "Night vision," in *Let There Be Night: Testimony on Behalf of the Dark*, ed. Paul Bogard (Reno: University of Nevada Press, 2008), 140.

microcosm and the macrocosm. Such enhanced ritual experience complemented the understanding of the cosmos, which seemed to witness and participate in the ritual performances.

Second, spatial movement shapes the emotional and affective response to space. We discussed examples of employing architectural form in the service of theatrics and staging, in order to reveal the sanctuary to the visitor in clearly defined stages. In ancient Greece, staged interior darkness was intended to guide religious experience. This was most intensely witnessed in oracular consultations, when direct communication with the god was expected to be imminent. The connection with nature was important here, asserted through the presence of groves, as well as the attempt to imitate natural darkness similar to that found in naturally enclosed spaces like caves. The cognitive processes associated with the experience of natural cave environments involve the sense of disorientation, accompanied by sentiments of anxiety from being in a confined space (natural or artificial), and the absence of visibility. Such dark cave environments, ideal for cognitive manipulation and sensory experience, are an "important causal force in the transcendental or imaginary thinking". (90)

Clearly, these features intended to alter the oracle seeker's frame of mind and perception, influencing cognition and emotions through low sensory conditions, in order to prepare them for contact with the divinity. This mechanism is witnessed in various oracular structures, where intense use of darkness achieved intense psychological control

90   Holley Moyes et al., "Darkness and the Imagination: The Role of Environment in the Development of Spiritual Beliefs," in *The Oxford Handbook of Light in Archaeology,* ed. Costas Papadopoulos and Holley Moyes (Oxford: Oxford University Press, 2021), 99.

through labyrinthine passages, underground descents, and narrow vaults. Oracular architecture required visitors to step down into the bowels of the religious structures, forcing them to look inward. Low sensory conditions and an induced emotional state prepared the consulters for contact with the divine. Cleverly constructed architecture confused visitors, tricked their senses, and ultimately, convinced them that they had arrived at a sacred space, where divinity was not only present but also willing to communicate and reveal itself. In this context, darkness was not only physical, but also cognitive, as a metaphor for the oracle seeker's uncertainty, intimidation, and anticipation, of the divine response.

The use and manipulation of darkness is the medium that facilitates this experience of the supernatural. Through the combination of carefully staged architectural form and darkness, ritual experience reached immense sensorial heights in ancient Greece. We are fortunate to be able to piece together all this material and cognitive evidence, to reveal the discernible statements that ancient monumental architecture makes about the world views of the society which constructed it.

BYZANTINE NIGHT
Subterranean Darkness as Productive Space
Maria Shevelkina

According to the extant *typika,* rulebooks produced by Christian monastic foundations in the Byzantine period, worship spaces were most often used for their primary purpose—liturgy—during the night and early morning. (91) Precious sunlight hours were reserved for labor critical to the proper economic functioning of the monastery. While it is incontestable that natural sunlight had a significant impact on the construction and design of Byzantine sacred space, much less attention has been afforded to these same structures and spaces in their primary nighttime use. Architectural studies have long begun their inquiries by examining plans and projections devoid of spatial atmosphere either by day or night. The assumption that daylight is the most potent period for achieving the greatest amount of visual information inevitably leads to daylight as the primary mode of apprehension. This study addresses an example in which architecture, spatial organization, and affective experience are driven and formed by the lack of daylight in the construction of Byzantine sacred space. I consider the significant chromatic power of wall paintings perceived by candlelight and in the dimness of the night as constructive of specific experiences and spatiality. Relevant references to liturgical sources that were enacted in the space indicate the crypt's particular nighttime use and its inherently powerful effect.

The subterranean crypt at Hosios Loukas in Stiris, Greece, built in the early eleventh century, is set directly beneath a towering cross-in-square *Katholikon* church. (92) The crypt is a low-ceilinged space with ten widely-set groin vaults, replete with narrative, figural, and ornamental frescoes created simultaneously with the mosaics above. Three large marble sarcophagi introduced in various centuries obstruct the floor plan, and a single arched window pushed up against the ceiling is the only opening in a small eastern apse. Embedded metal hooks interspersed throughout the vaults indicate the prevalence of hanging oil lamps that were likely added in later periods, given the off-apex perforation of the frescoes. Free-standing candle holders and low-level oil lamps were presumably the primary sources of artificial light in the early use of the space.

The space was mainly used for burial and healing rites. (93) Although cold, damp, and stony, the crypt functioned as a common space for monastics and laypersons alike, accessible to a larger amount of people than the imperially oriented *Katholikon* reserved for special feasts and iterant visitors above. (94) The *Katholikon* took advantage of unhindered access to daylight from at least three sides, literally illuminating the church structure through translucent marble revetments, glittering gold mosaic, reflective squinches and curvatures, and rows of windows in the drum and throughout the naos. (95) The soaring interior vectored its energy in an ascending spiral upward toward the anagogical heavens of divine illumination. On the other hand, the crypt below was a space tasked with facilitating a consistent flow of monastics and

91 John Philip Thomas and Angela Constantinides Hero, eds., *Byzantine Monastic Foundation Documents. A Complete Translation of the Surviving Founders' Typika and Testaments*, 5 vols., Dumbarton Oaks Studies, XXXV (Washington, D.C.: Dumbarton Oaks, 2000).

92 Nicolas Oikonomidès, "The First Century of the Monastery of Hosios Loukas," in *Social and Economic Life in Byzantium*, ed. Elizabeth Zachariadou (Ashgate, 2004): 245–255; Carolyn L. Connor, *Saints and Spectacle: Byzantine Mosaics in Their Cultural Setting* (Oxford Scholarship Online, 2016); Robert Weir Schultz and Sidney Barnsley, *The Monastery of Saint Luke of Stiris, in Phocis, and The Dependent Monastery of Saint Nicolas in the Fields, near Skripou, in Boeotia* (London: Macmillan and Co., 1901). 93 Carolyn L. Connor, *Art and Miracles in Medieval Byzantium: The Crypt at Hosios Loukas and Its Frescoes* (Princeton, New Jersey: Princeton University Press, 1991); Oikonomidès, "The First Century of the Monastery." 94 Bissera Pentcheva, "Eternal Victory: Byzantine Territorial Expansion and Constantinopolitan Liturgical Splendour at Hosios Loukas (Steiris, Greece)," *Journal of the International Society for Orthodox Music* 6, no. 1 (November 29, 2022): 1–70; Alicia Walker, "Pseudo-Arabic 'Inscriptions' and the Pilgrim's Path at Hosios Loukas," in *Viewing Inscriptions in the Late Antique and Medieval World*, ed. Antony Eastmond (Cambridge: Cambridge University Press, 2015), 99–123. 95 Carolyn L. Connor, *Saints and Spectacle: Byzantine Mosaics in Their Cultural Setting* (New York: Oxford Scholarship Online, 2016); Ernst Diez and Otto Demus, *Byzantine Mosaics in Greece, Hosios Lucas & Daphni* (Cambridge, Mass.: Harvard University Press, 1931).

96 John Chrysavgis, "Katanyxis: Compunction as the Context for the Theology of Tears in St. John Climacus," *Kleronomia* 17, no. 2 (1985).
97 Connor, *Art and Miracles*, 56.

pilgrims hindered by an inherent lack of light-filled clarity. The crypt embraced darkness and rendered it productive, acting as an indicator of the power embodied by nighttime—a power that today is mostly grounded in fear, but which the Byzantine crypt predicated on the proleptic 'compunction' or *katanyxis* of individualized healing. (96) The crypt's energetic productivity was rendered through various instances of convex spatiality, in which forms and atmospheres were inversely directed inward *into* the subterranean space, rather than upward or outward to the heavens.

The crypt of Hosios Loukas is accessible by a single entrance from the outside, down a wide flight of southern stairs. Monastics, pilgrims, and other liturgical participants entered into a relatively low-ceilinged space, only eleven feet high, into a rhythmically vaulted interior covered in geometric and vegetal ornamental motifs, as well as warrior martyrs, apostles, and holy men medallioned in each triangular groin. Deep blue stripes accent the stark white; rich ochres embellish emerald greens. The eastern space opens to a diminutive sanctuary with a stone templon barrier, altar, and prothesis niche. Sunlight enters here from the only window in the crypt, past an image of the Deesis painted in the narrow arch above. (97) The templon, which in all likelihood was originally outfitted with curtains, would hinder the passage of any exterior light entering into the depths of the interior. Directly opposite this intercessory scene is an ossuary vault in the west wall housing the dismembered remains of the monastery's former monastic inhabitants. Nine scenes predominantly from the Passion Cycle of Christ are fre-

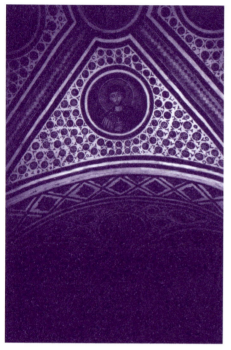

A NOCTURNAL HISTORY OF ARCHITECTURE   Byzantine Night   Maria Shevelkina

98 Jelena Bogdanović, "Framing Glorious Spaces in the Monastery of Hosios Loukas," in *Perceptions of the Body and Sacred Space in Late Antiquity and Byzantium* (Routledge, 2018).   99 Bogdanović, "Framing Glorious Spaces."

scoed in the eye-level lunettes against the outer walls: to the right of the Deesis is the Last Supper, followed by the Deposition of the Cross, Christ's Burial, The Incredulity of Thomas, another Intercession, The Koimesis of the Theotokos, The Entry into Jerusalem, the Crucifixion, and the Washing of the Feet. In these rounded planes, silvery figures draped in thick layers of pastel robes in front of mountains of subdued earth tones emerge from cold, dark-blue surroundings. Rustling bodies, sharp edges, and protruding forms catch the low light in gray and milky whites. Horizontal almond eyes flicker throughout the scenes, illuminated briefly by candlelight. As sight adjusts and incense dissipates, figures and narratives swell out from their stony surface into the tight quarters of the crypt's interior, like carved reliefs. The mass of bright highlights overlaying the darkened grounds pull the surface of the image forward, away from the wall, rather than receding into the background.

By the year 1011, fifty-eight years after the death of the eponymous Luke, the relics of the saint were housed in their final resting place in an elaborate shrine at the locus of the monastic complex's two main churches: the church of the Mother of God (formerly the church of St. Barbara), and the newly built *Katholikon*. (98) The expansion of the fifth bay of the southwestern exonarthex of the church of the Mother of God, merging with the north arm of the *Katholikon* of Hosios Loukas, accommodated the growing influx of pilgrims who came to venerate the saintly relics, hoping to avail of their healing powers. (99) The new monumental tomb was situated directly above the north wall of the subterranean crypt, where the saint's relics were likely interred initially. Currently, a non-Byzantine cenotaph marks this spot. (100) There is further evidence of a direct connection between the upper and lower sanctuaries, dating from the time of the construction of the crypt and *Katholikon* in 1011: the fresco in the northwestern lunette of the crypt depicting the falling asleep, or *Koimesis* of the Mother of God. Bissera Pentcheva has recently written on the two main feasts of the monastery: the falling asleep of St. Luke on February 7 and the translation of his relics or *anakomidē*, which was performed as the inauguration of the new *Katholikon* on May 3, 1011. (101) Given the grand expansion and new construction of the monumental churches above, including an enlarged area for a funerary chapel across from the saint's tomb, what was the need for such an elaborately fashioned crypt, replete with vigorous and expansive frescoes painted in the same year? And why deliberately deposit the relics of St. Luke directly above their former resting place in the crypt? Furthermore, why insert the scene of the falling asleep of the Mother of God into a standard cycle of the Passion of Christ, which usually did not include this particular apocryphal event? (102) My study contends that while the tomb above fulfilled the needs of those pilgrims who passed through the monastic compound during the day, the crypt was crucial for enabling the physical and spiritual healing of monks, local laypersons, including women, and those seeking intensive care in the night. In fact, people of all kinds were often present in the Monastery, which included a hostel for travelers. (103) As a known center for healing, Hosios Loukas regularly admitted women pilgrims who sought therapeutic services. (104) Demons were exorcized through incubation (sleeping near a holy tomb or directly beneath it), and various other quasi-medical *therapeia* practices were accomplished by lengthy rituals. (105)

The most common rite likely performed in the crypt was the burial of resident monks. (106) Commemorated on the third, sixth, ninth, and fortieth day, and a year after passing, death-related services were frequent. They also occurred three years after burial, when bones were removed from the *chora* cemetery and reburied in the ossuary. (107) According to the Goar's Great Euchologium, services for burial, death, and commemoration called *akolouthiae* were separate for laypersons, monks, and priests, multiplying the number of death rites performed. (108) Instructions indicate that after washing and preparing the body, processing, and lighting candles, services took place around the body on a bier in the middle of the naos if they were monks or in the narthex if they were laymen and priests. Monks were then brought either to the cemetery or the funerary chapel before burial. Time-based rites were believed to match the stages of the soul's separation from the body as well as Christ's Passion over three days and ascension to heaven on the fortieth day: physical rites retained metaphysical allegory. (109)

Perfuming the body with fragrances and dressing it in burial clothes was a female task, meaning women were explicitly present in the monastic space throughout many days of the year. (110) This particular female presence is mirrored by the crypt frescoes in the image of the three Maries approaching Christ's empty tomb under the cover of nighttime with oils for burial, as well as frescoes of

100 Bogdanović, "Framing Glorious Spaces." 101 Pentcheva, "Eternal Victory." 102 Brian E. Daley, trans., *On the Dormition of Mary. Early Patristic Homilies* (Crestwood, New York: St. Vladimir's Seminary Press, 1998), 86. 103 Oikonomidès, "The First Century of the Monastery," 254.

104 For example, an elderly woman of Boeotia "went to the monastery of the Saint, entered the sacred precinct, and prostrated herself at the holy tomb." For a discussion of miracles at the tomb of Hosios Loukas, see Connor, *Art and Miracles*, 93–101. 105 Connor, *Art and Miracles*, 56–57, 93. 106 Dorothy Abrahamse, "Rituals of Death in the Middle Byzantine Period," *The Greek Orthodox Theological Review* 29, no. 2 (1984): 125–134, esp. 132; Connor, *Art and Miracles in Medieval Byzantium*, 91; Elena Velkovska, "Funeral Rites According to the Byzantine Liturgical Sources," *Dumbarton Oaks Papers* 55 (2001): 21–51, esp. 41. 107 Connor, *Art and Miracles*, 91. 108 Connor, *Art and Miracles*, 84; Sharon E. J. Gerstel, "Painted Sources for Female Piety in Medieval Byzantium," *Dumbarton Oaks Papers* 52 (1998): 89–111, esp. 102. 109 Velkovska, "Funeral Rites," 39–40; Nicholas Constas, "'To Sleep, Perchance to Dream: The Middle State of Souls in Patristic and Byzantine Literature," *Dumbarton Oaks Papers* 55 (2001): 91–124, esp. 103: cf. *Apostolic Constitutions*, 8.42.1: "Celebrate the 3rd day of those who have fallen asleep with psalms and prayers, on account of the one who rose on the 3rd day" and Eustratios, *Refutation*, 29: "the 3rd day memorial is a *typos* of the 3rd day resurrection, the 9th of the post-resurrection appearance of Christ on the 8th day plus one, and on the 40th day a *typos* of the ascension." 110 See Velkovska, "Funeral Rites," 254 for preparation of the body. Symeon of Thessaloniki discusses the symbolism of the baptism of the deceased (PG 155, col. 676, Heading 361: 1.5-9) as cited in Athanasios K. Vionis, "The Materiality of Death, the Supernatural and the Role of Women in Late Antique and Byzantine Times," *Journal of Greek Archaeology* 4 (2019): 256.

111 Ephrem Lash, trans., *Kontakia: On the Life of Christ. St. Romanos the Melodist* (New Haven: Yale University Press, 2014), 177.
112 According to the Evergetis *Typikon*, cited in Connor, *Art and Miracles*, 85-88. The practice echoed pre-Christian graveside feasts, and such funerary meals were taking place at least until the twelfth century, according to Niketas the Areopagite, Metropolitan of Thessaloniki (PG 3, col. 997), cited in Vionis, "The Materiality of Death, the Supernatural and the Role of Women in Late Antique and Byzantine Times," 259–269, esp. 257.   113 Such as the miracles through the oil in the light over the coffin of Evaristos the Studite on the fortieth day of his death. Abrahamse, "Rituals of Death," esp. 127, 129.

the Mother of God's mourning at the Deposition and the Burial, and finally her own *Koimesis*. The enormous angel poised on the marble stone rolled away from the tomb represents an entryway unbarred for the Maries and all women. Ushering them closer with a mountain-high wing, the angel privileges women with an intimate knowledge of rank and divinity obtained out from the darkness of the early morning visit to the tomb. (111) The scene of the angel at the tomb is an excellent example of the relief-like form of the imagery, with the thick frothing whites of the robes swirling directly out into the viewer's space.

The burial rite was considered a joyous event, celebrating the beginning of the devotee's ascension to God. The feast was marked by the distribution of *Kolyvos* prepared by women: sweets of boiled wheat with dried fruits and honey as a part of the *Pannychis*, which was celebrated in the funerary chapel using the tombs as feasting tables. (112) Miracles involving light occurred in the days following a saint's death. Sanctity was marked by a radiant glowing from the corpse's face. (113) The depths of a subterranean crypt of Hosios Loukas would often have been illuminated not by sunlight but by the divine glow of the deceased and the warmth of a joyous festal celebration replete with specially prepared foods. The nighttime crypt served as an intimate space of communal congregation, garnering a distinct sense of closeness and commonality in death, mourning, joy, and sorrow.

Liturgically, the crypt also functioned as a space of mourning and compunction for the individual soul, either the soul deceased or the one still toiling through life. Particular hymns performed in this space would have directed

A NOCTURNAL HISTORY OF ARCHITECTURE   Byzantine Night   Maria Shevelkina

114 Mother Mary and Kallistos Ware, trans., *The Lenten Triodion* (South Canaan, Pennsylvania: St. Tikhon's Seminary Press, 2002), 125.

the viewer to an intensified state of inner contemplation, facilitated by the proximity of the crypt's structure, especially the forest-like nature of the columns. In the cover of the night, the crypt allowed for individuals to hide and rest from the watchful eye of the demanding sun. There is no centralized dome and no image of the Pantokrator anywhere in the space, nor is there a fully centralized area of any kind. The small sanctuary apse is hidden from view when participants are situated against the north wall beneath the Saint's tomb or at the entrance to the south. In the following, I will briefly point to a few pertinent liturgical moments that would have facilitated the crypt's individualized, interiorized experience when performed during the nighttime matins.

The Lenten Triodion's death-related hymns are heavily dependent on the intercession of the Mother of God, the powerful draw of light during a distinct period of darkness, as well as an acceptance of death's mystery. During Friday evening's Vespers of the Saturday of the Dead, the singers try to make sense of their inevitable death: "I lament and weep whenever I see death and look upon our beauty, formed according to God's image, lying in the grave disfigured and inglorious, its outward form destroyed. O strange wonder! What mystery is this concerning us? How have we been delivered to corruption? How have we been yoked to death?" (114) The hymn is sung in the first-person plural, pulling individuals into a similar shared state which includes the multitude of saints on the vaulted ceiling of the crypt who join in on the prayers. The Saints on the vaults face in all four cardinal directions, becoming accessible to participants from any point within the crypt. As a group, participants face the repulsive image of the corpse, formerly an iconic reflection of divine condescension, but must accept the enigma of bodily corruption ordained by God. Their spatial and atmospheric surroundings push them deeper into inner contemplation. The Mother of God is then called on in the refrain to intercede as the faithful pass from bodily life to ensouled death, hoping to rest "…in Paradise, where the choirs of the saints and the righteous shine as the stars of heaven." (115) Studding the undulating ceiling of the crypt in circles, these saints are not far from their living monastic counterparts, who themselves exude a shining glow as "sons of light." (116) The saint's intercessory assistance is yearned for specifically in the pre-dawn' *Katavasia* prayer, immediately before the rising of the sun: "My spirit seeks Thee early in the morning, O God, for Thy commandments bring us light before Thy coming: Shine with them upon our minds, O Master, and guide us in the path of life." (117) As the mystery and questioning of death mounts throughout the night into the hymns for the Martyrs, the co-dependent dichotomy of sorrow and joy is paralleled by darkness and light: "What pleasure in this life remains unmarked by sorrow? What glory can endure upon this earth unchanged? All is feebler than a shadow, more deceptive than a dream; for death in a single moment takes all things away." (118)

The frescoes in the crypt intensify the shimmering dullness of dispersed light and color perceived through a veil of incense, softened by clouded tearful eyes in the midst of compunction. The dark gray wall's atmosphere diffuses throughout the confined space. While unalloyed brightness and lucidity are never achieved, surfaces are progressively layered toward lighter tones, producing the illusion of a relief-like structure that swells out from the wall. From the depths of a darkened blue emerge clay-colored mountains, their peaks sharpened by jagged white forms extending into the crypt's interior space. Intense olive greens and woodsy ochre hues are tempered by the silvery atmosphere of the weak glow of candles and oil lamps. Textiles and bare flesh are rendered with abundant swaths of sinuous white, often dissolved by a wine-hued pink, marking them as reflectors of a light realized only from the interior of the space rather than the sunlight from the orb in the sky.

The cold subterranean Crypt mitigates the imagined scorching flames of Hades but slightly retains its memory. While hell's flames burn without light, the crypt conserves illumination through its flickering candles and pastel colors superimposed over a hardened darkness. In the seventh step on the monastic mystical ordering the *Ladder of Divine Ascent* from the sixth century, John Climacus exhorts: "Never stop imagining and examining the abyss of dark fire…the limitless chaos of subterranean flame, the narrow descents down to underground chambers and yawning gulfs, and other such images. Then lust in our souls may be checked by immense terror, by surrender to incorruptible chastity, and receive that non-material light which shines beyond all fire." (119) The literal subterranean crypt at Hosios Loukas is a metonymical stand-in for the effect desired by Climacus' drive toward salvation: the crypt facilitates the need to fully experience the power of death, heightened by the darkness of night.

115 Mother Mary and Ware, trans., *The Lenten Triodion*, 128.
116 Mother Mary and Ware, trans., *The Lenten Triodion*, 129.
117 Mother Mary and Ware, trans., *The Lenten Triodion*, 134.
118 Mother Mary and Ware, trans., *The Lenten Triodion*, 143.

119 Colm Luibheid and Norman Russell, trans., *John Climacus. The Ladder of Divine Ascent* (New York: Paulist Press, 1982), 137.

The *Koimesis,* or falling asleep of the Mother of God, is instructive of the affective experience instigated by the nighttime rituals of the crypt; its imagery extended formally and symbolically into the subterranean space. In accordance with John Chrysostom's directive, "the coffin is so arranged that it faces east, indicating in this way the coming Resurrection." (120) Mary's head is lifted at an almost ninety-degree angle, her body shrouded in the same unembellished dark blue and gray himation and maphorion, flattened horizontally across the scene, mimicking the layout proscribed for a burial rite in the crypt. The apostles crowd at Mary's head and feet, rendered in "somber shades of gray, green, blue and brown." (121) Slightly off-center, Christ hovers over Mary: he too is dressed in darkened garments, while the Theotokos' swaddled child-like soul is accented with bright-colored twill. Unlike the dark and mountainous backgrounds of the other scenes, the *Koimesis* of the Theotokos is rendered within a partial interior closed in by a wall, with masonry buildings on either side, pushing the scenic events in closer proximity to the claustrophobic interior of the crypt. According to Pseudo-John the Theologion, the event was filled with heightened senses: her body was aglow, emitting a beautiful perfume, and the song of invisible angels surrounded her tomb for three days. (122) In addition to the days of commemoration of the dead discussed above, the *Koimesis* feast was the only day on which women were explicitly welcomed into the monastery. (123) The feast called for nighttime processions around the monastery and throughout the surrounding area. (124) Later *typika*, such as that in the *Kecharitomene* convent' from the twelfth century, specify that for this particular feast, in addition to generous distributions, fresh fish for the table, and the purchase of rose-essence and incense, "crater lamps must be removed, and the silver chandeliers with many lights must be hung up and the silver pot-shaped lamps and silver crater lamps, and all of them should be filled with oil and water, and lit…and candles with cotton wick of one litra must be fixed in front of the holy icon of the Mother of God set out for veneration…" (125) The royal Isaac Komnenos, author of the *Kosmosoteira typikon*, had a particular zeal toward the *Koimesis*, honoring it "more splendidly than all her other feasts, by the lighting of all the lamps, and by an assemblage of a greater number of priests and deacons in the sanctuary," and proscribed a hundred *kyrie eleison* for chanting. (126) As with the healing incubation recorded in the crypt at Hosios Loukas, Isaac Komnenos knew the *Koimesis* was a space "highly favored by the grace of divine inspiration" and therefore required a "sleepless lamp to be lit perpetually through the year with mastic oil" beneath the image of the feast. (127) Through the celebration of the *Koimesis,* we stand to gain a better understanding of the crypt's atmosphere of interior light and protruding convexity, vectored toward the individual feeling of either joy or sorrow induced by such nighttime rituals. Furthermore, the affordances proscribed to the *Koimesis* feast indicated a mass of visitors and people, including women, who would have descended into the depths at night to crowd into the low-ceilinged intimate space under the cover of darkness and enclosure.

In celebration of her divine ascension, the Theotokos invites the participants to partake in a great feast,

120 Connor, *Art and Miracles*, 54; Engin Akyürek, "Funeral Ritual in the Parekklesion of the Chora Church," in *Byzantine Constantinople: Monuments, Topography, and Everyday Life*, ed. Nevra Necipoğlu (Leiden: Brill, 2001): 89–104, esp. 94.   121 Connor, *Art and Miracles*, 40.   122 José María Salvador González, "Iconography of The Dormition of the Virgin in the 10th to 12th Centuries. An Analysis from Its Legendary Sources," *Eikón Imago* 11, no. 1 (2017): 185–230, esp. 188.   123 Thomas and Hero, eds., *Byzantine Monastic Foundation Documents*, 496.   124 Thomas and Hero, eds., *Byzantine Monastic Foundation Documents*, 787.

125 Thomas and Hero, eds., *Byzantine Monastic Foundation Documents*, 697.   126 Thomas and Hero, eds., *Byzantine Monastic Foundation Documents*, 803.   127 Thomas and Hero, eds., *Byzantine Monastic Foundation Documents*, 827.

symbolized in burial rites with the *Kolyvos* sweets: "To this perfect spiritual banquet of minds, the fleshly mother of the eternal Mind invites us. The royal table is ready, and the subject of our discourse today is enlivened and swelled by God's mysterious action. All this radiant beauty, shining beyond the power of words in the faces of the guests at the banquet, suffuses our surroundings today." (128) The body of the Theotokos' is laid on the tomb in preparation for the banquet, and everyone is suffused with the reflected light emanating from the oil lamps continuously lit in front of the *Koimesis*. Angels, spirits, monks, priests, laymen, and laywomen are invited in together on this day: "Let us simply celebrate," says Andrew, "with shining hearts and splendid rites, the memory of the holy entombment of that tabernacle where our life began. Together with this visible world, let all intelligent creatures, all in heaven and all on earth, who have gathered for the feast, honor the Queen and lead the procession that will involve our whole race." (129)

This brief foray into the sensual and liturgical enactment of the crypt at Hosios Loukas introduces the possibilities for pre-modern nighttime spatial activation. An imperial monastery well-studied in its daylight instantiations, the power and energy of the main *Katholikon* directed toward imperial and sun-centered forces also included a space for inducing authority during the night. Functioning as a central point of access during nighttime hours and for nighttime rituals, the crypt embraced not only regular monastic inhabitants but also pilgrims, local laypersons, and especially women congregating in the nighttime and early morning hours after the passing of the day's work. It was thus intentionally fashioned as an intimate space, allowing for individualized interior contemplation as well as communal joy and sorrow. Lived darkness was materially imitated and amplified by the cold stony nature of the subterranean space. Emphatic reflection of the exterior heightened the individual senses and facilitated spiritual growth. Intentionally darkened frescoes with bright overlaid swaths of paint extended into the interior, initiating an atmosphere of dense closeness and fricative surfaces, enlivening the darkness and giving power to the night.

128 Daley, trans., *On the Dormition of Mary*, 111. 129 Daley, trans., *On the Dormition of Mary*, 113.

A FASCINATION FOR THE MOON IN JAPANESE AESTHETICS AND ARCHITECTURE
Murielle Hladik

The full moon	明月や	*meigetsu ya*
Around on a pond	池をめぐりて	*ike wo megurite*
All the night through	夜もすがら	*yo mo sugara*
	(Bashō) (130)	

In Japanese culture, the contemplation of moonlight (*tsukimi* 月見) appears as a leitmotif in art, painting, architecture, literature and especially poetry. (131) Associated with shadow and night, the moon, with its dim glow, is a motif regularly celebrated by poets in the Far East. In this article, I will discuss firstly the history and genealogy of this attraction to the moon; secondly, the semantic aspects of the moon's reflexivity and reflection in a poetic and philosophical sense; thirdly, the moon as contemplated through architectural ruins or a rustic hermitage lodge. In the fourth section, the architectural device is set up to take maximum advantage of the moon's nocturnal observation—notably through the example of the very famous Katsura Villa and its "platform for contemplating the moon" (*Tsukimi dai* 月見台)—and finally, in the epilogue, the resurgence of the moon in contemporary art.

Contemplating Nature Illuminated by the Moon (tsukimi 月見)

This interest in the moon was already present in Chinese poetry. The moon is often a metaphor for the beloved, or for the distance between two loved ones, creating a "virtual triangle" in which the two lovers communicate symbolically, or at least through the poems they sometimes exchange despite separation. The moon is both near and far: though far away in space, it appears identical to all human beings; it is close to them by virtue of the link between the lunar cycles and the cycles of life or the tides. Kōzen Hiroshi wrote about the moon in Chinese poetry:

---

130 Matsuo Bashō (松尾芭蕉 1644–1694). Throughout this article we adopt the Japanese convention of putting the patronymic name before the first name. 131 See Murielle Hladik, "Lumière, éclat et dissimulation. La lune dans l'art, l'architecture et la littérature au Japon," *Revue Art Asie Sorbonne. La Nuit en Asie,* eds. Marie Laureillard and Edith Parlier-Renault, no. 4 (2021), https://124revue.hypotheses.org/6485, accessed November 30, 2022.

Although the moon is an object of changing shape, alternately waxing and waning, the reason why most moons in poetry manifest themselves in the form of a circle is that its perfect shape acts as a symbol of the 'perfect circle' of gathering people close at heart, relatives or friends. (132)

The moon, contemplated by poets, was associated with famous places in China, such as Mount Lao 嶗山, Mount Huangshan or Yellow Mountains (黄山), Mount Lu (盧山) or Dongting Lake (洞庭湖), to quote only the best known. Similarly, it was also associated in Japan with famous places (meisho 名所) such as Ōsawa Pond (大沢池) at Daikaku-ji Temple (大覚寺) in Kyōto, the Sarusawa-ike pond (猿沢池) in Nara, or the Ishiyama-dera (石山寺) located in Ōtsu in present-day Shiga Prefecture. Among these, the Ōsawa pond and its moon gazing promontory, located at the Daikaku-ji temple, with a raised walkway around the pond (*chisen kaiyūshiki-teien* 池泉回遊式庭園), is one of the most popular. The tradition of moon gazing at Ōsawa Pond dates back to at least the Heian period (794-1185) in Japan, and has given rise to many ceremonies accompanied by poetic jousting. It started in a villa that Emperor Saga (嵯峨天皇 785–842) had built for himself here, and from where the retired Emperor Go-Uda (後宇多天皇 1267–1324) later ran his cloistered government. The artificial lake (Ōsawa-ike 大沢池) is thought to be one of the oldest Heian-era ponds still in existence today, designed in reference to the model of Dongting Lake (洞庭湖) in China, famously mentioned in ancient Chinese poetry. A structure of such size, nearly 2.4 hectares, is impressive for its time: the lake was created by damming a stream that is believed to originate from the Nakoso waterfall. The vast pond lends itself to boat rides and poetic jousting during "moon gazing": *tsukimi* (月見), literally "looking at the moon" or *o-tsukimi* (お月見) or "moon gazing" *kan-getsu* (観月). The place is famous for contemplating the autumn or harvest moon: 中秋の名月 (*chūshū no meigetsu*), on the 15th day of the 8th month of the ancient lunar calendar, called Jugoya (十五夜) (Mid-Autumn Festival). Before it turned into a poetic celebration meant to admire the special beauty of the autumnal red moon, the ritual of moon gazing was principally a religious practice linked to the changing seasons and cycles of harvest and renewal.

Contemplation of the full moon was often mentioned in poems as a "seasonal description" (*kigo* 季語) associated with autumn; but the moon also appears in poetry as veiled or incomplete. The poet Yoshida Kenkō 吉田兼好 (1283?–1350?) is sensitive to the beauty of the veiled moon, partly shaded by the curtain of a rain shower or the passage of clouds, the moon in its incompleteness arouses an emotion like no other:

> The moon that appears close to dawn after we have waited for it, moves us more profoundly than the full moon shining cloudless over thousand leagues. And how incomparably lovely is the moon, almost greenish in its light, when seen through the tops of the cedars deep in the mountains, or when it hides for a moment behind clustering clouds during a sudden shower! (133)

Kenkō emphasizes process. A preference is given to the beginning or the end, rather than to a finite and unchangeable result. The beginning suggests and contains in essence, the germ of what is to come, while the end evokes what has been, but is now

---

132 Hiroshi Kōzen, "Trois aspects de la lune dans la poésie Tang: Wang Wei, Li He, Li Shangyin," *Études chinoises* 19, no. 1–2, (2000) :167, [Mélanges de sinologie offerts à Jean-Pierre Diény (II)], https://doi.org/10.3406/etchi.2000.1292, accessed November 30, 2022.   133 Urabe Kenkō, *Essays in Idleness: The Tsurezuregusa of Kenkō*, trans. Donald Keene (New York & London: Columbia University Press, 1967), [fragment 137], 118. The poet Yoshida Kenkō 吉田兼好 (1283?–1350?) is also know as Urabe Kaneyoshi (卜部兼好) or Kenkō.

gone: the "not-yet" and the "already-no-more". It is about capturing ephemeral beauty just before it fades away, for it is at the beginning and end of a cycle that beauty is found: Are we to look at cherry blossoms only in full bloom, the moon only when it is cloudless?
...
In all things, it is in the beginning and in the end *that are interesting*. (134)

Moon and its Reflexivity

The moon provides us with indirect light, a reflection of sunlight. However, long before science was able to explain this phenomenon, the moon already exercized a profound effect on humans. On this theme of "reflection", semantic associations focus on a dialectic relationship between image and reality / real and imaginary worlds / dream (*yume* 夢) and reality (*genjitsu* 現実).
Many Japanese poems and paintings evoke the reflection of the moon on water. The leitmotif of the moon and its inaccessible reflection appears, in Chinese and Japanese paintings, as a metaphor of illusion. Thus, the famous motif of the monkey plunging its paw into the water to try to catch the fragile lunar disc is found in Chinese paintings; the same theme of the *"Monkey trying to catch the moon"* (猴子撈月) is reinterpreted by Hasegawa Tōhaku (長谷川等伯, 1539–1610) at the Konchi-in Temple (金地院), located within the precincts of the Nanzen-ji (南禅寺) in Kyōto. If the image of the moon's reflection on the water is an illusion, then all images are illusions, as perhaps all "reality" is an illusion. The moon will thus be used as a metaphor for the complex relation between illusion and reality, as well as a symbol for Buddhist ideas of comprehension and, finally, illumination (*satori* 悟り).
In French, there is a semantic and phonetic proximity between "reflet" (from low-Latin, *reflexus*) and "réflexion" (from low-Latin, *reflexio*) or to reflect (c. 1300 lat. *reflectere*), with a double meaning, firstly: "to reflect back in a different direction"; secondly (c. 1672), "to reflect on oneself", "to collect oneself"; then, by extension, to think, to reflect, to seek, to concentrate, etc. Surprisingly, in Japanese, there is a semantic proximity between the verbs utsusu and utsuru: 移す (*utsusu*), to transport, to transfer and the reflexive verb 移る (*utsuru*) to transport oneself, to be transferred—映す (*utsusu*) to reflect, to reflect/ 映る (*utsuru*) to reflect, to reflect oneself (in water, in a mirror)—and 写す (*utsusu*) to copy, to reproduce / 写る (*utsuru*) to be photographed, to be projected. We can thus observe a proximity between reflection, displacement and transfer. Finally, there is a semantic proximity between *utsuroi* うつろい and *utsuwa* (器/うつわ) the receptacle, or in a concrete sense, container, vessel.

134 Kenkō, *Essays in Idleness*, 115.

Appearance and Disappearance of the Moon: Transparency of the Ruin

The figure of the moon is a recurring leitmotif in poetry, with light passing through the remains of a dilapidated architectural ruin. The interpenetration between inside and outside and transparency, which are characteristic of the figure of the ruin in the West, are echoed in the *topos* of the hermitage pavilion with its collapsed roof, where the light of the moon penetrates through the cracks. With the ruin, the absence of a roof and the disappearance of partitioning devices, the gaze penetrates inside the space just as in these scroll paintings (*emakimono* 絵巻物) seen in plunging axonometry, where the roof is erased just as if "torn off by the wind" (*fukinuki-yatai* 吹抜屋台).

The moonlight penetrating through the broken roof of the hermitage pavilion becomes a poetic *topos*. As soon as the thatched roof is no longer maintained, rain and wind penetrate the interior, eventually leading to collapse. However, precisely with the collapse or partial destruction of the roof and then of the wall sections, we move towards an assimilation of the artefact into nature. The ruin will prolong the transparency of architectural object or device and the interpenetration between inside and outside.

The leitmotif of the moonlight entering the interior of an abandoned house appears more prominent during the eighteenth century, in the brush of the master of a new genre of fiction, Ueda Akinari (上田秋成 1734–1809). His *Tales of Rain and Moon* (*Ugetsu monogatari* 雨月物語) consist of a series of nine fantastic tales, including a short story called "The House in the Reeds" (*Asagi ga yado* 浅茅が宿). In this story, the narrator, returning to the place where he had abandoned his wife nearly seven years earlier, at first believes he sees her again under the shadow of night. Under the brilliant and fantastic light of the moon, he then sees a woman of fabulous beauty who leads his senses astray. Unfortunately, the next day, in the early morning, he realizes that it was only a dream: it was a ghost or a demon that led his senses astray. The house he thought he had found intact during the night is now a ruin overgrown with vegetation, where no one lives:

> … The roof had been torn off by the wind, and he could see the waning moon lingering dimly in the sky. The house had lost its shutters. Reeds and plumed grasses grew tall through gaps in the decaying floorboards, and the morning drew dripped from them, saturating his sleeves. The walls were draped with ivy and arrowroot; the garden was buried in creepers—even though fall had not come yet, the house was a wild autumn moor. (135)

In such an abandoned place, the narrator finds only desolation. All that remains of his wife's body, who died a few years earlier, is a poem and a mound, erected by a faithful servant, before which he laments from her loss. Thus, according to the teaching of Buddhism, or according to the *mujō* (無常) term "impermanence", all things and all humans are doomed to disappear. Ueda Akinari reinterprets many classical literary sources in his short novels. The very title of the short story *Asagi ga yado* (浅茅が宿 "The Dwelling in the Reeds" / or "The House in the Thicket") is a direct reference to the famous *Tale of Genji* (*Genji monogatari* 源氏物語) (136) which has a chapter named

---

135 Akinari Ueda, *Tales of Moonlight and Rain* (雨月物語, *Ugetsu Monogatari,* 1776), trans. Anthony H. Chambers (New-York: Columbia University Press, 2008), book 2, 15–16.   136 Murasaki Shikibu, *The Tale of Genji,* trans. Edward G. Seidensticker (New-York: Alfred A. Knopf, 1977). *See* Akio Abe, Ken Akiyama and Gene Imai, *Genji monogatari* 源氏物語, in: *Nihon koten bungaku zenshû [Complete Works of Japanese Litterature]* vol. 13 (Tōkyō: Shōgakkan, 1972, 1995), (26th reprint), 337. *The Tale of Genji* is a famous medieval text, probably one of the first novel written by a woman, Murasaki Shikibu (紫式部 v. 973–1014 or 1025).

"A Ruined Villa of Tangled Gardens" (*Yomogi.u* 蓬生). Although the refined world of the Heian period disappeared many years ago, it still reappears within the quotation. Thus, in writing—where the work of *quotation* or *intertextuality*, to put it in contemporary terms, functions—different temporal layers are superimposed, different strata of writing that the erudite reader will be able to understand through layers of time.

A new layer of transposition can be seen through the beautiful eponymous film *The Tales of the Wave after the Rain Moon* (*Ugetsu monogatari* 雨月物語), directed in 1953 by Mizoguchi Kenji (溝口健二 1898–1956). Mizoguchi's film plays with ambiguities, moonlit *chiaroscuro*, where the main character has trouble distinguishing between truth and falsehood, *simulacrum* and reality. During his waking dreams, he is drawn in by a beautiful, seductive and perverse woman, who is none other than a ghost or demon (*oni* 鬼), following the same narrative framework as Ueda Akinari! Mizoguchi's shots and framing plunge us into a poetic universe where the past and the present intertwine; the depth of the night gives off a vaporous atmosphere crossed by foggy glows, sailing on troubled waters, where at times the moon still appears veiled by clouds.

Contemplation of the Moon (tsukimi 月見) and Architecture

In China we found special architectural devices for the contemplation of the moon. Many round windows and doors are dedicated to moon viewing, such as in the famous Chinese scholar's gardens in the city of Suzhou (蘇州市), located in Jiangsu province.

In Japan, the Shisendō (詩仙堂) hermitage, founded in 1641 by the intellectual and poet Ishikawa Jōzan (石川丈山 1583–1672), in the north-east of Kyōto, has a space dedicated to nocturnal moon gazing, and with its thatched roof, it is admired for its informal and rustic character. Above the building, in the high tower, named (嘯月楼 Shōgetsurō), is a small space dedicated to poetic writing, pierced by a round window for moon gazing. A description of the building in the *Nenpu Chronicles* 年譜, written shortly after the death of Ishikawa Jōzan, describes the tower for contemplating the moon, dedicated to writing poetry and filled with books and poems (137).

137   Minkai Sun 孫旻愷, *Ni.chū.kan ni okeru insei.teien no kōsei to zōei ito ni kansuru kenkyū* 日中韓における隠棲庭園の構成と造営意図に関する研究) [*Studies on the composition and intentions for the construction of the gardens of hermitage in Japan, China, and Korea*] (PhD diss., Chiba University, 2015), https://ci.nii.ac.jp/naid/500000963215, accessed November 30, 2022.

In the gardens of Jishō-ji (慈照寺, lit. "Temple of Shining Mercy"), better known as the Silver Pavilion (Ginkaku-ji 銀閣寺), the raked sea of silver sand is also famous for reflecting the light of the moon. Walking through the garden propels one into another world, the moon being associated with dreams and the afterlife. In front of the pavilion, a large expanse of dry silvery sand symbolizes the sea, in which the light of the moon can be reflected, while a truncated sand cone symbolizes Mount Fuji in miniature.

Katsura Villa
Finally, the very famous "Platform for contemplating the moon" (*Tsukimi dai* 月見台) of the imperial Palace of Katsura, the "detached palace of Katsura" (*Katsura-rikyū* 桂離宮) located in the extension of the palace, the old Shoin (*Ko-shoin* 古書院), is undoubtedly the most blatant example for the aesthetic appeal of moonlight. A specific space, a real architectural device consisting of a bamboo-covered platform beyond the engawa (縁側), is thus dedicated to the contemplation of the moon, facing the lake, and most probably intended for poetic jousting.

The very name of the Katsura Villa is associated with the Katsura (桂) tree, a redbud "with moon leaves" (Latin name: *Cercidiphyllum japonicum*) that a Chinese legend would associate with the moon. Based on an analogy between the round leaves of the tree and the shape of the satellite planet, this legend claims that a redbud (Katsura 桂) grows on the moon. Katsura (桂) is also the name of the river (桂川 Katsura-gawa) flowing adjacent to the villa, part of which was diverted and channeled to create the artificial pond and gardens.

The construction of the detached Katsura palace is associated with multiple literary references borrowed from the classics of Chinese literature, such as the anthology of Bai Juyi's poems (白居易; 772-846, in Japanese Po Chū-i); but also from the classics of Japanese literature, such as the *Tale of Genji*. This intertextuality or interweaving of multiple literary references led the architect Isozaki Arata to write:

> Katsura [can be seen] as a textual space, in which one may detect a polysemy of architecture. (138)

There is a direct reference to the concert performed under the moon, on the fictional site where the Prince Genji had built his own palace, in the chapter "The Wind in the Pines" (*Matsukaze* 松風) of the *Genji Monogatari*:

> 月のすむ川のをちなる里なれば桂の影はのどけかるらむ
>
> Far away, in the country village of Katsura, the reflection of the moon upon the water is clear and tranquil. (139)

The Katsura villa is considered one of the most accomplished and most referred-to examples of Japanese architecture. Its interpretation has been a popular subject in literary studies, and one may refer to Inoue Shōichi's essay, which literally *deconstructs* the history of its various layers and multiple reinterpretations: *The Re-invented Myth of the Katsura Villa* (*Tsukurareta Katsura rikyû shinwa* つくられた桂離宮神話 (140)). While the myth of the "rediscovery" of Katsura Villa is commonly attributed to the German architect Bruno Taut (1880–1938) who first visited the villa in 1933, other Japanese architectural historians such as Kishida Hideto (141) (岸田日出刀 1889–1966) have described Katsura Villa as early as 1929.

---

138 Arata Isozaki, *Japan-ness in Architecture,* trans. Sabu Kohso (Cambridge, Mass. / London: The MIT Press, 2006), 256. 139 Shikibu, *The Tale of Genji*, chapter 18, 328. 140 Shōichi Inoue, 井上章一, *Tsukurareta Katsura rikyû shinwa* つくられた桂離宮神話 [*The Invented Myth of Katsura Imperial Palace*] (Tōkyō: Kōdansha gakujutsu bunko, 1997), (Kōbundō, 1986). 141 Hideto Kishida, 岸田日出刀, 過去の構成 (*Kako no kōzō*) [*The Composition of the Past*] (Tōkyō: Kōseisha-shobō, 1929); Hideto Kishida, 過去の構成 (*Kako no kōzō*) [*The Composition of the Past*], (Tōkyō: Sagami-shobo, 1951) (Reprint 1938, 1951).

The German architect Bruno Taut is closely associated with this 'rediscovery' or 're-reading' of the Katsura Villa by modern architects. In his comments and notes after his first visit in 1933, and then in his sketches made on his second visit in 1934, alongside his sketch of the former palace, Ko-shoin (古書院), and the platform for the moon-viewing (Tsukimi-dai), he wrote:

Why is there no line of the house extended to the garden? Because each element—house, water, boat-landing, tree, stone, has a life of its own. It only searches for good relations, like a good society. (142)

Katsura's "platform for contemplating the moon" (Tsukimi dai 月見台) is linked to the history of Japanese media and photography, as it was photographed by the great master Ishimoto Yasuhiro (石元泰博 1921–2012). Ishimoto Yasuhiro's pictures that illuminate the 1960 book written by Tange and Gropius, *Katsura: Tradition and Creation in Japanese Architecture* (143) not only present the ancient traditional shoin-zukuri (書院造り) architecture as an example of early minimalism, but also give rise to the myth that modernism, with its values of lightness and modularity, was embedded in Japanese culture long before its reinvention in the West.

Finally, the Gepparō Tea Pavilion (月波楼), the *sukiya-zukuri* style "Wave and Moon Tower Pavilion" (数寄屋造り), is dedicated to the contemplation of the moon and its inimitable reflection in the water... Yet, unfortunately for us, any common man or woman, would never be allowed to stay for a night tour of the Katsura Villa! A film, produced by NHK, was shot at night (桂離宮 知られざる月の館 [Katsura-rikyū—*The Unknown Moon Villa*], (144) in 2010) thanks to an exceptional permission from the office in charge of Japan's imperial buildings. This film offers fantastic night views of the Katsura Villa, lit only by the light of the moon. Finally, a graphic simulation, made especially for this film, with a view from the "moon-viewing platform" perfectly illustrates how the entire villa was designed on an axis with the moon, in order to admire it at all hours of the night, from rise to set, as well as its symmetrical reflection on the surface of the pond. The entire orientation of the villa, with its diagonal offset, is based on a south-east axis offset by 19 degrees, in order to facilitate contemplation of the moon during the autumnal equinox. (145) Other details may catch one's attention, such as the mica powder that is used in the printing of Japanese *fusuma* papers (襖 sliding walls, stretched with paper) decorated with armorial patterns of paulownia flowers (*kirimon no karakami* 桐紋の唐紙), a motif reserved for the imperial family; this powder gives a slight silvery sheen intended to delicately reflect the light of the moon or candlelight. The moon character (*tsuki* 月), the emblem of the Katsura Villa, also appears in stylized form on the bronze handles, on the chased wooden parts above the sliding panels (*ranma* 欄間). Finally, the moon circle motif still appears on the famous asymmetrical shelf known as the "Katsura shelf" (*Katsura dana* 桂棚) of the new palace (*shin-shoin* 新書院).

142 "Gedanken nach dem Besuch in Katsura," in *Bruno Taut, Natur und Fantasie*, note 2, 314. Quoted by Manfred Speidel, "Japanese Traditional Architecture in the Face of Its Modernisation: Bruno Taut in Japan", 106.   143 Walter Gropius, Kenzo Tange and Yasuhiro Ishimoto [Photography], *Katsura: Tradition and Creation in Japanese Architecture* (New Haven: Yale University Press, Tōkyō: Zokeisha Publications, 1960); Yashuhiro Ishimoto, 石元泰博, *Katsura-rikyū* 桂離宮, [*The detached Palace of Katsura*] (Tōkyō: ed. Rikuyosha, 2010).   144 NHK 桂離宮 知られざる月の館 [" *Katsura-rikyū*—The Unknown Moon Villa "] (2010), NHK Production.   145 Osamu Mori 森蘊, *Katsura rikyū no kenkyū* 桂離宮の研究 [*Studies on the Katsura Villa*] (Tōkyō: Tōto Bunka Shuppan, 1955). There, we would find a radical difference where the entire orientation of the buildings would be set on the axis of the falling moonlight, contrary to the West, where churches and cathedrals—as well as their stained glass rose windows—would be oriented according to the sunlight.

Epilogue—Light and Shadow / Contemporary Art

In 1933, Tanizaki Jun.ichirō (谷崎潤一郎 1886–1965), made us aware of the beauty of darkness and shadows in his masterful essay *In Praise of Shadows* (*In.ei raisan* 陰翳礼讃). All of the spatial and architectural devices of the traditional Japanese house, with its sliding panels covered with semi-transparent paper (*shoji* 障子), its exclusive openings towards the garden, or its wooden shutters (*amado* 雨戸), would highlight the shade and the delicate gradation of shades and greys. The Japanese house, furnished with successive skins and envelopes, would be like a garment on a body, offering different degrees of light and shadow with the help of various screens. Tanizaki describes his aesthetic experiences, including the beauty of lacquer, which can be appreciated only in weak light:

> Lacquerware decorated in gold is not something to be seen in a brilliant light, to be taken in at a single glance, it should be left in the dark, a part here and a part there picked up by a faint light. Its florid patterns recede into the darkness, conjuring in their stead an inexpressive aura of depth and mystery, of overtones but partly suggested. … A moment of mystery, it might almost be called a moment of trance. (146)

Lacquer is applied by Japanese craftsmen in successive layers, creating a profound effect of depth. For Tanizaki, only indirect light, subdued by paper lanterns, or even moonlight and darkness have an aesthetic quality that direct sunlight would never be able to provide.

During the Nuit Blanche in Kyōto in 2014, I had the pleasure to collaborate, as curator in thirty different places, temples and traditional houses, deeply anchored inside the city of Kyōto. The Kyōto Nuit Blanche provided an opportunity for encounters between French and Japanese contemporary artists, designers, craftspeople and to demonstrate high-level Japanese know-how. During the exhibition "*Shadow of Time*" (時間の影 *jikan no kage*) curated for the Kodōkan temple in Kyōto, we exhibited the works made by the Japanese artist Ōfune Makoto (大船真言) as well as works by the French artists Anne and Patrick Poirier. During this very special night, a Noh theater performance in situ, at the Kōdōkan temple, illuminated only by candlelight, was an occasion for the contemplation of the beautiful moonlit scene.

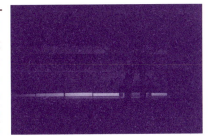
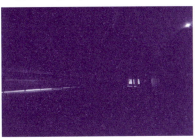

Furthermore, during the exhibition "*Materiality-Immateriality*" for the kyoto ddd gallery (October 2016), I invited the designer Nosigner, who presented a 3D moon printed in 2011. This moon, a symbol of hope and rebirth, commemorates the huge full moon that shone in the sky just after the terrible events on 11 March 2011, when a tsunami, an earthquake and nuclear accident in Fukushima devastated eastern Japan). Nosigner's work evokes images of the craters of the moon, but also the idea of renewal and hope for reconstruction. Furthermore, during the exhibition "*On the Art of Building a Teahouse*" (147) at the

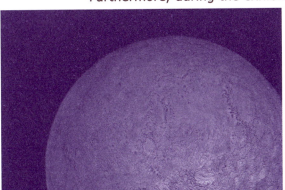

146   Jun.ichirō Tanizaki, *In Praise of Shadows*, trans. Thomas J. Harper and Edward G. Seidensticker (Sedgwick, Maine: Leete's Island Books, 1977), 14–15.   147   Murielle Hladik & Axel Sowa, *On the Art of Building a Teahouse—Excursion into Japanese Aesthetics / Von der Kunst ein Teehaus zu bauen—Exkursionen in die japanische Ästhetik* [Preface by Eva Kraus] (Nuremberg: Neues Museum, Verlag für Moderne Kunst, 2017), [Exhibition catalog].

Neues Museum in Nuremberg, curated together with Axel Sowa, Nosigner's moon was revealed inside an experimental pavilion built by the Atelier Bow-Wow (Kaijima Momoyo & Tsukamoto Yoshihatsu). The prototype, an assembly of prefabricated elements made from Japanese cypress wood (*hinoki* 檜), is fully demountable and would be readily made available for refugees after destructive events such as earthquakes, tsunamis, typhoons, etc. For architects and designers, too, the moon, both one and many, is a symbol of constant renewal.

Conclusion: Real and Unreal

Very different from our western appreciation for the sun's luminosity, the contemplation of the moon requires special knowledge and a more contemplative life. Thus, the attraction for the light of the moon is a constant throughout Japanese history, and runs through painting, poetry, architecture, design and even contemporary art. The moon has a poetic and metaphorical dimension that touches all beings—the "ten thousand beings (万象 *banshō*)" as in the philosophical terminology of the Zen Buddhist Monk Dōgen (道元 1200–1253):

心月孤円	The full moon uniting with the heart /
光吞万象	by its light all beings are illuminated
光非照境	Light does not illuminate things / and things do not exist by themselves
境亦非存	When light and things disappear, then what happens? (148)

Dōgen employs the image of the moon and its reflection on the water, as found in the Indian, Chinese and Japanese classics, but beneath Dōgen's brush, the moon (*tsuki* 都機 / 月), appears primarily as a metaphor for "emptiness" (Sanskrit Śūnyatā, Jap. kū 空). The poetic, philosophical and aesthetic appeal of the moon is so important for the Eastern mindset that a real architectural device has been dedicated to its contemplation. Sometimes these were round windows in the gardens or within hermitage retreats of China or Japan, which allow men or women to contemplate the lunar satellite while drinking or writing poems. Katsura's device, a very simple bamboo platform facing a pond, is perhaps the most fascinating because of its simplicity and horizontality. The platform is a surface on which light is reflected, as is the lake. The person, a spectator standing there, is only the 'receptacle', the one who receives the light, the one who subjectively composes a new poem in the continuity of those more ancient poems that have already been written several centuries ago.

The moon, illuminated by the sun, gives off itself only a reflection, an indirect light. If from a scientific point of view, it has lost its distant and inaccessible dimension — we can say that we have, with Neil Armstrong, "walked on the moon"—, it continues to inspire legends and to arouse contemplation and fascination.

---

148 Composed by Panshan Baoji (盤山宝積 720-814), a Chinese Ch'an Master, quoted by Dōgen in the 23rd fascicle "the Moon" (*Tsuki* 都機) of the *Shōbōgenzō* (正法眼蔵). See Orimo, Yoko, *Le Shōbōgenzō de maître Dōgen. La vraie Loi, Trésor de l'Œil* 正法眼蔵, *Un guide de lecture de l'œuvre majeure du bouddhisme Zen et de la philosophie japonaise* (Vannes: Sully, 2003, 2014).

CHASING DARKNESS
Night and the Performance of Metaphor in Seventeenth-Century Rome
Maarten Delbeke

Introduction: The Night of Error

On the first Sunday of Advent, 1617, the Italian community in London was treated to a sermon by an exceptional preacher. Marcantonio de Dominis had been a Jesuit and a bishop before he came to England and converted to Anglicanism. [149] Some years after he delivered the sermon, he would return to the Catholic fold and be condemned for heresy. On this occasion, however, De Dominis was still eager to weigh his newly found faith against the old. For the sermon, De Dominis chose his theme from the *lectio epistulae* for the first Sunday of Advent of the Roman Missal, verse 13 of Paul's Letter to the Romans: "Nox Praecessit, dies autem appropinquavit"; "The night is almost over, the day is almost there", highly appropriate as a forecast of the birth of Christ, the arrival of a new day, in the deep of Winter.

De Dominis builds his sermon on the proposition that the verse refers to three kinds of night: the nights of ignorance, sin, and negligence. [150] To these three, De Dominis adds a fourth: error. He proceeds by explaining in detail the nature of each of these nights, and how they can be overcome. Ignorance is a lack of knowledge of Divine things, such as was the condition of Jews and Gentiles. De Dominis asks: "what else is the night but the absence of sun?" [151] The second night is that if the abundance of sin in which both Jews and Gentiles languished, and

[149] "De Dominis Marcantonio," Dizionario Biografico Treccani, https://www.treccani.it/enciclopedia/marcantonio-de-dominis_(Dizionario-Biografico), accessed February 21, 2022. [150] Marc' Antonio De Dominis, *Predica: Fatta La prima Domenica dell'Auuento quest'anno 1617* (London: Billius, 1617), 14. [151] De Dominis, *Predica, 27.*

which De Dominis detects in his own days again in the customs of the Roman court of the papacy: "o horrible night, o palpable shadows, o intolerable blindness!" (152) The third night is that of negligence and numbness, that is the neglect of faith when it is already available. (153) By far the most attention is lavished on the fourth night, that of error; "a night all the more dangerous, since deplorables think that only they enjoy the Light, and want that all the others that not adhere to them are in shadows." (154) This is of course the night of the fallacies and delusions of the Roman Catholic church and encompasses four doctrinal errors, mainly concerned with the supremacy of the pope. It is a night of false light.

The bulk of De Dominicis' sermon is devoted to explaining how these four types of night can be overcome, and day is reached. As such, it presents night as deeply undesirable, both a negative and a temporary condition that is thus available as a metaphor for a state of error and confusion. Yet in its insistence on the persistence of darkness, De Dominicis' sermon treats this negative not just as something residual. It is a force, for evil for sure, but an agent nonetheless which should be counteracted. Moreover, the state of night assumes various guises, from the absence of light, the presence of darkness, a condition of blindness to finally even the appearance of light itself; a false light, so De Dominicis states, is worse than the deepest darkness. The absence of true light reveals an unsettling presence.

152 De Dominis, *Predica*, 25.   153 De Dominis, *Predica*, 28.   154 De Dominis, *Predica*, 30.

Chasing Darkness — Maarten Delbeke

In the natural world, the opposites of night and day are locked into an endless cycle, where one precludes the presence of the other. This dynamic turns the opposition of night and day into an at once accessible and powerful metaphor. Envisioning how night imposes its presence when light disappears, and how this presence is challenged by the emergence of light, allows us to associate a precise set of binary values to each part of the cycle. In an early modern Christian context, the values of light are identified with the role of Christ as the redeemer of humanity, expressed in the identification of Christ with the sun, and of light with truth. (155) The self-evidence of this metaphor makes it available for explanation and elaboration.

At the same time, that same self-evident quality opens up an enormous potential for manipulation. What does it mean when night and day co-exist, or one irrupts into the other, or indeed day turns out to be night? What does it mean when, as in De Dominicis' sermon, light may be present but remains unseen, or true dawn is usurped by a false one? Such disruption is by definition the result of artifice, and a potential index of the supernatural or otherwordly, for good or for bad. This artifice, in turn, signals the investment of considerable energy in the transformation of a given situation, be it a particular setting or the world as a whole, and betrays an intention: to mislead, shock, convince or, in the religious and cultural context that concerns us here, convert.

155 Fabio Barry, "Lux and Lumen: The Symbolism of Real and Represented Light in the Baroque Dome," *Kritische Berichte* 4 (17 January 2022): 22–37.

This essay explores some examples of how metaphors of night and day are activated during the 17th century. After discussing an example of how the cyclical relation between night and day is given metaphorical meaning, and how these meanings serve to convey specific messages, I will illustrate how the manipulation of day and night is used to perform these ideas. By turning day into night and vice versa, attention is drawn to their inherent metaphoricity up to the point that they are literally made present. Key to this performance is the apparent artificiality of the manipulation, and the exceptional effort that makes it possible, aspects which underscore the importance of the messages that are being performed. And precisely because of its declared artificiality, the manipulation of night and day acquires one final layer of meaning; it performs the performance of metaphor itself. The opposition of night and day is a metaphor for evil and good, error and truth, Christ and Satan, but it also describes the very anatomy of metaphor: with a metaphor, insight emerges when the veil of an initially obscure image is lifted and becomes a source of illumination, just like light emerging from darkness, or when true light supersedes false splendour, like the emergence of truth from confusion. What this series of examples suggests, then, is a persistent and ambiguous presence of 'night' in 17th-century forms of expression, both as a force to be opposed, and an element inherent to the human condition of communication and understanding.

Night as an Efficient Metaphor

The sermon of De Dominis activates the metaphorical potential of the night by holding out the hope that light will emerge in the midst of Winter, right when darkness is at its deepest and longest. Some decades after he delivered his sermon, another ex-Jesuit used the same metaphor to explain how a preacher should use the Advent to illustrate that "God chose to have the Savior born right when human malice was at its most extreme." (156) The author in question is Emanuele Tesauro, who compiled an extensive treatise on metaphorical language, the *Cannocchiale aristotelico*, first published in 1654 and then, in an expanded version, in 1670. As part of the treatise, Tesauro explains how the preacher should use metaphors to make his sermons more effective. In this particular case, the preacher can associate the depth of human depravity with the circumstances of the birth of Christ: "midnight at the Winter solstice, when the nocturnal shadow has joined its maximum length, and the sun begins to turn towards us, to lengthen the days, and shorten the night." This circumstance establishes a metaphor in which "shadow stands for sin, the sun for the messiah, and daylight for grace." The preacher can then formulate his "witty argument": "that the sun of grace should be born when human malice was at its most extreme."

156 Emanuele Tesauro, *Il cannocchiale aristotelico: o sia idea dell'arguta et ingeniosa elocutione che serve à tutta l'arte oratoria, lapidaria, et simbolica esaminata co' principij del divino Aristotele* (Savigliano (Cuneo): Editrice artistica piemontese, 2000).

What is interesting about Tesauro's metaphor is less the comparison at its heart than the various strategies he proposes to visualize it. He advises the preacher to stage a conversation between the three seasons other than winter venting their jealousy at not being selected to host the divine birth. Then he recommends inserting a short astronomical discourse into the sermon, and having the audience marvel at the divine decision to have the sun travel on an elliptical rather than a circular course around the earth (sic) so that seasons change and nights and days shorten and lengthen: "Such story can be adorned so lively and represented with such expression, that the uneducated understand it, and the educated enjoy it." Finally, Tesauro invites the preacher to drive home the point, by recalling that there is no natural phenomenon that is not the "figure" of some supranatural mystery. So if "light and shadow grow and diminish", and seasons change, and Christ is born at the point of deepest darkness, right when the sun is about to return to us, it must signify that "this heavenly sun, is returning to us, to chase with the rays of grace the shadows of sin."

What Tesauro adds to the previous brief discussion of De Dominicis' sermon is how the metaphor of night and day allows for a process of visualization, and how elements of this visualization make the metaphor effective. Tesauro emphasizes that the opposites of night and day stand in a cyclical relationship and that therefore the emergence of light against darkness can be predicted. The deepest dark sits at the opposite of the brightest day. As a fixed natural phenomenon, this cycle appeals to various spheres of knowledge and experience: from the intuitive, basic awareness of the daily cycle and the course of the seasons, to an expert understanding of the astronomical principles underlying it, and an awareness of its global dimension; dayrise is the local manifestation of a universal order. This gives rise to an almost self-evident association of the natural with the supra-natural: the natural world and its laws point to a higher, supranatural sphere, of which it is the image. As a consequence, the metaphorical charge of night and day is a fact; not a construct that needs to be proven, but a layer of reality that needs to be revealed, a truth that can be illustrated.

Night as the Image of Figural Expression

As an almost naturalized metaphor, the alternation of night and day can be understood as an image of metaphorical language itself: the day emerges from what was initially covered and obscured by night, just as a metaphor first veils an idea with an image only to allow it to shine forth more powerfully. In baroque theories of literature, it was commonplace to consider figurative language as a form of light, luster, or sheen. (157) With this understanding came the admonishment to apply such ornament in ways suitable to the subject matter. Metaphors have the capacity

157 Jon R. Snyder, *L'estetica Del Barocco*, Lessico Dell'estetica 17 (Bologna: Il Mulino, 2005).

to enlighten and please the reader by evoking powerful images, but they can also obscure the author's meaning by drawing attention away from the message in hand or providing a false light of misunderstanding. Exactly this balance opens the door to a deliberate play with obscurity. The mid-seventeenth century saw a proliferation of theories of metaphor—often developed by means of examples rather than conceptualization—which combined the long tradition of hermeticism with Aristotelian poetics in order to gauge the value of obscurity in communication. (158) In the late 17th century the French Jesuit Claude-François Ménestrier provided a synthesis of such theories and examples in his *La philosophie des images énigmatiques* (1694). It is part of what he called a "philosophie des images": a theory of how images work, which extends from language over emblems to dance, tournaments, funerals, … This philosophy contends that everything (word, image, gesture, movement, object, … both artificial and natural) is an image and that it therefore bestows significance. As such, Ménestrier's philosophy further expands and generalizes Tesauro's conception of metaphor, to which it was deeply indebted.

Within this range of images, "images énigmatiques" push the potential inherent obscurity of metaphorical language to its limit. An enigmatic image is "an ingenious mystery that claims to cover with veils a different meaning than the one, which these words and figures present naturally." Ménestrier sees obscure expression as a stylistic means with many uses; it can involve the fabrication of an ingenious expression which produces aesthetic pleasure or be a

158 Florence Vuilleumier, *La Raison Des Figures Symboliques à La Renaissance et à l'âge Classique: Études Sur Les Fondements Philosophiques, Théologiques et Rhétoriques de l'image*, Travaux d'humanisme et Renaissance, no. 340 (Genève: Droz, 2000).

delightful game that appeals to curiosity and ingenuity, as in a riddle. But the enigma can also serve as a first line of defense against the profane and ignorant by protecting and enhancing the higher truth it encapsulates.

The model that *La philosophie des images énigmatiques* proposed for all enigmas is biblical mystery:

It is religion that has consecrated the enigma by the obscurity of its mysteries, which are above the penetration of the human spirit. God, as the prophet says, hides in the shadows to instil respect in man, and his adorable shadows are to him like some kind of Temple where he resides in his immensity. "And [God] made darkness his covert, his tabernacle round about him: dark waters in the clouds of the air", This obscurity is not in him, it is above him, that is to say, in the weakness of our minds. It is a veil that he puts between him and us, similar to that luminous cloud that blinded the disciples on Tabor at the Mystery of the Transfiguration, and on the Mount of Olives when the Lord ascended to Heaven. This is how all the obscurities of our religion are veils similar to those of the Temple of Jerusalem, which covered the sanctuary to maintain respect amongst the people. Our whole religion is therefore enigmatic. The mystery of the Trinity, the Incarnation of the Divine Word, the Eucharist, the Justification, and Predestination, are enigmas, of which we will only discover the true meaning thanks to the lights of glory. It is this great day that should instruct us perfectly in the realm of light. All our knowledge in this life is nothing but obscure nights and enigmas that are difficult to develop. (159)

159 Maarten Delbeke, "La philosophie des images énigmatiques: a Philosophy of Images at the Crossroads Between Poetics and Controversy," in *Images d'action*, ed. Annette Kappeler, Jan Lazardzig and Nicola Gess (Paderborn: Wilhelm Fink, 2018), 231–241.   160 Delbeke, "La philosophie des images énigmatiques," 231–241.

As I have argued elsewhere, there is an inherent ambiguity in Ménestrier's insistence on the religious origins of all enigmas, as it risks elevating mere metaphorical games to the level of religious revelation and tainting revelation with the ambiguity of play. (160) Still, the passage quoted here makes clear that obscurity, shadow and night are an inherent part of the human condition. Humanity is condemned to an imperfect knowledge of higher things, as these are veiled or covered. The enigma confirms the circumstances of communication enunciated in Paul's first letter to the Corinthians "videmus per speculum in aenigmate" ("We now see as through a mirror darkly") (1 Cor. 13, 12). Conversely, pure and true light is not of this earth, but supranatural. Only in heaven "we will [...] discover the true meaning." This implies that humanity's earthly condition is characterized by a permanent process of negotiation. Manifestations of the divine in this world are like irruptions of light into darkness, while the earthly sites of the divine are covered and obscured in order to maintain respect and awe, as with the veil in the Temple. The enigma is the linguistic equivalent of this negotiation, and this equivalence suggests a fundamental analogy between the basic structure of the enigma and the relation of obscurity to light. The 'image' is a form of obfuscation that stands ultimately in the service of illumination and truth.

Ménestrier's theory of the enigma emphasizes the artifice integral to both obscurity and light. These are not just natural phenomena with an almost inherent metaphorical charge, but the actual manifestation of metaphoricity in the natural world. If the origin of this metaphoricity is divine, it provides a model for the human production of images and metaphors as well. As such, night and day do not just allow to visualize certain concepts and ideas, but almost embody how revelation works in opposition to the darkness that is inherent in our human condition. As much as night carries negative metaphorical connotations, on this second level, it acquires a positive value, as a means of engagement with truth intrinsic to human understanding. This ambiguity of night—as a signifier of sin and error, and a veil that ultimately facilitates insight and faith—is exactly what Ménestrier tries to balance in his *Philosophie des images énigmatiques*, in order to make darkness productive in human communication as a form of artifice.

Artificial night as the scene for revelation

It is also this ambivalence that lends a particularly performative aspect to the use of night and shadow in various media, be they sermons like the one pronounced by De Dominicis or suggested by Tesauro, or the enigmas discussed by Ménestrier. Insight is obtained when the metaphor is performed, in speech, writing, images or scenography. The manipulation of night and day enacts the manifestation of truth. Perhaps the most well-known 17th-century Catholic examples of such performance are the installations built for the so-called *quarant'hore* (40-hour) adoration of the sacrament. Adopting a devotional practice that developed in the mid-16th-century in Milan, it was instated in Rome in 1592 by Pope Clement VIII (r. 1592–1605) as the perpetual adoration of the sacrament, in a cycle that commenced in the Cappella Paolina in the Vatican on the first Sunday of Advent (November 30, 1592), and then carried over to a chain of churches in Rome. (161)

The devotion called for an installation where the Eucharist is set up on a darkened altar underneath a veil, flanked by candles. Clement VIII specified that the installation should remain sober, with no excess of lights and other scenographic means. Yet from the first decades of the 17th century onwards the installations for the *quarant'hore* became ever more spectacular, as can be witnessed from printed representations that emerged from the 1630s. There is an interesting verbal description available of a scenography in the Oratory of St Francis Xaverius and the Virgin Mary, where from 1620 onwards a *quarant'hore* installation was built, not for Advent, but the week of Carnival, as a competing spectacle:

It has a beautiful façade with a portico that is ample, but closed, and vaulted; and under the pavement one descends in another, subterranean one, where the arena opens for more remote and secret penitence to those who desire salvation. Here at the start of the profanity of Bacchanals thanks to a sacred installation (*apparato*) the days from which sanctity has been banished are being sanctified, as [the oratory] opens into a luminous theater, where

161 Mark S. Weil, "The Devotion of the Forty Hours and Roman Baroque Illusions," *Journal of the Warburg and Courtauld Institutes* 37 (1974): 218–248, https://doi.org/10.2307/750841, accessed November 8, 2023.

amongst an array of angels the divinity is shown, which hides under the most candid veils of transubstantiated substances. There Rome … learned the unknown mastery of the reflection of hidden lights when ingenious art … invented ways so that sunlight can be seen to the shame of this most splendid planet, and with more advantage, even in the darkest bosom of the blindest night. Because the artificial light is placed behind dense matter that hides its source, and because the light is opposed to some colourful drawing, behind it one sees illuminated without knowing from which source this light descends, with marvelous artifice that which is in the air the splendor of the sun, its rays and the succession of the light. And so one enjoys the most graceful perspectives, where one sees hills, valleys, woods, forests, cities, seas, which seem to be very far away due to the variety of the lights, and the eye is often deceived by the enticing object, which it reckons to be natural, while it is part of art. (162)

As the description suggests, the cycle of night and day used by De Domenicis and Tesauro to illustrate the triumph of Christ over sin is here at once recreated, condensed and literally imagined through artifice. This artifice concerns both night and day. First, the visitor is induced into artificial darkness, "the darkest bosom of night", created to celebrate an equally artificial day. Its artificiality is signalled by the invisible origin of the light. If outside we can see the sun, here illumination is provided by a hidden source. And in contrast to the real world of sin outside, the scene revealed here is one of perfect harmony. At its center sits a second source of light, the sacrament, hidden under its own cover.

162 Maarten Delbeke, "An Unknown Description of Baroque Rome: Michelangelo Lualdi's Galleria Sacra Architettata Dalla Pietà Romana Dall'anno 1610 Sino al 1645," *Bulletin de l'Institut Historique Belge de Rome* 74 (2004): 61–271.

The description allows us to read this *quarant'hore* as a spatial and visual manifestation of Ménestrier's enigma: the light of revelation lifts the veil of the darkness which had first enveloped the visitor. The apparent artificiality of this process draws attention to its mechanics, which both suggest the presence of their creator and the requirement of active participation. The bodily movement of entering the underground oratory prefigures the mental and psychological movement of insight and conversion. In that sense, night remains present in the discovery of day; it tinges the illusion and reminds the visitor of the imperfect world outside.

Crucial to this experience of revelation is its extraction from the natural cycle of night and day; it becomes possible to experience night at noon, and day in the deepest night. The *quarant'hore* interrupts the natural cycle for the 40 hours that Christ's body remained in its tomb, between the crucifixion and the resurrection, to create a scene that is suspended in time. This suspension hints at a struggle between night and day on the altogether different, eschatological temporal scale than its natural counterpart. The seemingly endless artificial day experienced in the scenography prefigures the final triumph of light. At the same time, it remains out of reach, as it disappears as soon as the visitor leaves the theater.

The same mechanism is at work in the sumptuous ephemeral installations set up on the occasion of funerals or *esequie*. When prominent citizens died, they were celebrated by means of catafalques erected in the churches of their nation or religious order. This, too, involved an elaborate scenography, where the darkened surroundings of the church interior were contrasted with insignia, medals and figures, mostly skeletons that lit up in the darkness, thanks to candles and torches. A fine example can be gleaned from the richly illustrated *relazione* of the decoration of the Santi Giovanni Evangelista e Petronio church in Rome on April 9, 1644, for the *esequie* of Ludovico Fachinetti, a prominent member of the local Bolognese community. (163) In the crossing of the church stood a monumental catafalque, framed by an interior built of dark cloth, which carried an elaborate decorative program celebrating the life and virtues of the deceased.

If the *quarant'hore* established a temporary uninterrupted day, the *esequie* enveloped the visitor in night. Night is, of course, a funerary symbol. In his *Mondo Simbolico*, a compendium of 'imprese' or images for the benefit of preachers or designers of exactly this kind of installation, Filippo Picinelli proposes 'obscure night' as the image for death, combined with the motto "VERTETUR IN DIEM" ("it will turn into day"), as a metaphor for the expected resurrection. "It serves to mean that for all the horrors of the calamities undergone now, a clear day of happy satisfaction will succeed." (164) Again this eschatological dimension is made present by immersing an astonished crowd in an environment that escapes the natural cycle of night and day. The *relazione* of the Fachinetti catafalque hints at this irruption by pointing out how the church was flooded with visitors: "when the lights were lit, the

163 Sebastiano Rolandi, "Funerale celebrato nella Chiesa de' Bolognesi in Roma dall'Illustrissimo Senato di Bologna al Signor Marchese Lodovico Fachenetti ambasciatore residente per quella città appresso nostro signore Urbano VIII. A ix. aprile MDCXLIV," in *La festa barocca (Corpus delle feste a Roma)*, ed. Maurizio Fagiolo dell'Arco and Marcello Fagiolo (Roma: Edizioni De Luca, 1997), 321–325. 164 Filippo Picinelli, *Mondo simbolico formato d'imprese scelte, spiegate, ed' illustrate con sentenze, ed eruditioni, sacre, e profane* (In Milano: nella Stampa di Francesco Vigone, 1669), https://doi.org/10.3931/e-rara-48697 accessed November 8, 2023.

door was kept open continuously, and immediately the church filled up with people. The most eminent cardinals, and most illustrious prelates, who intervened in this mournful spectacle, entered through the neighboring house, where a very convenient opening was made so they could escape the crowd, which continued to increase." (165) The catafalque allows for a communal experience of night outside of regular time, reminding each visitor of their own temporary mortal condition.

Coda: Black Marble

The pavement of the Cornaro chapel in Sta Maria della Vittoria in Rome frames two black marble roundels. In each of them a supplicating skeleton appears, looking upwards. These representations of the souls in purgatory, awaiting their final judgment, sit at the bottom of an ensemble that thematizes the irruption of divine light in the earthly realm, by means of scenographic devices similar to those employed in the ephemeral installations mentioned earlier. But now the scenography is permanent. The chapel is an elaborate device to give material expression to the workings of divine light. (166) The two manholes juxtapose to the light from above a materialized night, suggesting the illusion of peering into the eternal night of purgatory that seemingly extends itself underneath the church. The cycle of day and night is frozen in marble, locked in an eternal performance of the drama of human salvation.

165 Sebastiano Rolandi, *Funerale celebrato nella chiesa de'Bolognesi in Roma ... al Signor Marchese Lodovico Fachenetti ...* (Roma: Ludovico Grignani, 1644), 35.   166 Fabio Barry, "Im/Material Bernini," in *Material Bernini*, ed. Evonne Levy and Carolina Mangone (London: Routledge, 2016), 39–69.

Unless noted otherwise, translations are the author's.

URBAN SLAVERY AT THE THRESHOLD OF NIGHT
The Architecture of Nightfall in Nineteenth-Century Rio de Janeiro, Brazil
Amy Chazkel

167 Arquivo Nacional (Rio de Janeiro, Brazil), Códice 327–10 (Polícia da Corte, OE, Vols 1–2, CODES). 168 Soraya Almeida and Rubem Porto Junior, "Cantarias e pedreiras históricas do Rio de Janeiro: instrumentos potenciais de divulgação das Ciências Geológicas," *Terrae Didatica 8*, no. 1, (Rio de Janeiro: Universidade Estadual de Campinas, 2012), https://www.ige.unicamp.br/terraedidatica/v8-1/pdf81/s1.pdf, accessed November 8, 2023.

Brazil became independent in 1822, freed from Portuguese colonial control and governed by a constitutional monarchy where all were equal before the law. As was the case in other nations that were constituted under a national charter based on liberal Enlightenment principles but failed to abolish slavery, Brazilian governing officials and slave owners struggled with how to handle the ubiquitous presence of enslaved people while maintaining the rule of law. The post-independence Constitution of 1824 explicitly upheld masters' property rights and provided no explicit rules for dealing with slaves. The governance of slavery was assigned to proprietary private jurisdiction, municipal ordinances, and criminal law. An extraordinarily rich body of scholarship reconstructs the social history of slavery in nineteenth-century Brazil under these conditions that also defined much of the Atlantic world, showing that slavery was not a contradiction to urbanism, industrialization, and the growth and spread of capitalism but rather was an integral part of these processes. And nowhere was the coexistence of nineteenth-century modernity and slavery more striking than in Brazil's capital city, Rio de Janeiro, which had an enslaved population so large that it made up nearly half of Rio's inhabitants in the first decades after independence.

In 1824 the commander of the Royal Guard of the Police, an early military police corps in Rio de Janeiro, alerted a judge to some serious concerns that arose when his soldiers had reported to him. "In a stable at the Pedreira de Conceição," a rock quarry just outside the city center, he writes, "there is a large number of runaway slaves who, with the consent of the person in charge, sleep there every night. With that prudence with which Your Excellency always carries out your service, [you shall] send a police escort to apprehend as many slaves as you can find there, and also arrest whoever is in charge of the stable." (167) The Pedreira da Conceição that served as a clandestine nighttime refuge for "many runaway slaves" was also intimately connected with the growth of the city. Granite extracted from this quarry became the stones that paved the streets, the city's public fountains, and its buildings; the roads to and from it in the eighteenth century became the first urban streets. Stones from here were used in the eighteenth century to construct the church, São Francisco de Paula, whose towerheld one of the city's two bells whose sound demarcated the beginning of night. (168) Fugitives from slavery might have found a way to blend into the busy city during the day. At night, though, a curfew directed officially at enslaved people but in practice at anyone of African descent subjected those in the streets after the evening bells to police stops, flogging, or arrest. This document is typical of the fragmentary information that survived to tell the story of the daily experience of the physical world that the city's enslaved inhabited. Historical research into the nocturnal experiences of the enslaved, by necessity, depends on the accumulation of anecdotes preserved in documents occasioned by the moments their private lives became public: curious asides noted by foreign travelers about the strange places where barefoot and "slightly clad" slaves were found taking their rest, newspaper announcements seeking their return when they ran away, and indignant orders by police to arrest them. (169) Today we are allowed these rare glimpses of enslaved workers trying to seize moments of respite or evade captivity altogether because they spent the night out of doors. Most of Rio's enslaved residents in the decades after independence took their rest in spaces that were, by design, outside the reach of the prying eyes of travel writers and patrolling police. Legally prohibited from living independently from their masters or overseers or from walking around the streets after the evening curfew bells, slaves' routine experiences of the city at night rarely found their way into the archive. This essay on nineteenth-century Rio only tentatively and speculatively enters the domestic realm; instead, it lingers in the doorway and reflects on the thresholds between house and street, private and public life, day and night, and, ultimately, architectural and socio-legal history.

Acknowledging life after dark as part of the history of built space means going beyond considering the play of light on and in buildings; it calls upon us to acknowledge the social experience of daily temporality. In modernizing cities everywhere in the nineteenth century, local governments restricted people's movement in public space during certain hours. These restrictions were only roughly bounded by sunset and sunrise; they invented the night as a socio-legal phenomenon and not just an astronomical one and were only loosely connected with the human inability to see in the dark and the need to sleep. (170) Appreciating the historical importance of daily temporality involves, first, understanding the hidden, informal, and dissident uses of space, like the granite quarry that became an encampment for fugitives from slavery, or how

169 Several foreign travelers who published accounts of their time in Brazil comment on the "slightly clad" slaves. See, for example, the abolitionist text by Thomas Fowell Buxton, *The Slave Trade and its Remedy* (London: John Murray, 1839), 91.

170 I develop this argument in "The Invention of Night: Visibility and Violence after Dark in Rio de Janeiro," in Gema Santamaría and David Carey, eds., *The Publics and Politics of Violence in Latin America* (Norman, OK: University of Oklahoma Press, 2017), ch. 7.   171 Bryan Palmer, *Cultures of Darkness: Night Travels in the Histories of Transgression [From Medieval to Modern]* (New York: Monthly Review Press, 2000), 6.   172 Jean Verdon, *Night in the Middle Ages* (South Bend, IN: University of Notre Dame Press, 1992), 1–2.

people slept in hallways, on floors, and more broadly the uses that formal architectural plans did not anticipate or make allowances for. It involves, too, reflecting on how public restrictions at night might have reached into the private recesses of people's lives, particularly into the interior spaces of the homes where the enslaved were compelled to flee before the last toll of the curfew bells.

Historians have taken up the question of daily time and the social and cultural importance of the difference between day and night. Nightfall is like a "frontier zone," as one classic study argues: people push beyond borders to find new opportunities for social advancement and wealth and to evade surveillance and social constraints. Others consider the night as a time of fear and danger as well as freedom and liberation from diurnal restrictions and routines. (171) By now, it is no longer revolutionary to see the night as a legal and a cultural construct that is "independent from the notion of darkness." (172) The growing cohort of scholars of the nighttime have shown that the world after sunset—as a social, political, legal, and indeed also architectural construction—while related to its astronomical context is also a human creation fashioned both to control and protect workers and to impose public order. The urban architecture of night in nineteenth-century Rio de Janeiro encompassed the city's church bell towers and doors with locks, along with clocks, bells, street lamps, and candles in niches in the sides of buildings. In a more figurative meaning of the term, Rio's architecture of night also included the edifice of municipal ordinances and police edicts that shut some of the city's residents inside each evening at curfew.

Over five million enslaved Africans were trafficked to Brazil from 1501 to 1850, comprising around 38% of the total slave traffic to the Americas. In 1821 on the eve of Brazilian independence, 46% of the population of Rio de Janeiro was enslaved. As a Portuguese colony, Brazil had become thoroughly addicted to the forced labor of captive Africans and their descendants. When it became an independent country, slavery endured the legal, political, and social transition fundamentally unaltered. The forced labor of captive Africans and their descendants was a central feature of urban life throughout Brazil, but Rio de Janeiro was the principal port in the South Atlantic slave trade. The city served as the seat of the colonial government (headed by a viceroy) and then the capital of independent Brazil. Slavery lasted until 1888 in Brazil, longer than anywhere else in the Americas. It endured long enough to intersect with urban modernity to an exceptional degree, overlapping with the beginnings of industrial factory labor, for example, and the commercialized entertainment that brought denizens to Rio's streets, theaters, and cabarets at night. During this period, artificial illumination made after-dark mobility in the city's public spaces a normal part of urban life. In fact, enslaved workers and so-called ""freed Africans" (*africanos livres*), people who had been illegally trafficked to Brazil after 1831 and nominally emancipated but actually kept as forced laborers, were the ones who lit and extinguished Rio's whale oil- and gas-fueled street lamps. It was because of—not in spite of—this nighttime mobility that fears of the enslaved moving about the city and blending in with the crowd created a perceived crisis. Municipal policy and local culture were marked by a fear of slave rebellion, an anxiety about fugitives, and by the slave-owning classes' increasingly racialized fear of people of African descent in general. While colonial and post-independence national and local authorities were slow to impose an urban design on Brazil's capital city, the use of public space was nonetheless of intense concern to governing elites and urban residents.

In Rio, as in many other cities throughout the world, the quotidian rhythm of activity occurred against the backdrop of a prohibition against entering the streets at night, a prohibition in Rio's case that was aimed at enslaved people but, in practice, affected all city dwellers of visibly African descent, at the arbitrary discretion of patrolling police officers. Rio's police chief issued new policing regulations in an edict (*edital*) published in January 1825. Anyone, whether slave or free, who encountered a law enforcement official had to submit to questioning. Among its several provisions, the edict established a curfew: After 10 pm in summer and 9 pm in winter, patrols could search anyone out in the streets "for illegal weapons or instruments that could be used in a crime." The bells of the São Francisco de Paula church and the São Bento convent were to ring for a full half hour, "without interruption," to announce the hour to all. This curfew only applied to slaves, implicitly to free persons of African descent, and, on occasion, to foreigners. The edict reads: "After the evening church bells have stopped ringing, it is prohibited to linger without an obvious motive on corners, squares, public streets; to whistle or to give any other signal. This prohibition extends to Blacks and people of color even before this hour, but after it becomes dark." Future police commanders expanded the hours but did not revoke this edict until 1878, and the city of Rio remained under a curfew for more than half of the nineteenth century. This explicitly selective regulation applied to slaves but offered exceptions to those with written proof of special permission from their masters to be out at night. The policy fell most heavily, then, on free people of color who could not obtain permission from a master to be out after dark. Captive laborers routinely found themselves on the streets at night doing their master's bidding in dumping household waste, drawing water, delivering messages and objects, and, ironically enough, tending to the oil and then the gas lanterns that had to be lit and extinguished each night after the curfew bells had already tolled. (173)

The urban infrastructure that supported the curfew included the street lamps that lit the way for patrolling police and the bell towers that signaled the beginning of the nightly lockdown; the curfew also depended, of course, on the existence of the places where those subject to it would return for the night. Houses in the residential nucleus of the city stood tightly lined up alongside the narrow, often sinuous roads. Unlike the farmhouses (*chácaras*) in the farther-flung neighborhoods on Rio's outskirts, urban residences in the city center in the early and mid-nineteenth century were strikingly uniform in their architectural style and layout: a door and window on the street, with a central living space in the front of the building (*sala*), small rooms (*alcovas*) along the side of a narrow hallway that extended the length of the building,

173 On both arrests for curfew violations and exceptions to it, see Amy Chazkel, "Toward a History of Rights in the City at Night: Making and Breaking the Nightly Curfew in Nineteenth-Century Rio de Janeiro," *Comparative Studies in Society and History* 62:1 (January 2020), 106–134.

174 Zephyr Frank, *Dutra's World: Wealth and Family in Nineteenth-Century Rio de Janeiro* (Albuquerque: University of New Mexico Press, 2004), 34; Frank cites Luccock, *Notes on Rio de Janeiro*, 119; Emanuel Araújo, *O teatro dos vícios: transgressão e transigência na sociedade urbana colonial* (Rio de Janeiro: José Olympio, 1997), 73–77.

175 Robert Burford, *Description of a view of the city of St. Sebastian and the Bay of Rio Janeiro* (London: J and C Adlard, 1823), 7, 154.

and on the top floors, if there were any, a small balcony. Other divided spaces on higher floors might include a study, more sleeping chambers (alcovas), and a kitchen. By day, the inside and outside of residential buildings conversed with each other only enough for smoke from kitchen fires to escape and for some daylight to enter. Houses protected themselves against the sun as much as they welcomed it in, shielding their homes from the destruction of furnishings, the radiant heat, and the unwanted glances of passersby.

When the evening curfew bells signaled the time for compulsory shutting in for Rio's enslaved population, how did they make use of the interior space of the home? Social historians of slavery and urban life in nineteenth-century Brazil have discovered fragmentary information about how people, and including the enslaved members of the household, used the domestic space they inhabited in nineteenth-century Rio. Postmortem inventories for those well enough off to have property to bequeath sometimes describe the layout of houses that were part of the estate. Travelers' accounts and literary works allude to shopkeepers who often slept in an alcove in the back of their shop while their servants and slaves slept on the floor behind or on top of the counters or sometimes inside a walled garden adjoining the back of the house. (174) The lower floor in a typical urban residential building only rarely served as a living space. It was most often used as a storefront, warehouse, or stable, or, according to one British traveler in 1823, was ""occupied by the slaves, cattle and for domestic purposes." (175) Only the city's largest houses had slaves' quarters on the ground floor, and most households included at least one enslaved person. In the homes of the poorer and "middling" classes, enslaved household members instead found makeshift places to rest in corridors, alleys, warehouses, and on the beaten earth of the bottom floor of a multistory house.

We know so little about how people used the interior space of households in nineteenth-century Rio and how these uses fluctuated with daily cycles of light and darkness because the documents that might have allowed us a detailed view of people's daily acts reflect the state's limitation to the public realm. At the threshold of the private home, the state ran up against the traditional authority of the father of the family and the constitutional principle of the "inviolability" of the domicile. What went on inside the household was the domain of patriarchal privilege, and only under narrowly defined circumstances could the police or other authorities enter. Police records, municipal ordinances, and administrative documents were largely silent when it came to what went on inside the home. The socio-legal night was a function of nineteenth-century Brazil's liberal legal regime. In urban Brazil, the threshold of the house was both an architectural detail and a powerful legal abstraction. And by night, this simple piece of wood assumed dramatic meaning in demarcating the outer boundaries for those subject to the curfew.

The difference between night and day was a resource for ordering the use of and access to public space in Rio de Janeiro in the decades after independence. The interior design of the residential homes and shops that housed Rio's population, however, was a black box of the law, left to the private domain and to the improvisation of those who owned and lived in them. In Rio, while the curfew was in effect, the home became the forced refuge for captive laborers. It is clear that night altered the way that private space was allotted and its relationship to the public realm, but it is far less evident just how; to reconstruct this history, researchers who gravitate toward the police and government documents favored by social historians of crime and slavery need to engage in a conversation with historians of architecture and interior design. To begin to answer the question of how the night transforms architecture, we need to recover the intentional process of planning built space and its dissident uses, the materials, knowledge, and biases that conditioned this process, and the ways in which this knowledge ramified through society and how it has been transferred between generations.

The Bohemian writer Franz Kafka's early twentieth-century novel *The Trial* contains a short parable in which the author uses architecture to evoke a hopeless search for justice despite the appearance to the contrary. The tale begins, ""Before the law sits a gatekeeper." A "man from the country" approaches an open gate. His desire is simply to "gain entry into the law," in the earnest belief that it "should always be accessible for everyone." The gatekeeper engages the man in conversation but refuses to allow him to enter. The man waits years and grows old and weak, learning the minute details of the gatekeepers appearance and manner, while the gatekeeper bars him from passing through the open gate, "yet." As the tale ends and the man lies dying, he asks why no one else had approached the gate to gain entry to the law in all those years. The gatekeeper crouches down to tell the man that the gate had been his alone, and now, the gatekeeper says, "I'm going to close it." Scholars of the social lives of the law have perennially called upon Kafka's parable, which lets us see into the mind of someone subject to the law's terrifying power and the capriciousness of those who control access to it. (176) The Brazilian historian Eduardo Spiller Pena in his important book on the legal history of slavery borrows from Kafka's tale to point to the patent absurdity of the idea of equality before the law in nineteenth-century Brazil, despite the persistent fiction that the law is an "open door" through which citizen-subjects can pass. Social and legal historians have shown that not only masters but also jurists and lawyers were more interested in protecting the hierarchical order and sanctity of private property than in freeing the enslaved, acting as gatekeepers to control who entered through that door.

Whatever its symbolic meaning, sometimes a door is, indeed, an actual door, too; a physical feature of a building designed to open and close and to serve as a physical barrier to define the space of a household. The field of architectural history can situate the study of urban slavery in the materiality of the real world and reconstruct what it was like to exist in built space, what resources architecture afforded, and what barriers it imposed. This incomplete and still open-ended inquiry has tried to highlight the urgency of finding a way to understand how the most oppressed members of households used domestic space in the context of the dramatic and

176 Eduardo Spiller Pena, *Pajens da casa imperial: Jurisconsultos, escravidão e a lei de 1871* (Campinas: Editora UNICAMP, 2001), 21–59.

177 Sandy Isendstadt, *Electric Light: An Architectural History* (Cambridge, MA: MIT Press, 2018).

long-lasting restrictions on moving around the city after nightfall. Artificial light is a building material akin to wood and stone, the architectural historian Sandy Isenstadt compellingly argues. (177) Perhaps, then, darkness provided scaffolding for the power structure in urbanizing Rio de Janeiro. The socio-legal nighttime effectively created architectural and urban space. Laws, buildings, plazas, and artificial illumination all formed part of an urban infrastructure that sustained the racialized process of the criminalization of everyday life outdoors. We have yet to apprehend which interior architectural features may have contributed to this process from the other side of the house's threshold.

NOTHING BUT A FEW SIGNS, LIKE STARS IN AN IMMENSE BLACK NIGHT
Clandestinity and Night-faring Practices in the Underground Railroad
Lucía Jalón Oyarzun

Framing the Connection Between Light, Darkness and Surveillance (178)

The first urban lighting system appeared in Paris at the same moment as the modern police did, in the late 17th century. The lamp posts or *reverberes* were an expression of the power of Louis XIV, the Roi Soleil or Sun King, source of life (and power) himself; and the penalty for intentionally breaking one of them was to be sent to the galleys for life. If you attacked light to regain the night, you attacked the king, but most importantly, you attacked and rebelled against his control. (179) This control could only be understood through the inextricable linkage between light and surveillance.

In his *Poetics of Space*, Gaston Bachelard wrote how "tout ce qui brille voit", or everything that casts a light, sees, (180) that is, everything that casts a light generates a sphere of control defined by the space that gets illuminated. If we look at the 1863 map of the lighthouses of Great Britain engraved by R. H. Laurie, we can see how the space produced by a light is one defined by reach and intensity. How far does it reach, how much intensity is lost along the way? Light does not operate through clear limits or lines, on the contrary, it creates a field of scopes and intensities which requires special spatial tools

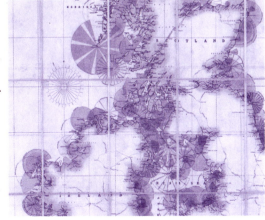

178   This article is part of an ongoing research that continues the author's PhD dissertation, "Excepción y cuerpo rebelde: lo político como generador de una arquitectónica menor / Exception and the rebel body: the political as generator of a minor architecture"' (PhD diss., UPM, 2017), http://oa.upm.es/48250/, focused on the potentialities of minor architecture to study the conflicts between the spatial production linked to the exception as political device, and the spatial production of the rebel body. Now, it is part of a post-doctoral research project carried out at EPFL, and oriented around the question of clandestinity and underground activities as minor spatial practices.   179   For a longer exposé on this topic, see Jalón Oyarzun, 273–86.; for the connections between the night and night-faring practices and the shared political and architectural agency of bodies, see Lucía Jalón Oyarzun, 'Night as Commons: Minor Architecture and Dayfaring Citizens', *Scapegoat: Architecture / Landscape / Political Economy* 10 (2017): 57–70.   180   Gaston Bachelard, *The Poetics of Space* (Boston: Beacon Press, 1994), 34.

to work with. Furthermore, we need to consider how that light that sees also *touches* the illuminated object, it has a material effect on it, it can interfere in its movement, its disposition, and its actions, as shown for instance in the anti-aerial systems used in the Second World War. With this in mind, we cannot consider the progressive expansion of daylight's rule in modern and contemporary experience without an analysis of the simultaneous development of control and surveillance.

The links had been there for quite a while, *vigilance* has for a long time implied the dominion of the night. We find a family of words in Latin that allows us to frame these links further. First, there was *vigil,* denoting an officer responsible to watch out for any danger during the night, *vigilia,* which was how each of the four parts in which Romans divided the night was named, in correspondence to the four night-watching turns of those night officers, and the verb *vigilare,* which meant to watch and guard the night, thus being awake and alert. To watch and surveil was a key activity of the night which made more vulnerable our senses, and thus our collective being. The original root for all these words was in fact *vigeo, vigere,* from the Indoeuropean *weg*, to be lively and strong (which is also at the origin of the English verb to *watch*). (181)

If we move forward in this *light-veillance* entanglement, we arrive at the *panopticon*, where we see a central eye—that of the king, the state, …—which was emerging already in the Parisian lamps controlling their surroundings. If we focus not so much

on its abstract figure, but as seen in some of its built instances, we see that central element appearing almost like a lighthouse in the middle of a sea of darkness (or dangers), which the light (and sight), just by potentially being there, is enough to overcome. Now, if we go forward in our search for the links between light, darkness and surveillance, we are faced with the architectural functioning and spatial consequences of a new figure, that of the *oligopticon*, defined by Bruno Latour as a multiplication of eyes that do not see very well, but which, by their sheer number, give nonetheless a precise image of a given situation. (182) It is the equivalent in our societies of control to the disciplinary societies' *panopticon*. The *oligopticon* quantifies, measures, and constructs a form of technological topography where each body or action is located, identified, measured and linked up with others in a single entity. The *oligopticon* can be thought of in a double dimension. It has, of course, an optical functioning, where every single living or non-living entity is translated into a measurable object, and a second, haptic dimension, where it is the touch of that vision that modulates and shapes behaviors. (183) These technological topographies show it is no longer the eye of a subject, be that human or institutional, but of a networked field of visibility that emerges where the agent that sees (and touches) is a machine, and where the information obtained and transmitted is of a computational nature. (184)

181 "Vigía", Diccionario Etimológico Castellano en Línea, http://etimologias.dechile.net/?vigi.a; *A Latin Dictionary,* Lewis and Short (New York, Oxford: Harper and Brothers, Oxford University Press, 1879), s.v. "Vigilo", http://www.perseus.tufts.edu/hopper/text?doc=Perseus:text:1999.04.0059:entry=vigilo.
182 Bruno Latour, *Reassembling the Social an Introduction to Actor-Network-Theory* (Oxford; New York: Oxford University Press, 2005), 181.   183   We have defined this as the *soft touch of capitalism*, or an *algorithmic touch*, in Lucía Jalón Oyarzun, "La Apariencia de Un Toque Humano, o El Diseño de La Pasividad Hiperactiva," *Revista de Occidente*, no. 453 (February 2019): 49–64.   184   On this networked visibility and agency, see the work of Geoff Cox and the Center for the Study of the Networked Image (CSNI), Centre for the Study of the Networked Image et al., 'Affordances of the Networked Image', *The Nordic Journal of Aesthetics* 30, no. 61–62 (2 July 2021): 40–45.

[185] For a more detailed analysis of this condition, see Lucía Jalón Oyarzun, "Cuerpos Anestesiados y Estéticas de Lo Clandestino En El Interior Totalizante Del Capitalismo Contemporáneo," (Lecture, IX Curso de introducción al arte contemporáneo: INTERIORES, CENDEAC, Murcia, May 2019, https://www.youtube.com/watch?v=xciqyimUlNI, accessed November 8, 2023.) [186] Hannah Arendt, *The Human Condition* (Chicago: University of Chicago Press, 1998), 51.

If we go back to Bachelard's formula and we make the experiment of inverting it, to show that "everything that sees, casts a light" we can explore these eyes as a source of light where the *oligopticon* produces a homogenous field of vigilance and *exposure*, with every single body always in the open, available, reachable, in a new form of internalized exterior or exposed interior. [185] In *The Human Condition*, Hannah Arendt already wrote about "the implacable bright light" brought by constant presence and exposure—what today we would call the need to be always ON, 24/7 connected—while a sphere of darkness and non-exposure was essential for the survival of any healthy political community. [186]

As we have already mentioned, this connection between light and surveillance is not inconsequential. In parallel to the emergence of this implacable field of light, control and exposure, we can trace the process whereby the night was progressively being erased. [187] The urban lighting systems in Paris, London and many cities around the world grew and improved, electricity arrived and along with it a control revolution that would come to shape our informational present. Meanwhile, slowly but steadily, our hours of sleep decreased, and the skies disappeared behind the glow of our expanded nocturnal activity. By now, several cities and institutions have appointed night mayors and other officials with not so straight-forward titles whose role is to manage this new time that must be consumed in our race towards a plentiful 24/7 existence.

However, the night remains, just as nature remains autonomous behind illusions of its control or disappearance. [188] And our physical constraints remain as well, physical limits that mean that if we don't sleep for a certain number of days we do, quite simply, end up dying. And through the millions of blue lights illuminating the sleepless night, or as the old expression said, "burning the midnight oil", the night still disturbs us, individually and collectively, positively or negatively.

French philosopher Denis Diderot wrote of how "the night conceals forms and gives horror to noises; even if it is only that of a leaf, in the heart of a forest, it sets the imagination in motion." [189] Darkness unsettles our physical experience. As it limits our sight, it puts the weight on our other, often underused, senses so that for each movement or noise felt, our imagination fills up the gaps with unexpected (and quite often dangerous) causes. By night, the corporeal map of our surroundings is faultier. The modern era has turned us into retinal beings, discarding and undervaluing our haptic condition; accordingly, by night we feel more vulnerable, a vulnerability we do not conceive as an asset, on the contrary, it is often presented as a weakness. However, we know that only those who have a trusty map of their environments inscribed on their body through experience, i.e. by making themselves available to the world, will know how to interpret noises or textures, will link signs to their embodied experience and will be able to thus navigate the night autonomously. That much was clear in those Parisian streets of the 17th century. Whoever broke the *réverbères* did it because they knew they had more chances of moving successfully in a neighborhood known *by heart,* that is, through maps written as affective images in his body, than the policeman who came from outside, depending on forms of abstract knowledge and *merely* his eyes. [190]

[187] A growing field of night studies has shown this transformation in several studies, we list here just a few references that we consider an accessible but still critical approach to the topic: Jonathan Crary, *24/7: Late Capitalism and the Ends of Sleep* (London; New York: Verso Books, 2013); Alain Cabantous, *Histoire de la nuit: XVIIe-XVIIIe siècle* (Paris: Fayard, 2009); Simone Delattre and Alain Corbin, *Les douze heures noires: la nuit à Paris au XIXe siècle* (Paris: Albin Michel, 2000); Craig Koslofsky, *Evening's Empire: A History of the Night in Early Modern Europe* (Cambridge; New York: Cambridge University Press, 2011); Wolfgang Schivelbusch, *Disenchanted Night: The Industrialization of Light in the Nineteenth Century* (Berkeley: University of California Press, 1988). [188] As well stated in the works of Carolyn Merchant, *Autonomous Nature: Problems of Prediction and Control from Ancient Times to the Scientific Revolution* (New York: Routledge, 2016); or Andreas Malm, *The Progress of This Storm: Nature and Society in a Warming World* (London: Verso, 2020). [189] Denis Diderot, *Diderot on Art. The Salon of 1767*, ed. John Goodman (New Haven; London: Yale University Press, 1995), 126. [190] On the notion of invisible maps, see Lucía Jalón Oyarzun, "Nightfaring & Invisible Maps: Of Maps Perceived, but Not Drawn," *The Funambulist*, no. 18 (2018): 40–43.

In what follows, we want to consider this night-faring knowledge as a minor spatial knowledge linked to clandestinity, capable of expanding the repertoire of a minor architectural practice. Departing from the work of Gilles Deleuze and Félix Guattari on the minor literature of Franz Kafka, of Michel Foucault on the importance of minor knowledges against normalized disciplines, and of architects like Robin Evans, John Hejduk, Jill Stoner or Jennifer Bloomer, we propose to define minor as an open set of spatial practices and plural know-hows based on the immanent differentiating agency of bodies (or their inexhaustible power of variation). These practices feed on the circumstantial and experimental, operating in the narrow margins and blind spots of major languages, structures and knowledges, and unsettling them. While minor architectures work with and within materially limited spaces, tools and conditions, they manage to bring forth affective amplitude: they enlarge the world through forms of plural material entanglement. Departing from this minor understanding of architecture, what can that person breaking the *réverbère* in Paris and its will to safeguard night and darkness around them tell us about the connection between embodied spatial knowledge and minor spatial practices?

Clandestinity as the Production of Darkness

"Our encryption is the real world". This is how Mr Robot, in the TV-series of the same name, replies to Elliot's astonishment as he induces him into his hacker cell by bringing him to meet the rest of the team at an old arcade in Coney Island. As he arrives, Elliot, a half-alive hacker who survives through self-inflicted numbness, is shocked to see they all work there together instead of hiding behind encrypted digital identities. Mr Robot conveys that, while IPs and codes make everything traceable, there's a depth, fuzziness and granularity to "the real world" that *encrypts* much better. It is a little scene, at the beginning of a series that would have a lot of twists, however, it helps us point with clarity at the relations between hiding, secrecy and clandestinity and night-faring knowledges as minor spatial practices.

Clandestinity, understood as the articulation of spaces of secrecy and invisibility, is traversed by a singular form of architectural knowledge centered on embodied practices, playing with lines while understanding of scopes and areas of affection. A set of know-hows founded on a fine-tuned awareness of the fuzziness and material qualities of that "real world" referred to by the Mr Robot character. While this notion holds further theoretical folds, here we will merely underline this preliminary definition through a quick overview of cases where this relation between space, secrecy and invisibility comes to the fore. For instance, we can observe how migrants use in a minor way the major syntax of our societies of control's regime of visibility and spectacle, articulating intermittent strategies of exposure and invisibility in the Straits of Gibraltar, erasing their individual fingerprints while they

collectively overexpose themselves to gain protection. (191) Meanwhile, the collective dimension of secrecy, the need for complicity that collectively weaves the underground space, is laid bare in the construction of shelters and hiding places at the Warsaw ghetto during the Second World War or those where the Spanish "moles" hid during the Civil War and the more than 30-year-long dictatorship that followed. (192) Finally, we can see the importance of the apparently meaningless detail whenever and wherever survival is at stake in the Polaroids taken by the Stasi in the flats they searched, as recovered by Simon Menner in his project *Images from the Secret Stasi Archives or: what does Big Brother see, while he is watching?* These images were used to see how things were before their search so as not to leave any trace, allowing us to reflect on that persistent "clandestinity of private life" as formulated by Guy Debord, "about which one never possesses more than derisory documents" (193). We see then the existence of a spatial knowledge impossible to represent, but alive, embodied and situated. A knowledge based on the reading, interpretation and simultaneous inscription and erasure of traces, where space becomes defined by an ecology of signs, an active interrelation of affective exchanges involving and embedding a variety of material bodies. While in Mr Robot we see this production of darkness in relation to the technological topographies of control societies and the *oligopticon*, where everything casts a light until there's nothing left to distinguish, we can trace this idea of clandestinity (or en-*crypt*ion) as a form of spatial practice with a longer history, and one in which the role of the night was essential to create confusion around one's own figure. In the following pages, we seek to analyze this in relation to some of the night-faring practices evident in the Underground Railroad network threading the North-American continent during the 19th century.

The Underground Railroad

The Underground Railroad was a network of people, practices and landscapes that connected the United States with Canada and other free territories during the 19th century. It helped bring an estimated 135,000 fugitives to freedom. Although certain narratives showed it as a deeply organized network linked to the efforts of the Northern abolitionists, even depicted in some images as an actual railroad, recent research has produced a more accurate description, showing it as "a diverse, flexible, and interlocking system …, a model of democracy in action," not a conspiracy, as it "operat(ed) in most areas with a minimum of central direction and a maximum of grassroots involvement". (194) Furthermore, it was mostly "free … African Americans who were not enslaved, (and who) were the bedrock of this

FAC-SIMILE OF UNDERGROUND RAILWAY ADVERTISEMENT
(From "The Western Citizen," July 13, 1844)

191 On this topic and its architectural analysis, we refer to UPM, 2019Antonio Giráldez López, "El dispositivo frontera : la construcción espacial desde la norma y el cuerpo migrante" (PhD diss., UPM, 2019), https://oa.upm.es/63846/, accessed November 8, 2023.   192 For a thorough analysis of the *topos* or moles, see Jesús Torbado and Manuel Leguineche, *Los topos* (Madrid: Capitán Swing, 2010).   193 Guy Debord, "Critique de La Séparation," in *Œuvres* (Paris: Gallimard, n.d.), 546.   194 Fergus M. Bordewich, *Bound for Canaan: The Epic Story of the Underground Railroad, America's First Civil Rights Movement* (New York: Amistad, 2006), 5–6.

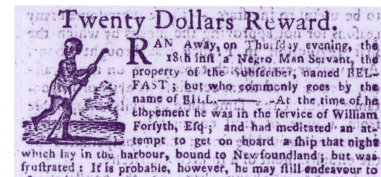

movement…" (195) The infrastructure was large, and the actors diverse, because it was not just about making a safe passage for the fugitives, it required the carrying of messages and information too, as well as the legal aid to defend those escaping as well as those helping them, getting money and funding, "as well as an even wider pool of family members, friends, and fellow parishioners who although they might never engage personally in illegal activity, protected those who did and made it possible for them to continue their work." (196)

While the first African slaves were taken to Virginia in 1619, the enslavement of the native population and slaves coming from Spanish colonies was already a reality during the previous century. In the 1640s the first notices of slaves fleeing their masters emerged and by 1700 they could often be found in American newspapers. In the first two decades of the nineteenth century the clandestine movement worked mostly on a case-by-case strategy, however, through them, a series of lines and strategies started to be drawn up and practiced throughout the territory. It was only around the 1830s that an organized system emerged. This coincided with a deepening of the social divisions over the question of slavery. The South passed the 1850 Fugitive Slave Act, to harden the measures that could be taken to recapture fugitives and punish the accomplices helping them in their flight, which meant that a more active and efficient organization within the network was needed, creating safe routes and systematic practices of movement and communication.

That period was the most active moment of the network, extending its reach across several states and thousands of kilometers. It was also at that moment that the idea of an "underground" started to emerge, symbolically connected to the invention of the actual railroad. Linked to that growing organization a new vocabulary emerged to describe the different actors, routes and strategies used to traverse the territory. It was the vocabulary of a new spatial practice that was being mastered. And so, there were *agents* whose role was managing information and organizing strategies, *conductors* who "transported or guided fugitives from slave territory, …across major bodies of water, or through hostile northern territory", and *station masters* who kept safe-houses along the way. (197) Terms describing bundles of things were used to refer to groups of fugitive slaves, for instance "loads of potatoes, parcels, bundles of wool, (or) bushels of wheat".

Although there have been some efforts to fix the network of stations and routes, as shown for instance in the Wilbur Siebert's maps from his 1898 study on *The Underground Railroad*, these attempts were for the most part proof of our inability to work with fuzzy spatialities (198). The spatial lineament of the Underground Railroad, as well as of many other clandestine and minor practices, were not roads or points, but ecologies of signs. Something we can better see

195 J. Blaine Hudson, *Encyclopedia of the Underground Railroad* (Jefferson, North Carolina: McFarland & Company Inc., 2006), 7. 196 Bordewich, *Bound for Canaan*, 6. 197 Hudson, *Encyclopedia*, 8. 198 Tom Nurmi, "Shackle, Sycamore, Shibboleth: Material Geographies of the Underground Railroad," in *Cartographies of Exile* (New York; London: Routledge, 2016), 115.

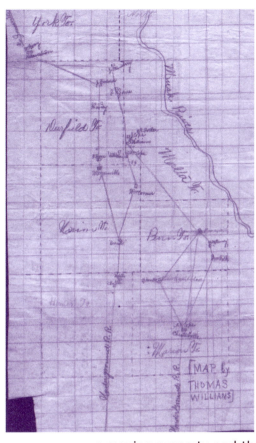

in some of the hand-drawn maps Siebert collected. Ecologies of signs that worked alongside practices of reading, learning, interpreting, narrating, sharing, embodying, or (re)enacting those signs. The underground railroad is a clear example of a transcalar spatial entity which overflows traditional spatial tools and demands us to do better as spatial and material practitioners, because, as Fergus Bordewich has said, "the essential nature of the Underground Railroad lay in the character and motivation of the people who made it work, *not in bricks and mortar*..." (199) The Underground Railroad needs to be understood in relation to the spatial practices at work to sustain slavery and the extension of a capitalist world system. Slaves were considered chattel, and the racialized body carried the exception within it wherever they went. They were a moving property and the legal codes of the time, as explained by Walter Johnson, "expanded the territory of captivity beyond state lines to inscribe servitude within the body itself. In the eyes of the law, it no longer mattered how far a slave might travel (...) his body was already written, spoken for, *signed*". (200)

Around the plantation, the engine of Southern economy, organized around the master's house and the slave quarters, emerged a larger carceral landscape, a "patterned

ecology of slaveholding agro-capitalism". (201) The labored land surrounding the slave's daily existence was "the determining parameter of his condition", while the open lands created fields of hypervisibility where the slaveholder and their official enforcers—from the elevated position of a horse-rider—dominated all their subjects' movements, who on their side "could not see any place to run" or hide to. (202) However, at the edge of the plantations, "there was another sort of landscape. In uncleared woods and undrained swamps, (...) the spatial premises of the Cotton Kingdom, the structured and mutual formation of body and landscape called 'slavery', disintegrated". (203) Through "practical navigation rather than ordinal abstraction," slaves got to develop a singular form of embodied knowledge of this "off-the-grid landscape in the course of their daily work"; and they would use it to "hunt, trap, and fish to supplement their rations". (204) This embodied knowledge of an alternative geography hidden to the slaveholder would prove essential in their flight, as few slaves "had ever seen a map". (205) This alternative geographical knowledge was supported as well by shared stories and memories which helped produce a counternarrative to the efforts of the slaveholders to impress on slaves, in the words of Frederick Douglass, "a belief in the boundlessness of slave territory, and of their own limitless power."

199 Bordewich, *Bound for Canaan*, xv–xvi, our emphasis. 200 Nurmi, "Shackle, Sycamore, Shibboleth," 111. 201 Walter Johnson, *River of Dark Dreams: Slavery and Empire in the Cotton Kingdom* (Cambridge, Massachusetts: The Belknap Press of Harvard University Press, 2013), 210. 202 Johnson, *River of Dark Dreams,* 221. 203 Johnson, *River of Dark Dreams,* 228–29. 204 Johnson, *River of Dark Dreams,* 230–31. 205 Bordewich, *Bound for Canaan*, 113.

This psychological enclosure sought to foreclose the night as well. It was after all the best accomplice in any flight attempt. Darkness short-circuited the hypervisibility otherwise at the service of the slaveholder, allowing for freer movement. The night became a space with specific characteristics, dimensions, and uses. Even if freedom lay far away in a vague notion of the North, the night was a necessary threshold to the path towards it. To block it, white people sought to scare the black population by instilling in them a fear of supernatural stories of ghosts and spirits that haunted the hours of darkness. (206)

In the event of an escape, would-be fugitives would first try to reach those peripheral landscapes of forests and swamps and wait for the night to come. The day was a space-time defined by vulnerability, while the night offered safety and transformed that vulnerability into an asset: an increased awareness allowed for a better interpretation of material signs essential to navigating in the night, such as the stars. Researcher Tom Nurmi writes about the novel *Blake,* written by Martin Delany, where "the hero Henry draws for his fellow runaways a map of the stars organized around 'the North Star, the slave's great Guide to Freedom!'" (207)

However, lack of knowledge about abstract navigation methods meant that would-be fugitives needed to master their physical senses far beyond the visual to turn their body into compasses. Aurality and touch were essential to manage the encounters with topography. The fugitive Charles Ball remembered how, "at dark, I again returned to the road, which I traveled in silence, trading as lightly as possible with my feet and listening most attentively to every sound that I heard." (208) Sound signals were an important part of the railroad codes. For instance, prearranged signals were used to detect a friend or foe in the road. One fugitive told how: "As a signal of our meeting in safety he would give the signal crying out, 'yea! yo!'" (209) A sound signal created a common spatiality, a connection between two isolated bodies, a bond capable of orienting the body in darkness. Thus, for the station masters and conductors, using sounds to codify encounters was essential.

Touch was another important bodily orientator, if we go back to Delany's novel, we see that when the stars could not be seen, haptic navigation had to be used, and "you must depend alone upon nature for your guide. Feel, in the dark, around the trunks or bodies of trees, especially the oak, and whenever you feel moss on the bark, that side on which the moss grows is always to the north." (210)

We see then, how the night leads to an affective reading or navigation of space that goes beyond the visual and includes an extended material realm. The body orients itself by an exchange of affective intensities with a world that is rendered even. The superiority of the human being is no more and the trees, the stars, the bodies moving through the forest are all at the same level, their signifying or signaling expressions equally meaningful. Learning how to read material signs to move through the unexpected was a minor knowledge needed to escape the slaveholder's major languages, writings and readings. The night reading had to be made by "physically interacting with objects", and in the process, new crossings between "the somatic and (the) semantic"

206 Gladys-Marie Fry, *Night Riders in Black Folk History* (Chapel Hill: The University of North Carolina Press, 2001). 207 Nurmi, "Shackle, Sycamore, Shibboleth," 119–20. 208 Quoted in Johnson, *River of Dark Dreams,* 233. 209 Quoted in Johnson, *River of Dark Dreams,* 234. 210 Martin Delany's novel *Blake* quoted in Nurmi, "Shackle, Sycamore, Shibboleth," 120.

emerged, (211) by listening in Toni Morrison's words "with his fingertips, to hear what, if anything, the earth had to say." (212)

We see this minor haptic knowledge at play in the narration of Levi Coffin, an American Quaker living in Newport, Indiana, whose house became one key station of the network:

"Where there was a fork in the road there was a nail driven in a tree three and a half feet from the ground half way round from front to back; if the right hand road was to be taken the nail was driven on the right hand side; if the left was the road the nail was to the left. If there were fences and no tree, the nail was driven in the middle of the second rail from the top, over on the inside of the fence, to the right, or left as in the trees; if neither tree, nor fence was near then a stake, or a stone was so set as to be unseen by day, but found at night. When fugitives started on the road they were instructed into the *mystery*: when they came to a fork in the road, they would go to the nearest tree, put their arms round and rub downwards, and which ever arm struck the nail, right or left, that was the road; and they walked on with no mistake. So with fences, but the stakes, or stones had to found with their feet, which was tolerably easily done." (213)

The ability to read these signs was key as most of the paths and decisions taken were defined by non-planned encounters, where care, vigilance and alertness were the guide: "the frequency with which people got seriously lost and disoriented along the way (was) striking… (Because) enslaved people's mode of geographic knowledge handicapped them when they left familiar, memorised ground." (214)

Aware of his vulnerability, the fugitive needed to turn it into a tool, operationalize it to read those encounters with care and allow for unexpected signals to come in. All those knowledges were inscribed, written into, the fleeing body. They were instructions that had been told by conductors and station masters, but there were also memorized narratives of these semiotic systems given by other fugitives. This minor knowledge was inherently cooperative, and made to be shared in an embodied way, through oral and practiced means. This secrecy through embodiment was important because as Frederick Douglass put, it was essential to leave no traces: "Let us render the tyrant no aid; let us not hold the light by which he can trace the footprints of our flying brother." (215)

By erasing their footprints and making the network invisible to the disciplinary vision of the slaveholders, they were aiding the ones coming after them. We have written elsewhere about these kind of invisible maps, hidden because they remain unwritten in paper while they become inscribed in the body. They operate as affective images, traces left upon the body capable of orienting it as it communicates with the world, or in other words, as it creates a common ground, with the world.

Accordingly, to consider how minor spatial practices were shaped and transmitted it is essential to understand how landscapes worked as ecologies of signs. These traversed ecologies were more important than buildings, roads or houses, in the words of Gilles Deleuze and Claire Parnet, "nothing but a few signs, like stars in an immense black night". (216) These signals allowed for the experience of space to be rearticulated, creating "improvised material geographies that exploited, altered, and re-wrote the carceral

---

211 Nurmi, "Shackle, Sycamore, Shibboleth," 123–24. 212 Toni Morrison, *Song of Solomon* (New York: Vintage International, 2004), 279. It is interesting to make here a little side note to consider the connection between these haptic knowledges and Charles Barbier "écriture nocturne" or "night writing", which was at the origin of Charles Braille system for blind reading. It was a tactile system of reading where sounds are substituted by a series of raised dots within a grid. Connected to this, it is also worth to mention Lewis Carroll *nyctography*, a system to write and take notes with no light. The author of *Alice in Wonderland* invented it himself after often awakening in the middle of the night wanting to jot down ideas but without the need to go through all the process of lighting a light: "Any one who has tried, as I have often done, the process of getting out of bed at 2 a.m. in a winter night, lighting a candle, and recording some happy thought which would probably be otherwise forgotten, will agree with me it entails much discomfort. All I have now to do, if I wake and think of something I wish to record, is to draw from under the pillow a small memorandum book containing my Nyctograph, write a few lines, or even a few pages, without even putting the hands outside the bed-clothes, replace the book, and go to sleep again." Letter to *The Lady* magazine of October 29, 1891, quoted in "Nyctography", Wikipedia, https://en.wikipedia.org/wiki/Nyctography, accessed November 8, 2023. 213 Quoted in Nurmi, "Shackle, Sycamore, Shibboleth," 123. 214 Nurmi, "Shackle, Sycamore, Shibboleth," 112. 215 Quoted in Bordewich, *Bound for Canaan*, 239. 216 Gilles Deleuze and Claire Parnet, *Dialogues II* (New York: Columbia University Press, 2007), 61.

landscape" and made movement, caring, hiding and other practices alike possible (217). Even traditional architectural or urban elements like houses or roads needed to be acknowledged as part of these ecologies, as shields, blockers, or buffers.

All of this connects us with one final key question, that of clandestinity as production of the confusion and blurriness brought on by night and darkness. Clandestinity is not so much about the creation of invisibility, it could be better defined as the careful and lucid playing with visibility and invisibility. For instance, the railroad network itself was not itself always hidden or operating in the night, on the contrary, it mostly "ran underground" in the first Southern stages and became more active in plain sight as it got to the North. Likewise, the escape did not always mean to hide, as "many free African American communities afforded fugitives the rare opportunity to *hide in plain view*". (218) And even in the Southern carceral landscape, enslaved people knew how to "hide behind their own hypervisible appearance." (219) We see then the profound connection between clandestinity and night, not so much because its activities often occurred at nighttime, but because, even when they happened in daylight, they depended on the visibility of control and its technical devices to become subject to the same effects that night causes in the human sensorium: confusion, blurriness and ambiguity, thus showing clandestinity as a minor spatial practice capable of producing night based on a collective embodied repertoire of material knowledge to navigate through it.

---

217 Nurmi, "Shackle, Sycamore, Shibboleth," 113.   218 Hudson, *Encyclopedia*, 225.   219 Johnson, *River of Dark Dreams*, 227.

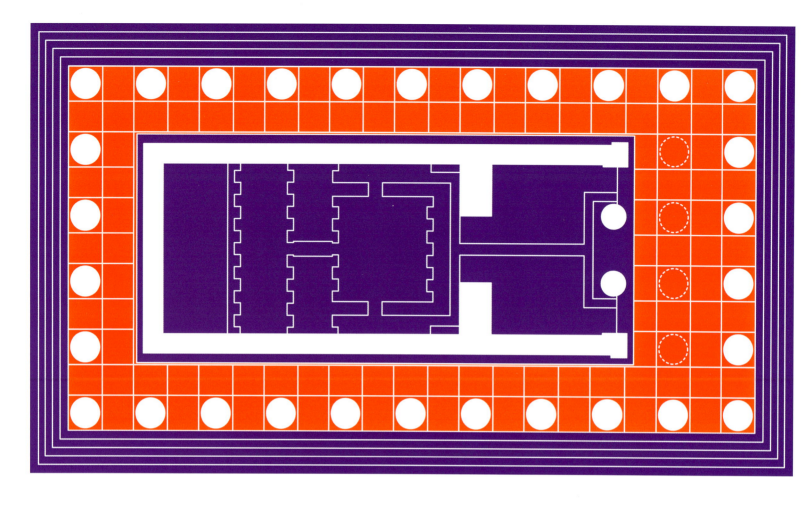

REFLECTING THE SUNSET FROM THE BURNING SANDS

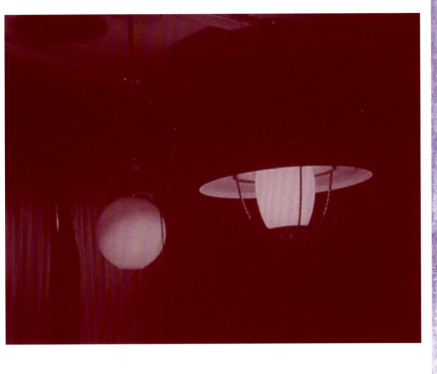

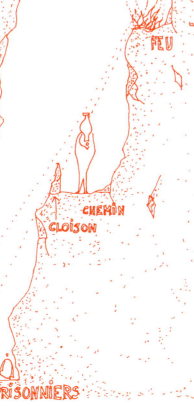

17. LA CAVERNE
(VII, 514a – 518b)

FEU
CHEMIN
CLOISON
OMBRES
PRISONNIERS

The Auditorium

Eberson's atmospheric concept in theater design is brilliantly reflected in the auditorium's blue plaster ceiling dome. The ceiling contains 96 twinkling lights, using 10-watt light bulbs with flasher units attached. On occasion fluffy clouds drift be that are projected from Brenograph machines hidden behind the organ screens. Eberson's magic touch is seen in the polychromatic ornamentation that zigzags across the proscenium, and by the broken symmetry of the free standing organ screens that jut out into the aisles on either side of the auditorium. Freestanding statues made at the Caproni Brothers Studios in Boston are attractively set in false balconies that line the outer walls.

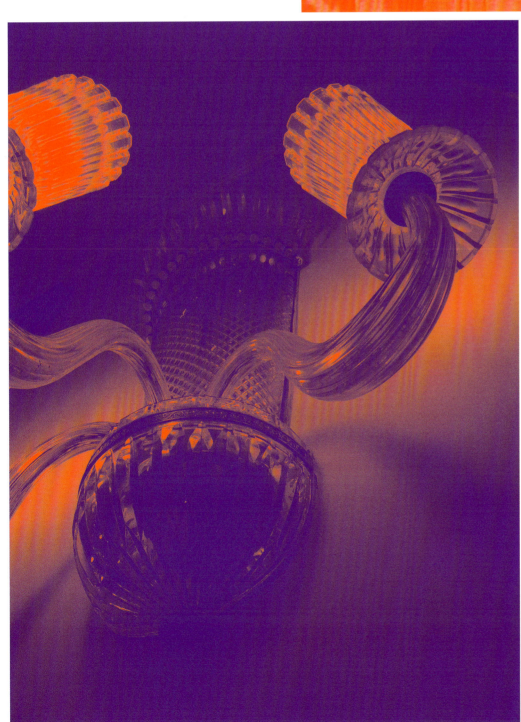

LIBERTY LINE.
NEW ARRANGEMENT---NIGHT AND DAY.

"ILLUSION IS THE THING"
Simulating Night at the Atmospheric Cinema
Carlotta Darò and Yann Rocher

A NOCTURNAL HISTORY OF ARCHITECTURE

In a history of the architecture of movie theaters that is distinguished by an illusionist and "fanciful" capacity of the enclosed space, associated with the technical apparatus of projection, the more specific history of atmospheric theaters deserves a separate chapter. Doubtless, in a form of continuity with the Palladian theatrical tradition (220)—which already simulated the opening of the sky on the ceiling of a closed dome, evoking, in reality, the Greek open-air theater with its classical scenes—it was in the 1920s that this theatrical type asserted itself in the sector of film production. The illusion of an infinite sky has been a theme dear to architecture since the Renaissance at the very moment when the first dedicated theaters re-enacted the ancient open-air models in closed interiors. The Baroque period was not to be outdone, since it multiplied church frescoes simulating the opening of the vault towards the celestial divinity. It is always a zenithal opening to the sky, invaded by a profusion of clouds, which hosts several scenes from mythology and religion. Among the techniques of dream creation and illusion, the image is worth less by its configuration than by its mobility, its internal dynamism and the extent of the imaginary variations to which it lends itself. (221) In this sense "it is certain that the cloud provides reverie with an incomparable material" writes Hubert Damisch. (222) The cloud confers a "pictorial" quality, as Wöfflin describes it, to the classical orthogonal tectonic space of the quattrocento, it allows a form of baroque ubiquity that will also be found as a supporting principle in early cinematographic projection rooms.

220   Even if the Teatro Olimpico in Vicenza, begun in 1580 by Andrea Palladio and completed in 1585 by Vincenzo Scamozzi, reproduced a Renaissance courtyard composed by a colonnade with statues surrounding the audience and a blue ceiling simulating an open sky, and thus seems to be ann obvious influence, Eberson never directly referenced this classical example in his writing.   221   Gaston Bachelard, *L'air et les songes. Essai sur l'imagination du mouvement* (Paris: José Corti, 1942), 212–214.   222   Hubert Damish, *Théorie du nuage, pour une histoire de la peinture* (Paris: Éditions du Seuil, 1972), 14.

The characteristic of atmospheric theaters is that they are designed to evoke a particular time and place through the use of spotlights, electric light and plaster mouldings and ornaments that reenact the feeling of being in the open air. Exotic set designs frame a stage hidden behind a draped curtain. The scenography generally forms the outline of the room and stands out against a simulated sky on the intrados of the room. In this way, atmospheric theater assumes the role of making the room a spectacle in its own right, a space that modernity and generic cinemas will soon neutralize: the audience discovers this interiorized cityscape through a magical ritual of fictitious nightfall and cinematic daybreak. Thus, electricity participates in the spectacle of the illusion. Indirect lighting is widely used to recreate outdoor gardens by reversing the natural order: light for the night represented by the room's décor and darkness for the projected show. (223) The architecture is then exposed to new laws, it explores new possibilities of the relationship between nature and artifice, between artificial nature and natural artifice. This game of illusion inhabits atmospheric cinemas at a time when the seventh art is investing in spaces that are by technical necessity enclosed, to be able to totally control the illusionary capacity of the projected film, without interference from the outside environment. It is a paradoxical form of project in which architecture challenges its own material properties through artificial illusionary devices. It is in this context of the rise of the illusionist spectacle and the intensification of a more open social and worldly life than the classical theater that the theme of night becomes central. Thus,

223 Anne-Elisabeth Buxtorf, "La salle de cinéma à Paris entre les deux guerres : l'utopie à l'épreuve de la modernité," *Bibliothèque de l'Ecole des chartes* 163, no. 1 (2005): 143.

the reversal of the cycle of light and darkness is a natural part of the ceremonial of the film show, inside a closed box that operates an artificial nightscape, simulating a luminous progression, a sunrise, which will give way to the lighting of the film once the show has begun. An artifice within the artifice, the former erasing the latter, that is the principle of atmospheric theater translated into light.

In order to grasp some of the meanings at stake in the atmospheric theaters and the artificialization of the sky, it is necessary to have a broader view of the history of theaters in relation to nature. This relation is often seen, by historians as well as designers, as a lost link, a kind of nostalgia for the continuity between the theaters and its natural environment, as exemplified by the open-air theaters from antiquity. In that sense, a theater architect and scenographer like Joseph Urban offers a relevant example. In his treatise *Theatres* written in 1929, he explicitly develops the idea that the main task of today's designers is to rebuild through performance venues antiquity's ideal link between architecture, audience, actor and nature, a process at the very heart of his project of the Musical Centre, supposed to "live or disappear through lights", and "like the theatres of the Greeks", to "enfold the beginnings of a drama in obscurity, and gradually disclose it to the audience". (224) The same diagnosis of a lost link is perceptible in the "Natural history of the theatre", an essay imagined by Theodor Adorno at the beginning of the thirties:

224 Joseph Urban, *Theatres* (New-York: Theatre Arts Press, 1929), s. p.

"Where today we have the gallery [...] the sky used to peer in on the theatre, and the play of the drifting clouds dreamily made contact with the human theatre beneath. Those who sat there were the spokesmen of the clouds in the trial of the stage action taking place below; the legitimacy of that action could be weakened or broken by their objections. [...]. The dome has long since closed over the theatre and now reflects the sounds coming from the stage, barring a view of the sky. But those who sit nearest to it [...] know that the roof is not firmly fixed above them and wait to see whether it won't burst open one day and bring about that reunification of stage and reality which is reflected for us in an image composed equally of memory and hope". (225)

This tension between stage and reality, blurring the theater with nature and considering them as an artificial autonomous entity, is a strong and useful reading key on atmospheric cinemas. And yet the separation from real nature is not a fatality as the *corral de comedias* and the Elizabethan theater perfectly illustrate in the first purpose-built permanent theaters, conceived as perimetral structures isolating a portion of the existing ground and the above sky. Indeed, like the traditional proscenium of the Renaissance, the atmospheric theater is based on the principle of an enclosed and artificial space, a principle which guarantees a comfortable condition for the cinematic illusion, suggesting to completely replay both nature and the city inside the building. The atmospheric night created within atmospheric cinemas could therefore be qualified, from this perspective, as a "lost night": the deliberate choice of

225 Theodor Adorno, "Histoire naturelle du théâtre ," *Musique en jeu* (1974) : 4.

reproducing a modernist sky by technical means as separated from the real night. On another note, at the same epoch, a second kind of hybrid atmospheric model appears. The drive-in formulates a model where the natural sky remains a part of the overall setup, even if it can be conditioned by a certain urban environment.

The absolute protagonist of this atmospheric effervescence was John Eberson, an electrical engineer of Austro-Hungarian origin (born in what is Ukraine today) who, after studying at the University of Vienna, migrated to the United States in 1901. Eberson worked first in an electricity company, and after a few years joined the Johnson Realty and Construction Company, a construction company specializing in theaters, promoting opera houses in small American towns, for which he became the designer. In 1908, John Eberson opened his own firm in St Louis, and in 1923 he created the first atmospheric cinema, the Houston Majestic, in Texas. Eberson designed this theatrical model more than a hundred times in the United States before and exported it to other countries such as South America and Australia, but also to France where he was a consultant for the creation of the Grand Rex in Paris in 1932. This career path makes Eberson one of the most important builders of scenic venues in history, alongside architects such as Fellner and Helmer in the 19th century. Eberson's designs have close antecedents such as Philadelphia's New Theatre (1794) with a ceiling painted as a daytime sky, in the manner of many eighteenth-century opera houses, and Chicago's Cort Theatre (John Pridmore, 1909) designed as an outdoor amphitheater with a sky, moon

and stars that were viewed through a trellis with hanging vines. Or the Winter Garden in Toronto (Thomas Lamb, 1913) is another striking anticipation, designed to simulate an outdoor scene with murals of plants, trellises and even a lamp post on the walls, while the ceiling was covered with real dried hanging leaves of beech and wisteria floating gently in the breeze produced by a fan. As part of this whimsical setting, the lights were transformed into lanterns and the columns into tree trunks. As a result, the stage area itself represented the sky with painted clouds and an illuminated moon.

Returning to the first genuinely atmospheric achievement, the Majestic Houston (1923), Eberson was both architect and set designer in his desire to recreate the illusion of an Italian piazza. Behind a neoclassical facade resembling a Roman palace, one entered the stage in a garden enclosed by asymmetrical walls of different sizes and dimensions with balconies and windows lit from within to simulate an internal life in contrast to the atmosphere of a simulated exterior. Fake tiles formed the roofs, trees and artificial vines were realistically placed on the facades. The ceiling was painted a dark blue, lit by a blue light that simulated evening twilight. The ceiling was perforated with bright lights that looked like stars. Moving clouds were projected on it. Just before the show, an orange light reproduced the sunset.

Even if the very first cinematographic projection rooms were of great simplicity—rectangular volumes with a stage to accommodate a piano and an auditorium filled with wooden chairs or benches—it is easy to find several other examples and contexts that may have inspired the emergence of atmospheric theaters. For several combined reasons, the scenography of the heavens featured in the atmospheric theaters has to be compared to a model invented more or less at the same time in Germany: namely, the modern planetarium. Planned to be built at the Deutsches Museum of Munich and as a prototype on the roof of the Zeiss factory in Jena, it is important to underline that the concept of Walther Bauersfeld is revolutionary in itself by the way it pictured the sky. If the famous engraving by Fischer von Erlach of the Hungarian imperial bath, or the even more famous Newton's cenotaph by Etienne-Louis Boullée, prove that the stars used to be represented in ancient times by perforating the domes, the electrified version of the planetarium reverses the very direction of light. No more natural sunlight depicting the other distant suns, but a central projection able to light up the vault and, most of all, to revolve. (226) These centrifugal and centripetal ways of lighting the sky are interestingly both present in the atmospheric archetype. In the Palace Theatre of Marion, for instance, the ceiling is punctually electrified to represent the stars, while a cloud machine displays the lower atmospheric layers. The Merced Theatre and the Akron Civic Theatre work nearly the same way, as does the Fox Theatre of Atlanta, which furthermore benefits from an additional system of flickering stars. These dramatic devices and effects, ever more impressive and immersive for the public, are not very far from the functioning

226 On these different aspects, see Yann Rocher (ed.), *Globes. Architecture et sciences explorent le monde* (Paris: Cité de l'architecture et du patrimoine/Norma, 2017).

of the planetarium which has alternated between a popular interpretation of the sky as a show and the scientific demonstration of it from its earliest beginnings. The models of heavens by Abbas Ibn Firnas or Erhard Weigel, both known for having provided weather effects in their respective cosmos theaters, are perfect examples of this. (227) Ultimately, cosmology—i.e. the order governing the atmosphere—is a relevant notion for understanding an entertainment space like the atmospheric cinema. Not only because each dome or vault in architecture, since at least the Roman Pantheon, calls for a cosmology. Not only because each performance venue, since the Globe Theatre of London, calls for a cosmology likewise. The theatrical repertoire and the scenography have often been concerned with models of representation of the sky, of the night, and more generally with what is called in astronomy the "frame of reference": the way of structuring the astronomical device according to a particular point of view within the cosmos. A significant example from this point of view is the Spectatorium designed by James Steele MacKaye for the Columbian Exhibition of Chicago in 1893. In order to achieve the most realistic performance of the discovery of America, MacKaye patents an incredible amount of inventions, among which a "Wind-making apparatus" and a "Nebulator" for rain and cloud effects. (228) But his quest for realism also concerns the representation of the night sky, as a reporter points out after seeing the model of the project:

227   Rocher, *Globes*, 46–47.

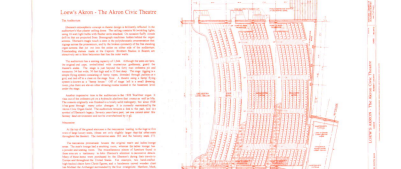

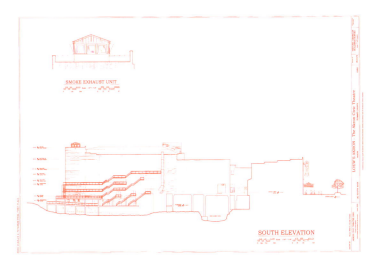

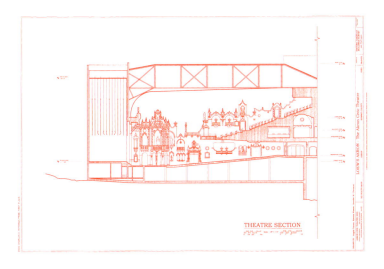

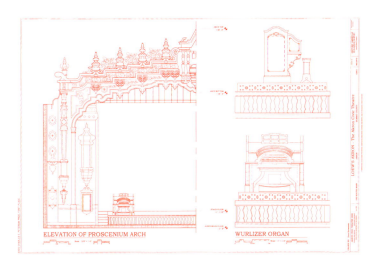

"By a peculiar arrangement [...] there is made to appear on this background of sky the constellations of the southern hemisphere, each star being given its correct magnitude by the light which attends it, and each being set at the proper place in the firmament from a chart furnished by the ablest astronomers of the day." (229)

In other words, despite their indisputable fanciful variations on the sky—as fanciful as the Egyptian cinemas of the same period can be –, the atmospheric theaters may be related to this dramatic science of the night representation. And one of the high representatives of this practical cosmology would then be Jules Moynet, whose words of *L'envers du théâtre* in 1873 sounds like a premonition of Eberson's invention:

"The sky is sprinkled with twinkling stars, admirably imitated by means of a series of little gadgets. A little square of tin, fitted at the center with an imitation diamond of colored glass is sewn on the back of the curtain. A tiny lamp fitted there sends its light through the facets of the diamond which is just opposite a hole cut in the curtain. The light twinkles as you look at it. This is quite a cumbersome thing, however, since it requires a light for each star. One could undoubtedly obtain the same effect with one or several sources of electric light." (230)

As a matter of fact, Eberson remains the most important creator of the 'atmospheric' type of theater through the amplitude of his production and the professionalization of his firm, which was to undergo further developments. But what exactly did the adjective 'atmospheric' mean in Eberson's conception and furthermore in the context of

228 Yann Rocher, *Théâtres en utopie* (Paris: Actes Sud, 2014), 62–67. 229 Joseph A. Sokalski, *Picturing illusionnism. The theatre of Steele MacKaye* (Montreal: McGill-Queen's University Press, 2007), 227. 230 Sokalski, *Picturing illusionnism*, 227–228.

his epoch? In referring to Gottfried Semper, Mark Wigley reminds us that a tradition in architectural theory directly connects the idea of atmosphere to the art of the stage and to theatrical effects. (231) To the German theorist "the haze of carnival candles" was to be the true "atmosphere of art". If according to Semper the destruction of reality, of the material, is prerequisite to artistic creation, this very destruction goes through a complete technical mastering. "Only complete technical perfection, only the judicious and proper treatment of the material according to its proprieties, and above all only the consideration of these proprieties in the act of shaping form can cause the material to be forgotten, can liberate the artistic creation from it, can elevate even a simple landscape painting to become a high work of art." (232) Architecture was indeed interconnected with décor, the outer surface and techniques capable of producing a specific atmosphere, one that can sublimate the reality of construction.

This very notion of atmosphere as (technical) effects, capable of erasing the material, is at the center of Eberson's creation. According to his writing, "atmospheric" was used to designate the various scenographic, decorative and technical contributions referring to other worlds, from Egypt to Persia, via Andalusia and the Mediterranean sky, and was also applied to service and circulation spaces such as halls, lounges, balconies, and mezzanines. Asymmetrical spatial organization was the order of the day to keep the public's interest at the highest level. If illusion was "the thing", any predictable effect of repetition was an obstacle to the magic of wonder theater, as the great lighting

231 Mark Wigley, "The Architecture of Atmosphere," *Daidalos* 68, 1998, 20. 232 Gottfried Semper, *Style in the Technical and Tectonic Arts, Or, Practical Aesthetics* (1860), trans. Harry Francis Mallgrave and Michael Robinson (Los Angeles: Getty Research Institute, 2004), 439.

expert put it. "Asymmetry is essential in a scheme of this kind because it gives the variety needed to keep interest high and, importantly, repetition would destroy that illusion—here the illusion is the thing." (233)

A commentator in the *Daily News* in 1929 described Eberson's versatility as a creator of modern theater, combining both classical pictorial skill with a mastery of the electrical potentialities of his time: "He was a man of great conceptions, realized in the smallest practical detail. He was more than an architect, however, in implementing his revolutionary innovations in theater construction, he followed in the footsteps of the great Michelangelo. Employing many arts, Mr Eberson is an architect, engineer, interior decorator, and wall painter, using artificial lighting as well as brushes to achieve his colour effect, and he applies all this knowledge to create his contribution to the modern theatre—the illusion of the outdoors." (234)

On another note, the illusion of the outdoors constitutes an additional similarity that brings us again to the modern planetarium, in terms of the structure of the sky itself, and of distance. Just like Bauersfeld's starry vault, but also like many georamas of the 19th and 20th centuries, the atmospheric theater faces the question of how to express infinity in an enclosed geometry. This specific problem finds a concrete answer in the planetarium through a double device. On the one hand, a 360° horizon, which usually symbolizes the countryside and nearby urbanizations thanks to a play of shadows, and on the other hand, a hemispherical screen welcoming the intangible stars provided by

233 John Eberson in Steve Levin, *A John Eberson Scrapbook*, Theatre Historical Society of America Annual no. 27, Chicago, 2000, 30.
234 Ernest Griffen, *Westchester County and Its People: A Record* (New York: Lewis Historical Publishing Company, 1946); Frances Mather, "Mostly About People," *Daily News*, May 4, 1929, 2.

the projecting method. In fact, Eberson's model is organized according to the same contrast between a peripheral and plastic foreground, and a distant and smooth second plan of the sky; except that the movie theater, unlike the centered space of the planetarium, is also built on a horizontal tension between the audience's cavea and the cinema screen. Basically, the atmospheric theater had to combine and accommodate two contradictory projections, two contradictory modes of representation within its space: the vertical frame of the open sky, and the horizontal frame of the cinematic window.

Night and day cycles are usually used for scientific purposes in cultural venues. In natural history museums, for example, the diurnal and nocturnal succession can certainly be spectacular. Still, it is above all a way to illustrate the biological rhythm of a given environment. In rare cases, like the Fleishmann Atmospherium-Planetarium in Reno at its opening in 1963, this idea can lead to an even more accurate simulation of night and day conditions, with a full range of phenomena including cloud formations, thunderstorms or rainbows. Comparatively, it appears that the nocturnal narration of the atmospheric theater fulfils the function of a gradual transition between the open sky and cinematic window. As night falls over the audience, day is dawning on the screen, assuming a theatricality of the auditorium itself, generally limited to the golden stucco and the raising of the curtain, the latter being preserved in the cinematographic ritual of today. This theatricality of the auditorium has often been the subject of debate in the history of theaters. Not only for the risk of overshadowing the theatricality of the show itself but also for its possible remaining presence during the show. In that respect, the nocturnal narration of the atmospheric theater certainly does not provide enough darkness to fully neutralize the exuberant forms of its architecture. Maybe this choice can be seen as a sort of spatial compensation to the frontal and pictorial condition of the cinema screen? From another perspective, the relatively simple apparatus of atmospheric cinemas was also considered to be inexpensive and convinced several theater owners to use it to promote the culture of the show to a wider audience. An electric panel controlling the lights could be operated by a single operator and the plaster mouldings were less expensive than the more rigid decorations of traditional theaters. Driven by a generous and egalitarian spirit, Eberson believed that he could educate masses of cinemagoers by immersing them in classic environments and experiences of grandeur for a minimal price. This combination of refined culture and economy resulting from technological advances in equipment and an innovative approach to construction using prefabricated elements was the secret of Eberson's success and allowed him to produce ever larger and more complex movie palaces across the United States for several years. (235)

At the beginning of the 1930s, at the end of the craze for the atmospheric, John Eberson and his son Dew turned to the construction of numerous theaters in the Deco style of the time, transforming the box of illusions into a

235 Celeste M. Williams and Dietmar E. Froehlich, art. cit., 575.

streamlined decorated space. Theaters were reduced in size, volumes were simplified, and plans were standardized, illusionist decorations gave way to other elements such as mirrors and acoustic panels. (236) We can assume that this process of simplification encountered economic, aesthetic, and technical needs, giving to movie theaters a kind of aseptic specialization that made cinemas more and more autonomous from other venues such as theaters and planetariums. Firstly, after years of exuberance and a pronounced taste for exoticism, the 1929 crisis came to impose a less conspicuous style by simplifying and standardizing the interior decoration, as illustrated by Norman Bel Geddes' search for a new functional, efficient, and economic theater model. (237) Secondly, this tendency met rising modern architectural ideals of simplification, erasing all figurative tendencies, and leading toward an abstraction of shapes. And finally, as movies are products of an art of illusion by projecting the spectator to imagined places and times through a unique bi-dimensional surface, their venues stopped offering visionary stages, rather becoming technical containers predominantly designed for the technical operation of sound and image systems. Moving images ended up completely capturing the attention of the public, thus making any other inputs such as zenithal heavens and exotic Mediterranean scenes unnecessary distractions from the cinematographic spectacle. In other words, with the normalization of the cinematic projection, movie theaters become neutral and standardized places progressively circumscribed by completely black walls. Indeed, the figurative night of the atmospheric theater was definitively replaced by the abstract night of the modernist venue.

236 Celeste M. Williams and Dietmar E. Froehlich, "John Eberson and the Development of the Movie Theater: Fantasy and Escape", 91st ACSA International conference, Helsinki, July 27-30, 2003, 577.
237 Norman Bel Geddes, "Industrializing the theatre," *Horizons* (Boston: Little, Brown & Co 1932), 140-158.

TOWARDS HAPPINESS AND EMOTIONS
Light in Socialist Realist Interiors in Poland
Aleksandra Sumorok

Issues associated with Socialist Realist art (architecture) have to a large extent become related to its perception and impact. The interior of a building was to be carefully directed, arranged, furnished as well as lightened. Artificial light in particular gained special meaning—it was easy to control, granted from above (by the authorities, the party), made available to everyone. Literally dazzling interiors were to confirm the fact that culture had become widely accessible and that its class habitus had changed. The problem of light in Stalinist culture is found in a number of contexts, e.g. the symbolic, political-propaganda, modernization and psychological ones that often overlap. Emphasis was openly put on the fact that architecture is not only a spatial form, but also a design of human behaviours that determines people's well-being and emotions. The then-popular slogan of the "engineering of the soul" included an extended definition of architecture and interior related to sociology and psychology. The interior was given a lot of rights connected with the possibility of creating (the right) emotions. One of the basic postulates of the doctrine concerned the necessity to create bright optimistic interiors filled with warm light. (238) Artificial lighting was thus carefully designed to affect mood and provide the desired contrasts (e.g. upper and lower zones), taking over the higher sphere associated with heaven and the sacred. Light was supposed to transform the interior into an "unreal" intangible structure. It became an element of stage design that directed suspense, built up meaning and had emotional appeal. Reading the luminosity of the interior is based on intertextuality. (239) It is because luminosity was co-created not only by design guidelines related strictly to architecture or the interior (there were not too many of them as far as the detailed programme was concerned) but also by literature texts that added definition to the problem. In the case of interiors, the ideological and symbolic sphere coexisted with that strictly architectural one. On the one hand, light was treated as an immaterial mystical factor. On the other hand, it was made present in the form of a very consistent and carefully designed lighting system—chandeliers, illuminated ceilings, etc. As it is rightly noted by Katerina Clark, the author of many important texts regarding Stalinist culture, "… The two dominant branches of the arts were linked in the one discursive system". (240) The case presented here has the character of a preliminary overview. The multitude of research perspectives that emerge in connection with light in a Stalinist interior require enhanced study. Reading the Socialist Realist interior in the context of light also definitely triggers a lot of new research areas.

238 Tadeusz Nowakowski, "Słońce w architekturze i urbanistyce," *Architektura*, no. 8 (1951): 251–255.   239 Wojciech Tomasik, *Inżynieria dusz. Literatura realizmu socjalistycznego w planie "propagandy monumentalnej"* (Wrocław: Leopoldinum, 1999).   240 Katerina Clark, "The 'New Moscow' and the New 'Happiness': Architecture as a Nodal Point in the Stalinist System of Value" in *Petrified Utopia. Happiness Soviet Style*, eds. Malina Balina and Evgeny Dobrenko (London-NewYork: Anthem Press, 2009), 199.

The Symbolic Dimension of Light

The question of the symbolic dimension of light in Stalinist culture has received academic attention. Researchers have so far emphasized the sacralization of space also in relation to light (Katarina Clark, *Socialist Realism and the Sacralizing of Space* (241)), the importance of light in the Leninist plan of monumental propaganda and in Stalinist culture (Julia Chadaga, *Light in Captivity: Spectacular Glass and Soviet Power in the 1920s and 1930s* (242)).

A very good example of a symbolic illumination practice are the pentagonal ruby stars installed in the 1930s on the towers of the Moscow Kremlin. They showed, in a symbolic manner, the luminous spectacle in the sky, especially at night; the triumph of technology; the overcoming of nature and night. They also made a clear biblical reference to the Star of Bethlehem, since they heralded the New Era that was to spring from the October Revolution. (243)

Light became one of the most important ideological dogmas "made present" in interiors. The notion of an alchemy of light and mysticism appeared, and "luminous metaphors" were widely used—broad streets turned into lines of light, and skyscrapers turned into palaces of light.

Electric light in particular gained a profound symbolic meaning. It contributed to overcoming evil identified as darkness. It referred to an archetype that had been rooted in culture for centuries.

Yet, these symbolic goals coexisted with practical ones concerning electrification as part of a modernization project.

Radiance, Optimism and Beauty

Light space has for ages significantly influenced the mental and physical well-being of its inhabitants. The possibility to program its reception and direct it towards creating a happy society became especially tempting at the times of Socialist Realist social engineering (244) and sensory psychomanipulation.

The persuasive character of Socialist Realist art and architecture was largely based on reinforced messages obtained by manipulating perception and directed above all at creating the impression of happiness and optimism (as the paramount categories of socialism). It is because architecture was to reflect a happy joyful life of the nation, full of energy and vitality. For example, the works of Alexey Shchusev, one of the most important "classics" of Soviet architecture, were described in the following way:

> Shchusev's works are characterized by [...] outstanding joy of life and youth. These features reflect the character of our socialist era, its inexhaustible powers and unstoppable progress—towards a more and more colourful, and happier life of the nation. (245)

Happiness was to be ensured by beautiful architecture filled with light and by its interior—the most common and direct transmitter of socialist content at the time, which

---

241 Katerina Clark, "Socialist Realism and the Sacralizing of Space" in *The Landscape of Stalinism: The Art and Ideology of Soviet Space*, eds. Evgeny Dobrenko and Eric Naiman (Seattle: University of Washington Press, 2003), 3–18.   242 Julia Chadaga, "Light in Captivity: Spectacular Glass and Soviet Power in the 1920s and 1930s," *Slavic Review*, no. 1, (Spring 2007): 82–105.   243 Chadaga, *Light in Captivity*, 103.   244 Edmund Goldzamt, "*Zagadnienie realizmu socjalistycznego w architekturze*," in *O polską architekturę socjalistyczną*, ed. Jan Minorski (Warszawa: PWT, 1950), 24.   245 A. Michajłow, "A.W. Szczusiew wybitny architekt epoki radzieckiej," *Architektura*, no. 2 (1951): 61.

everyone dealt with on a daily basis. In the following decades, emotions were to be acted on by, among others, mass media (especially television), while propaganda efforts did not focus on the promotion of (beautiful) material tissue (or creating a vision of such a tissue), but on the new, happy, quasi-consumerist lifestyle. (246) However, in the Soviet Union in the 1930s, and then in the Socialist states of Central and Eastern Europe after 1949, it was mainly beautiful architecture that was responsible for manipulating perception. However, it was also burdened with other tasks as well. Clark emphasizes that "The turn to 'beauty' meant a reaction against avant-gardism and a return to conventional tastes, but the foregrounding of the beautiful was also tied to other issues". (247) She also notes that "Soviet culture of these years might be discussed in terms of the Enlightenment". (248)

Rebuilding Moscow in the 1930s, and especially its new palaces and underground places (metro stations) literally became an Enlightenment project; "the 'new Moscow' was to be a city of 'light.' It was also, as a feat of modernization, aimed at increasing the well-being of residents, at bringing happiness (making people 'gayer')". (249)

Socialist Realism, which in the Soviet Union lasted for over 20 years, underwent various phases and development stages from the very beginning, i.e. since the 1930s—from monumentalized art deco to Neoclassicism and Neo-Baroque—these phases were different, but always subjected to the rule of monumentalism, increased decoration creating an "attractive" casing for the new Socialist Realist social reality. Light performed an important role in design right from the initial formation stage. Even before Socialist Realism had been decreed as the only permissible style, modernist (or, to be more precise, constructivist) designs submitted for competitions had emphasized the significance of light, e.g. the one by Alexandr Vesin for the Narkomtiazhprom Building (Ministry of Heavy Industry, 1934). (250) However, the luminosity of the still modernist architecture of the time mainly emphasized issues related to modernization, industrialization and changing the class habitus. (251)

While the doctrine was being popularized, the role of light underwent a gradual change towards a more symbolic, but mostly sensory dimension related to manipulating perception, and the will to ensure happiness and well-being. The phenomenon was exemplified in the Moscow metro stations. A modern means of transport, enriched with palace-like decorations, set the ideal of "modern" space combining what is "old" (traditional in terms of form) with what is "new" (in a technical and social dimension). The Moscow metro also represented the most important and coherent utterance regarding Socialist Realist interior design. (252) It established the canon of Socialist Realist interior design aimed at the creation of luxury spaces filled not only with expensive materials, marble, granite and detail but also saturated with light. Such underground palaces were to appear not only in the Soviet Union, but also in countries where Socialist Realism was imposed after 1949, e.g. in Warsaw and Budapest. (253) At the time, people wrote about the wonderful marble platforms and vestibule spaces of the Moscow metro, flooded with warm (sic) light. (254) The luminosity of this design was additionally praised in many poems (aimed at a broader audience from other socialist countries, consisting

246 Christe Evans, "Le « mode de vie soviétique » en tant que manière de sentir : émotion et influence sur la télévision centrale soviétique sous Brežnev," *Cahiers du monde russe,* no. 2, 2015, 543–570.   247 Clark, *The new Moscow,* 192.   248 Clark, *The new Moscow,* 194.   249 Clark, *The new Moscow,* 195.   250 Igor Kazus, "Architectural competitions in the Soviet Union during the 1930s and the formation of Soviet Art Deco and neo-classical styles" in *Sztuka Europy Wschodniej. Polska-Rosja. Sztuka i historia. Sztuka polska, sztuka rosyjska i polsko-rosyjskie kontakty artystyczne XX-XXI wieku,* eds. Irina Gavrash and Jerzy Malinowski (Warszawa—Toruń: PISSŚ, 2014), 268–275.   251 General slogans, imported in the form of ready-made formulas, were implemented in Central Europe gradually after 1948, after the rejection of the Marshall Plan. A number of political changes were then introduced in each of the countries of the so-called Eastern Bloc—a single party system, industrialization plans as well as Soviet-type modernization. An identical system imposed on different countries and economies brought different results for Poland, Czechoslovakia or Germany (the German Democratic Republic). Far-reaching changes also took place in the sphere of culture. There was a "soft" revolution at first, which became decreed with time, resulting in administrative implementation of rules of the doctrine in the whole field of culture, including interior design. Selected architects would become familiar with Socialist Realist architectural works directly in Moscow during "training trips." However, it should be noted that the Socialist Realist theoreticians who were assigned to "implement" the doctrine and give lectures on the new style had become well acquainted with forms of Stalinist architecture much earlier—already in the 1930s, or during the war. The architectural profession was subjected to control, design offices were nationalized and centralized, the system of architectural education was changed. The turning point for Polish architecture was the year 1949 when Socialist Realism was decreed.   252 Karen Kettering, "An Introduction to the Design of the Moscow Metro in the Stalin Period: The Happiness of the Life Underground," *Studies in the Decorative Arts* 2, vol. 7, (2000): 2–20.   253 "Konkurs SARP na projekty szkicowe stacji metra warszawskiego," *Architektura,* no. 3 (1953).   254 Józef Łucki, *Architektura metra moskiewskiego* (Katowice, 1951), 1.

of those who have not seen Moscow), e.g. the one written in Poland by Mieczysław Jastrun, about the Mayakovskaya metro station:

> You send out
> The rays of motion
> Rolling the underground sun,
> Continuous
> Inspiration. (255)

In the case of the metro, an underground construction, darkness identified with evil and the old order was defeated, both literally and symbolically. Light contributed to making the underground interior unreal, overcoming the dichotomy between day and night, and between what is above and below the ground. This fairy-tale mood was accessible to everyone, which is pointed out by Sheila Fitzpatrick:

> The first metro line was launched in the mid-1930s—its chandeliers, long escalators and spacious stations caused widespread admiration. (256)

The day-night/dark-bright dichotomy was to be overcome in interiors, especially in those located at the underground level. A good example from Poland is the Muranów cinema building in Warsaw (architect: Michał Ptic-Borkowski). The designers aimed to avoid creating the impression of being in a cellar, and remove any discomfort connected with staying underground, in rooms with relatively low ceilings. That is why the cinema, apart from rich artistic decoration, was equipped with various indirect and direct lighting solutions in the form of an illuminated ceiling or wall lamps.

Monumental tower blocks, described as buildings made of light, were also to be perceived by the proletarian as fairy-tale palaces or lanterns. These mainly included the seven monumental tower blocks ("vysotka") built in Moscow between 1938 and 1957, and the eighth such design in Warsaw, the Palace of Culture and Science in Warsaw, a "gift" from the Soviet Union that opened in 1955. These palaces were to offer a new type of life as well as fairy-tale beauty also related to light. Luminosity, however, was not ensured by glazed modern architecture (condemned at the time), but by traditional architecture with small windows, lit from the inside thanks to artificial light. It was frequently emphasized that the light emanated from the building in the evening, connecting the Palace with the city outside. (257) In practice, the emanation of radiance took on a more symbolic meaning, as the monumental stone (not glass) building emitted much more light outside than a modern one with walls made of glass panels.

Designing Luminosity and the Way of Feeling

According to doctrinal requirements in Poland after 1949, designers became "engineers of the soul" obliged to direct the thoughts of a socialist human being towards light and happiness. (258) They consciously used

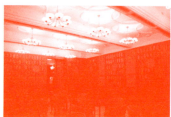

---

255 After: Tomasik, *Inżynieria dusz*, 99. Translated by Ewa Muszczynko for the purposes of the paper. 256 Sheila Fitzpatrick, *Życie codzienne pod rządami Stalina. Rosja radziecka w latach trzydziestych XX wieku*, (Cracow: Uniwersytet Jagielloński, 2012), 100. 257 "Przed Otwarciem PKiN," *Architektura*, no. 7 (1955). 258 Goldzamt, *Zagadnienie*, 26.

perception mechanisms and psychosomatic conditions as the instrument of persuasion. The main ideologist of Socialist Realism in Poland, responsible for the acquisition of doctrinal rules, Edmund Goldzamt, wrote candidly that "architectural forms do not trigger reasoning, but emotional associations: they create an artistic expression and not thought concepts". (259) The Socialist Realist form was thus mainly to be sensory, immediate and total in form, a "Stalinist Gesamtkunstwerk", as Boris Groys called it, although he was referring to issues slightly different than the sensory perception of an architectural work described here. (260)

According to the idea of a Gesamtkunstwerk, the whole interior, including its arrangement, structure, decoration, material, space and also light—capable of binding the whole composition, but mostly of affecting moods—was responsible for creating impressions and emotions.

A cardinal issue was to create bright, shiny and luminous spaces that would be easy to grasp. Light was to highlight/emphasize a "beautified", enhanced world (and interior) filled with pseudo-historical decoration that compensated reality, heralding/promising a better tomorrow. Consequently, dark interiors were considered pessimistic, non-noble and inappropriate. (261) A cultural code was additionally imposed on the entirety of light space—both on its physical and impression-based dimensions. The space was to induce a number of palace-related associations and underline the fact that palace glamour has become widely accessible, being a gift that evoked human faith in the New State. Light was combined with the "content" of socialist architecture informing one about the advancement of the socialist society, a change of its class habitus and a civilizational leap (industrialization, urbanization). Artificial lighting was strictly associated with the modernization dimension of communist states and turned into a symbol of progress, erasing differences between the city and countryside. In the early 1950s, one could read in Polish press that the light bulb "brings one the joy of living" and constitutes "a joyful sign of progress", contributing to a cultural advancement:

> Over vast areas of Poland, the electric bulb has already replaced the smouldering and firecausing kerosene or oil lamp that has so far been used in many of our villages. From month to month, and from year to year, there are more and more of these light bulbs that not only bring us the joy of living, but also raise the culture of the countryside household, ensure fire safety, make work easier and are conducive to cleanliness and hygiene. (262)

The light bulb itself mainly represented modernity and was responsible for transforming the state, while radiance became a broader term that was applied to representative interiors (or interior complexes) that were considered active, and responsible for shaping the mood and programming the impressions of large groups of people, e.g. halls, theater foyers, auditoria, cafes, restaurants, or train stations. Designing perceptions related to temperature, which strongly influences human well-being, became of key importance for such interiors. Light helped build the dichotomous break between warmth and cold, between what is individual and commonly available, intimate (warm)

---

259 Goldzamt, *Zagadnienie*, 24. 260 Boris Groys, *The Total Art of Stalinism: Avant-Garde, Aesthetic Dictatorship, and Beyond* (Verso, 2011).
261 Jan Minorski, "Nowe wnętrza Teatru Narodowego w Warszawie na tle współczesnych zadań architektury," *Architektura*, no. 5-6 (1950): 132–133.
262 Tadeusz Dobrowolski, *Oświetlenie elektryczne* (Warszawa: PWT, 1951), 3.

and sublime (cold). As a result, we deal with a range of often contradicting emotions—joy and solemnity, anxiety and tranquillity. Overcoming dichotomies, however, constituted an inherent feature of that period. It was postulated that a "pleasant mood" should be projected in interiors of the cultural, services and recreation sectors, using lamps (especially fluorescent ones) of warm white colour, while the interiors of state buildings should be saturated with rather cold light.

Sophisticated contrast between light and shadow was often applied to project warmcold impressions. It was especially popular to place an indirect light source on top in the form of a skylight and to darken the bottom. This method was used by Bogdan Pniewski, among others, in one of the most important state interiors of the first half of the 1950s in Poland, designed for the parliament and described in the official *Architektura* journal in the following way: So, the light, colours and shade intensity are distributed in such a way that it is darkest at the bottom and brightest, or rather brilliantly shiny, on top. Such an impression is largely contributed to by gray stucco columns that are narrower in their lower part and illuminated from the top, producing beautiful shading effects—as if washed with watercolour going down on their surface. (263)

Lighting the upper part of a room was associated with the concept of space verticalization that served to control the "higher" sphere that had so far been traditionally connected with the sacrum.

The luminosity of a Socialist Realist interior was created on the basis of various architectural and artistic tools. These not only included light fixtures, but also interior arrangement itself and the material or detail applied. The key aspect here, according to the postulate of the doctrine, was connected with projecting impressions, sensory and instinctive perception, as well as the sphere of direct emotional impact of the building and its interior on and through the human senses. (264) Light, through its direct impact, did not require complex thought processes connected with, for example, the right interpretation of iconographic representations.

One of the most important factors responsible for the intensification of radiance and its reception in an interior was the material used. Its texture and the surface treatment method applied make the recipient perceive an interior as warm (cosy, peaceful, intimate) or cold (not cosy, overwhelming, intimidating). During the period of Socialist Realism, reflective materials—polished stone (marble, granite), shiny lining with glossy surfaces, or metal, e.g. polished brass—were more often used in representative interiors. What is interesting, in accordance with the spirit of the time and the assumptions of monumental architecture, the impression of cold would often dominate an interior

263 Jan Maas, "Wartości plastyczne wnętrz gmachu sejmu," *Architektura,* no. 2 (1953): 37.   264 The problem of pleasure as part of socialist happiness was pointed out by Emma Widdis. Emma Widdis, "Sew Yourself Soviet: the Pleasure of Textile in Machine Age," in *Petrified Utopia. Happiness Soviet Style*, eds. Malina Balina and Evgeny Dobrenko (London-NewYork: Anthem Press, 2009), 117.

despite quantitative balance between the use of warm and cold elements (materials). The so-called warm materials, such as wood, would take on new properties when their surface was covered with a glossy layer of varnish. Mirrors were used as reflective surfaces in order to increase the luminosity of an interior—a method that had been known for ages. Materials used in such ways contributed to strong and uniform saturation of interiors with light.

Light spots sometimes did not contribute to achieving the effect of radiance, but brought out important values of the material, detail, decoration, or artistic wall arrangements, contributing to increased sensory perception. This was mainly achieved with the help of hidden light sources or wall lamps. Light-absorbing materials were also more willingly used at the time—ones that would not cause light reflections, such as ceramic lining or fabrics (curtains or carpets), additionally contributing to the impression of warming interior space and obtaining positive sensory experience.

The intensity of light experience in an interior was not only connected with the material, but with the entirety of the composition. The interior structure itself—transparent, without obstacles, not fragmented—would make lighting easier. Large rectangular rooms were preferred—ones that were easy to be evenly saturated with light. It must be remembered that the space of a Socialist Realist interior was to be subjected to the idea of building a classless society. Organized in such a way, it might have been perceived as overwhelming, uncomfortable and deprived of intimacy. Its function, however, was to reinforce the new social order that would ensure happiness and content in the long run.

The Art of Light. Light Fixtures.

In practice, however, most attention was paid to artificial lighting and light fixtures. In the first half of the 1950s, a number of handbooks were published in Poland on the nature of electric, artificial lighting. They would focus on practical issues, exploring the still fairly new phenomenon. Representative interiors were treated differently, as the dominance of aesthetic and sensory values was immediately assumed there. (265) At that time, representative interiors of the highest rank were commonly illuminated using ceiling skylights hidden in plafonds or suspended ceilings, and fluorescent lamps which would "lighten up" the interior and give the then desired effect of "raising". Light spots would perform different functions, highlighting, like a theater lantern, specific details or spaces.

A lot of attention was paid to the form of light fixtures themselves. At the time, highest-quality crystal, ceramic or mostly wrought iron chandeliers were produced. Sophisticated forms of ceiling lights, hanging chandeliers and wall lights were used. Attempts were made to adjust lighting to the function it performed in an interior. Designers themselves recall the process of creating Socialist Realist lighting systems as a type of experimental work in process. Halina Jastrzębowska, the co-creator of light fixtures for the Palace of Culture and Science in Warsaw, among others, emphasized many years later that the experience was totally new for the designers:

265 Ignacy Baran, *Oświetlenie wnętrz światłem elektrycznym: wskazówki i zalecenia* (Warszawa: PWT, 1956).

We started going anywhere we could find some antique chandeliers and learnt about their design, the correlation between form and light effects. By looking at them, we tried to figure out if anything new could be conceived... We had to look at how others had done this before us. (266)

Unique light experiences were mostly ensured by elegant crystal designs that additionally enhanced the impression of radiance. Perfect designs were created in Poland for example by Henryk Gaczyński and Wanda Zawidzka-Manteuffel for the interiors of the Warsaw Philharmonic or the Palace of Culture and Science. Hanging crystal ornaments were manufactured by the Józefina glass works, while the metal elements that the ornaments were attached to were made by the Brąz Dekoracyjny cooperative. Multi-level chandeliers were constructed using piled up glass bouquets or metal rings onto which crystal shades, ceiling lamps made using glass beads, or glass wall lamps in the shape of bouquets with mirror elements reflecting light were mounted. Glass candelabra of unique artistic form, used in the parliament building, for example, also constituted a palace-like decorative element producing light reflections.

Hanging chandeliers with visible metal constructions were also popular. They usually had a few arms, although sconces were also used.

Another special decorative element used in interiors were large ceramic chandeliers with complex forms. They were original and are most often associated with Socialist  Realism. The majority of spectacular designs of this type were created by Hanna and Lech Grześkiewicz who raised ceramic chandeliers to the rank of outstanding decorative art. They designed ceramic sculpture forms rather than light fixtures. In a lavish way, these resembled the shapes of five- or seven-arm candle holders, while their white surfaces were painted in floral patterns referencing folk art. (267) Unique ceramic chandeliers made by Mr and Mrs Grześkiewicz appeared in the most representative interiors, e.g. the Warsaw Philharmonic, the Palace of Culture and Science, and other palaces of culture in Poland (in Dąbrowa Górnicza or Świętochłowice), as well as in theaters (Dramatyczny, Studio or Lalka).

Overhead ceiling lighting that ensured even light saturation and, at the same time, the desired movement upwards and light-shadow gradation, was provided using modular skylights integrally combined with the architecture and adjusted to the size of the given interior. They consisted of an aluminium frame divided into square fields and shields made of frosted glass, which sometimes constituted separate light coffers.

Lighting issues were dealt with in a slightly different way in auditoria, where practical design issues were the main focus. Here, light complemented interior decoration but the uses of light fixtures did not constitute new decoration or add detail. (268)

266 Anna Demska, "Oświetlenie w Pałacu Kultury i Nauki," *Renowacje i Zabytki* 15, no. 3, (2005): 121.   267 Marta Rydzyńska, *Pracownia Grześkiewiczów, zarys monografii* (Warszawa: 2014) [manuscript], 25–31.   268 Czesław Konopka, "Teatr operowy," *Architektura*, no. 3 (1954): 62.

The issue of light took on a really unique meaning in the interiors of cultural centers located outside the city, in less urbanised areas, where the electrification process had only just begun. This is where the joy of light became especially clear and the building itself would sometimes be the only brilliantly lit one in the region. Designers themselves pointed out: "we have given them what they have not had so far". (269)

Conclusion

Conscious directing of light in Socialist Realist interiors definitely contributed to experiencing space more effectively and strongly. Sensory experience was meant to powerfully influence the emotions of the observer in the first place and to be part of persuasive strategies of Socialist Realist art. It must be emphasized, however, that after so many years it is difficult to unambiguously interpret the persuasive effectiveness of this type of sensory-emotional messages (individually conditioned and connected with a given place and time). It is hard to determine how social actors, the beholders of the works, actually reacted to the lighting policy imposed from above.

269   An unpublished conversation of architect Aleksander Franta with Aleksandra Sumorok, Katowice 2014. Owned by the author.

THIS DARKENED VILLAGE
Obermutten in the Extended History of Swiss Electrification
Chase Galis

Let's begin with a joke.
In 1973, the Swiss satirical magazine *Nebelspalter* published the following lines, documenting a fictional visitor's journey into the Swiss countryside:
The Tourist: "Does the village have electric lighting?"
The Local: "Only during a thunderstorm." (270)

270 N. O. Scarpi, "Anekdoten-Cocktail," *Nebelspalter*, April 4, 1973, 63.

As late as the 1970s, numerous villages in Switzerland remained without electric light. The country has often been referred to as an exceptional case in the development of electricity infrastructure for its speed of expansion and adoption—all supposedly motivated by the overwhelming support of the public. (271) When the reality of village life posed a contradiction to this heroic narrative, mainstream discourse targeted the unilluminated state of these rural locations as a point of critique. Literal darkness—that which is experienced without the aid of electric illumination—was equated to intellectual darkness, producing a strategy for characterizing villages in a state of disobedient regression. Drawing on this association, popular periodicals such as *Nebelspalter* began to present villages without electric light by relegating them to a subject of amusement, critique, and, at its lowest, the punch of a simple two-line joke.

The joke published in 1973 was not the only instance of *Nebelspalter* dedicating space in its printed magazine to the lack of electric light in rural villages. In 1966, a regular contributor writing under the pseudonym Philipp Pfefferkorn wrote an essay, "Wem ging da ein Licht auf?" reacting to the outcome of a public vote in the rural Alpine village of Obermutten. Included in the text is the following quote:

In 1946 and again in 1965, this darkened village rejected the attempt to install electric lighting. So much backwardness! Meanwhile...the Americans hope to land an astronaut on the moon in 1968. (272)

271 Contemporary historiography, written by scholars of technology including David Gugerli, have cited that Switzerland was "far ahead of any other European country at the turn of the century" in the production of electricity. Further, he attributes this success to public support for the development of electrical infrastructure, which had been built through discursive processes channeled through public periodicals among other media. David Gugerli, *Redeströme Zur Elektrifizierung Der Schweiz* (Zurich: Chronos Verlag, 1996), 7–11. 272 Philipp Pfefferkorn, "Wem ging da ein Licht auf?," *Nebelspalter*, November 23, 1966, 9.

This text finds its satirical edge by locating irony in the supposed asynchronicity between a village stuck debating the value of electric light and the ambition of the American space program. Both sides of this regressive-progressive dichotomy are diametrically positioned to characterize Obermutten as moving against the trends of expected progress. While the American space program looks to the future, the village of Obermutten, the author exclaims, demonstrates "So much backwardness!" The English term, *backwardness*, and its German equivalent, *Rückständigkeit*, carry the same positional connotation—that of literally looking back or looking at what is behind instead of at what is ahead. (273) By demonstrating that the topic of electric illumination had been repeatedly discussed and rejected in Obermutten, the author of this text suggests that the village was unable to follow a technological turn that had been widely accepted in other contexts earlier in the century. Obermutten remained in the past, behind the pace of innovation set by cities such as his contemporary Zurich.

Today's critical reader looking back on the November 23, 1966 issue of *Nebelspalter* may not only be surprised by learning of the existence of a village that was debating the merits of electric light in the 1960s but also by the fact that a widely-circulated, left-of-center satirical magazine was still using electric illumination as a fundamental metric of modernity. While the terms of debate in Obermutten should not be overlooked as an indicator of rural response to encroaching infrastructuralization, attending also to Pfefferkorn's interest in electric light can be used to demonstrate the techniques of a popular critical position condemning village hesitancy to modernize. It is these

273 This usage of the term "backwardness" echoes colonial rhetoric that had found its way into Switzerland by the turn of the 20th century—this is despite the country claiming to have absolved itself from participation in any formal colonial projects. Patrick Minder, *La Suisse coloniale : les représentations de l'Afrique et des Africains en Suisse au temps des colonies (1880-1939)* (Bern: Lang, 2011).

techniques in question—in particular, the leveraging of illumination and its blinding effects—that allow for the flattening of complex social, political, and economic processes into something like the *backward*.

Two Lamps

Pfefferkorn's *Nebelspalter* essay was published on the occasion of a public vote in Obermutten that finally accepted the proposal to install electric lighting in the village in 1966. Following the procedures of Swiss "direct democracy," the proposal was raised in a referendum for which the voting-eligible (read: male) population of the 115 village inhabitants would cast a ballot, and a simple majority would rule.

At the time of the vote, Obermutten belonged to the municipality of Mutten, located in the Canton of Grisons, where it was linguistically isolated as the only Swiss German-speaking municipality among predominantly Romansh-speaking communities. It is for this reason, in addition to its difficulty of vehicle access, that linguist Hans Rudolf Hotzenköcherle referred to Mutten by stating that it "is still one of the loneliest places I know in the *Deutschbünden*." (274) The municipality consisted of two primary settlements separated by four-hundred meters of altitude. Obermutten, the higher elevation of the two, is only inhabited during the warmer months of the year when a portion

274 *Deutschbünden* here refers to the German-speaking portion of the canton Grisons. Rudolf Hotzenköcherle, "Die Mundart von Mutten: Laut- und Flexionslehre," Beiträge zur schweizerdeutschen Grammatik 19 (Frauenfeld, Huber, 1934), 3.

of residents from Untermutten make the journey up the mountain with their families, animals, and equipment in tow. While Untermutten was electrified in the year 1910, the electrification of Obermutten remained the subject of debate until 1966 and beyond.

The proposal to install electric light in Obermutten had been discussed periodically in the years following Untermutten's electrification in 1910; however, it was not brought to a first referendum until April 1940 when it was ultimately decided to postpone the decision-making to a later date. (275) The vote would again be considered on the 25th of August 1946, six months after a devastating fire in Obermutten that had destroyed 37 buildings. (276) The disaster provided an opportunity to bundle electrification with reconstruction and perhaps even prevent further fires by removing a significant quantity of household kerosene lamps. (277) The referendum was initially approved in the meeting on the 25th of August and then, despite these compelling arguments, subsequently rescinded just over one month later. (278) This process repeated a number of times over the following two decades before the matter was voted on one final time in 1966. With the majority in favor, the village of Obermutten decided to electrify at the cost of 80,000 Swiss Francs, paid for by the municipality. (279)

Throughout the half-century of debate prior to the 1966 vote, the arguments supporting electrification had been structured around the benefit of artificial illumination for domestic and agricultural labor. In a televised Swiss news

275 "Gemeinde Protokolle 1935-1950, Gemeindeversammlung vom 21. April 1940" (Gemeinde Mutten, April 21, 1940), Kulturarchiv Thusis-Viamala. 276 "Grossbrand in Obermutten," *Neue Zürcher Zeitung*, April 26, 1946. 277 With financial and labor contributions supplied by the local carpenters, the cost of electrification at the time of reconstruction would have been approximately one-third of what it would otherwise have cost. "MUTTEN: Zum erstenmal elektrisches Licht in Ober Mutten," *Neue Bündner Zeitung*, 1966. 278 "Gemeinde Protokolle 1935-1950, Gemeindeversammlung vom 29. September 46" (Gemeinde Mutten, September 29, 1946), Kulturarchiv Thusis-Viamala. 279 "Endlich Strom in Obermutten."

segment from 1966 documenting Obermutten's moment of transition to electric light, a local farmer remarked that the new artificial illumination was "very bright" whereas, in the past, "you always needed two of those poor barn lamps to see anything at all." (280) Because of the slope-side, Alpine location of the village, buildings were typically built into the hillside. The northeast-facing facade looked into the valley and was built exposing the entirety of the building's multi-story elevation. For domestic buildings, this space was occupied by the *Stube*, providing ample natural light for daytime activity and familial gatherings. (281) However, the opposite side of the same floor—consisting of spaces dedicated to storage and cooking—was typically embedded into the hillside, restricting the placement of windows necessary to illuminate daily labor. (282) With the potential to support these tasks, electric illumination presented a clear benefit to domestic laborers. The same argument applied to agricultural work where barns were subject to the same architectural conditions and limited illumination. Proper light was required to make the work of early-morning and late-evening animal tending more efficient.

While the arguments in support of electrification were more-or-less aligned, (283) finding clear benefits in the potential for illumination to make daily work easier, arguments against electrification demonstrated much greater variation. The project's potential economic impact was among the most prominent reasons to cast a negative vote. The cost of electrification was considered at two distinct scales: that of the municipal budget and that of its burden on the individual user.

280 "Endlich Strom in Obermutten." 281 Willy Th. Höhn, "Das traditionelle bäuerliche Gehöft der Schweiz als Typenbau," *Schweizerische Bauzeitung* 19, no. 125/126 (November 10, 1945): 215–19. 282 Hans Rudolf Hotzenköcherle, "Der Vokalismus der Mundart von Mutten" (Frauenfeld, Huber, 1933), 12. 283 The legacy of this position has survived the several decades since electrification. One story, passed down through generations of Obermutten village leadership and again relayed by current resident Erwin Wyss, tells of the state of electrification debate in 1963 where ongoing discussion resulted in one farmer pleading "Oh, if one at least had light in the barn." Erwin Wyss, email message to author, March 9, 2023.

The total cost of electrification for the village, which accounted for the construction and installation of the necessary pylons and wires, came to approximately 80,000 Swiss Francs. In 1966, this significant sum was being considered next to other infrastructure improvement projects, including sewage upgrades, also costing 80,000 Swiss Francs, and the construction of a new road that would cost 150,000 Swiss Francs. In comparison, the annual municipal revenue, generated from a combination of taxes and wood sales from the local forest, was less than 50,000 Swiss Francs for the year. (284) Fear of draining the municipal budget proved to be a legitimate concern for the voting villagers. In addition to the strain on the municipal budget, individuals would have to invest upwards of one thousand Swiss Francs to connect the new electrical wires to their respective homes and to purchase and install fixtures and bulbs. (285) Beyond the installation cost, new electricity customers would also be responsible for paying the required energy supply rates. For residents of Obermutten, who had been experiencing increasingly precarious financial conditions, this presented an additional obstacle for personal use. (286)

Among other motivations for voting against electrification in Obermutten was the concern that electric light had ties to witchcraft. While the general concept of electricity had been conveyed to the rural public as early as the turn of the 20th century, (287) for some, the exact mechanisms of its transmission and subsequent conversion to electric light remained a topic of speculation. With no nearby material evidence of electricity generation to point to, some villagers

284 "Endlich Strom in Obermutten." 285 "Endlich Strom in Obermutten." 286 Beginning in the early decades of the 20th century, high-Alpine cattle raising became significantly less profitable as it was unable to keep up with the low production cost of industrial operations. Obermutten's dairy operation declined due to this trend, leaving its farmers with less stable incomes. "Endlich Strom in Obermutten"; Peter Moser and Beat Brodbeck, *Milch für alle: Bilder, Dokumente und Analysen zur Milchwirtschaft und Milchpolitik in der Schweiz im 20. Jahrhundert* (Baden: hier + jetzt, 2007). 287 Gugerli demonstrates various techniques and formats for educating the general public on the technologies of electrification—packaging complex principles into metaphors and clear demonstrations of potential use through public lectures, exhibitions, and propaganda disseminated beyond city borders. David Gugerli, *Redeströme Zur Elektrifizierung Der Schweiz* (Zurich: Chronos Verlag, 1996), 169–183.

categorized artificial illumination as a force rooted in the supernatural. Perhaps in a slightly less mystical interpretation, this sentiment could be seen to represent a lack of trust in distant sources of energy production. Inhabitants of the village were forced to ask where their electricity came from and how it was converted to illumination. Without knowing exactly what stood at the other end of the wire, the villagers' confidence in the technology remained weak. In the early days of Obermutten's electrification, it would not be uncommon to see two lamps hanging side by side: one kerosene and the other electric. This redundancy demonstrates both a readiness to switch back to the older technology—should it be needed—and also a reluctance to give up the act of illumination to a simple light switch.

The competing attitudes represented in the image of the two side-by-side lamps appropriately define the conditions of the debate over electrification. In the small village of 115 residents, many simultaneous and conflicting perspectives emerged and were re-staged with each subsequent referendum. Refusal to compromise supposedly incited intense arguments in community meetings. Then Municipal President Johan Elsa remarked: "We have a lot of disagreements. I argue with people a lot. The biggest concern is the … disunity that we have in the municipality." (288) The interpersonal conflict in Obermutten led to numerous political stalemates directed at electric light, among other subjects of public debate.

The fragmented action (or inaction) of Obermutten has made it a difficult case to locate outside of the dominant narrative of Swiss electrification. This ambivalence should be considered separate from formal movements of

288 "Endlich Strom in Obermutten."

resistance to electricity organized in the first half of the 20th century, which included staging protests, chopping down wooden electric poles, and boycotting electrification in general. (289) Without vocalizing a clear position on modern technological development—either in support or rejection of its further progress—the judgment of Obermutten was left open to interpretation. To an outside observer, such as the author of the mentioned *Nebelspalter* essay, the most obvious point of analysis remained in the binary of dark and light. Or otherwise stated, the decades-long hesitancy to artificially illuminate was considered an accurate representation of the village's *backward* conservatism. The flattening of social and political negotiating processes under the symbolic weight of illumination provided one strategy for dismissing complex value systems, shaping the case of "this darkened village" for a public audience disinterested in anything less sensational.

Infrastructure, Dark and Light

It is important to clarify a slippage of language present throughout the documentation of Obermutten and intentionally maintained in this text. Because electricity was intended to power only electric light when it was first introduced to Obermutten, the terms *electrification* and *illumination* were frequently interchanged. To restate this

289 Florian Blumer-Onofri, "Die Elektrifizierung Des Dörflichen Alltags: Eine Oral History-Studie Zur Sozialen Rezeption Der Elektrotechnik Im Baselbiet Zwischen 1900 Und 1960," *Baselbieter Heimatblätter* 58, no. 11 (1993): 5–7.

in a slightly different manner, illumination was frequently used as a stand-in for larger, more complex processes of electrification in the context of public debate and discourse. Electric light was the accessible end of what was, by the 1960s, a robust power network and the only point of direct engagement for the population of a rural village. Even the local wires, transformers, and meters fell into the domain of expertise embodied by the electrician.

The nearest energy supply to Obermutten was a hydroelectric plant on the Albula River, a significant engineering project that had once established the Canton of Grisons as a pioneer in the history of Switzerland's electricity infrastructure. Due to its alpine terrain, myriad glaciers, and resulting natural waterways, Grisons was viewed as a priority location for the development of hydroelectric power. Shortly after the turn of the 20th century, the city of Zurich, no longer able to produce enough electricity to sustain its increasing consumption, turned to Grisons, looking for new hydroelectric energy sources. An agreement was reached between the city of Zurich and four Grisons municipalities to grant water concessions over a portion of the Albula River. One of these municipalities was Mutten. In exchange for the concession, each municipality was offered electricity to be connected and supplied by the city of Zurich. (290) Upon completing the 30 Megawatt Albula power plant in 1910, Untermutten was connected and supplied electricity.

Obermutten's decision to install electric lighting in 1966 implicates the village as a participant in these structures. The expression of artificial illumination constitutes a form of representation, making visible the village's connection

290 Walter Baumann, *75 Jahre Partnerschaft zwischen Graubünden und Zürich: Wasserkraft und Elektrizität* (Zürich: EWZ, 1981), 31–44.

to the larger electrical system that lies behind it. Illumination—shining through windows and casting across public passageways—played an active role in making infrastructure visible at select points across the nocturnal landscape. Electric light, as Marshall McLuhan once claimed, "escapes attention as a communication medium…because it has no "content." (291) The content, he suggests, lies not in the technological object itself but instead in its surfaces of projection. This could be extended to say that electric light (as projected from a simple, incandescent bulb) is not something to see but to see with, providing a technologically-contextualized frame of visuality. It modifies the perception of its immediate environment from what would otherwise remain darkness to an illuminated space defined by the extent of its reach. The new technological perimeter outlined by the illumination of an electric light source characterizes those within its bounds as participants in the greater infrastructure of electrification. Illumination here performs as a *cultural technique*, (292) re-disciplining the agrarian settlement of Obermutten, whose nocturnal form was once defined by a more-or-less uniform darkness, to one ruled by a new visible radius of artificial illumination. Oral histories from the municipality of Mutten confirm that electric illumination produced differentiated spaces with consequences for interpersonal social relationships—some spaces were cast in light, and those who inhabited spaces that were not were cast out. (293) Houses that refrained from installing electric light—particularly those at the village perimeter—experienced both social and visual alienation. They came to represent

291 Marshall McLuhan, *Understanding Media: The Extension of Man* (London: Sphere books, 1967), 31. 292 Bernhard Siegert and Geoffrey Winthrop-Young, *Cultural Techniques: Grids, Filters, Doors, and Other Articulations of the Real*, First edition., Meaning Systems (New York, NY: Fordham University Press, 2015). 293 Erwin Wyss, *Diis Gsetz Isch Nit Inschas Gsetz: Lebensbilder Aus Dem Walserdorf Mutten* (Chur: Desertina, 2012), 178–197.

the hesitancy of adopting new technology and were lost in the nocturnal landscape against the contrasting illumination of the rest of the village.

Such visual differentiation—between dark and illuminated spaces—applies to the larger scale of the village itself. Returning to Pfefferkorn's *Nebelspalter* essay, the language used to describe the village's attachment to darkness should be paid special attention: "In 1946 and again in 1965, this *darkened* village rejected the attempt to install electric lighting." Darkened, or in German, *verdunkelt*, adopts an active mood suggesting that the noun following could be described as something *made* dark. In this phrase, the author assumes that the neutral state of village life is an illuminated one and that the act of remaining dark requires additional effort. By the 1960s, an inversion in assumptions made of the nocturnal environment had occurred. The night had become a space where electric light was not only anticipated but expected, and any attachment to darkness was viewed as an act of regression. What had once been considered an urban condition of ever-present illumination had crept into the countryside and was projected onto even "one of the loneliest places…in the *Deutschbünden*."

By the second half of the 20th century, electric light had been absorbed into everyday life to a degree that rendered it essentially invisible. It was noticed only through its absence—the shock of darkness to the modern subject. Despite this invisibility, electric light remained an essential component in the representation of electricity infrastructure read through its illumination of space. For Obermutten, its state of disconnect was made legible through darkness, shifting perception of the village to one of *backwardness.* This characterization was developed despite the municipality's fundamental support of hydroelectric projects earlier in the century. The village had not fulfilled its representational duty as a supporter of both national infrastructure and modern ideology, and the only explanation that Pfefferkorn could reach was that it inhabited a primitive ideological state.

The case of Obermutten is not anomalous here—many villages in Switzerland had not yet been electrified by the 1960s. What deserves critical attention is that Pfefferkorn's text in *Nebelspalter*, printed in 1966, still locates a point of critique—or what he stretches to irony—in the near century-old debate over electric light. The more than fifty years of social and political negotiation that had occurred in the village prior to its ultimate electrification were flattened into a universal characterization of regression by reading in darkness the *backward*. The representational dimension of electric light overshadowed nuances of technology acceptance and its extended trajectory, trading shades of gray for the binary of dark and light. Electric light provided an effective device for applying criticism to portions of the Swiss population seen to damage—both economically and representationally—the image of the nation as universally modern. The only point of resolution, as Pfefferkorn alludes, is turning a light on.

"INEXISTENT" ARCHITECTURE, CULTURAL "STAGINGS" AND THE INTERCONNECTEDNESS OF THE NIGHTCLUB INTERIOR

Cat Rossi

"Inexistent." This is the word the Italian architect Carlo Caldini used in 1972 to describe the architecture of Space Electronic, the nightclub he co-founded and designed with other members of the architectural collective Gruppo 9999 three years earlier in Florence. (294) Space Electronic was an architect-driven exercise in multidisciplinary experimentation: its programme in the late 1960s and early 1970s included live music, poetry, classical dance, theater, exhibitions, and a temporary architecture school.

Caldini's description of Space Electronic's architecture as "inexistent" is curious. Space Electronic was absolutely a real, physical place. It was situated in an old engine repair garage that had been abandoned following the flood that devastated Florence in 1966. Visitors arrived through a narrow ground floor entrance and went down a ramp into a rectangular, black-painted space with a chequered laminate floor. Another ramp led up into a large, double-height space. Furnishings were mostly salvaged, including refrigerator casings used as temporary structures and 200 washing-machine drums used as seating. Fixed elements included a stage and mezzanine seating. A parachute and white cloth banners hung from the ceiling, and stretching across the space was a rig hosting speakers, lights, a slide carousel, Super 8 film projectors, and overhead projectors.

This equipment is the key to Space Electronic's "inexistent" architecture. Space Electronic only came into existence when the projectors and speakers were switched on, and the intangible qualities of light and sound activated the space, something which the architects and collaborators experimented with through multi-layered projections of shapes, patterns, films, and images cast over performers and spectators alike.

Space Electronic is one of a handful of nightclubs designed and run by architects associated with Italy's Radical Design movement in the late 1960s and early 1970s, which also included the Piper in Turin, designed by future members of Gruppo Strum in 1966, and Bamba Issa, which was opened by Gruppo UFO on the Tuscan coast in 1969. All were created by architects rebelling against the modernist and market-driven conventions of their profession, including the types of spaces they were meant to build.

Caldini's idea of "inexistent" architecture is one of the earliest attempts to define nightclub architecture, and it has echoes in later conceptualizations. "Inexistence" also features in architecture critic Aaron Betsky's description of Studio 54, which opened in New York in 1977. Its owners, Ian Schrager and Steve Rubell, employed the design studio Experience Space to transform the former opera-house-turned-television-studio into the peak of disco architecture. Betsky, who used to frequent the club as a

294 The club was conceived by Gruppo 9999 members Fabrizio Fiumi and Carlo Caldini. Other members of the group, initially known as Gruppo 1999, were also involved at the start: Paolo Coggiola, Paolo Galli, Andrea Gigli, Mario Preti, and Giovanni Sani. They co-ran the club with local friend Mario Bolognesi. Emmanuele Piccardo, *Radical Piper* (Busalla: Plug_In, 2016), 126.

student, describes in 1997's *Queer Space* how "Instead of walls, floors and ceilings" there was "only rhythm and light". (295)

These ingredients are what the architectural historian Ivan López Munera would more recently describe, with Studio 54's successor Palladium as his case study, as 'discotecture', a term to describe 'the relationship between sound and lighting systems in the creation of a new kind of architecture'. (296) These voices all assert the "inexistence" of nightclub architecture, a concept that is useful in exploring the specificity of nightclub interior architecture. This essay will, however, argue that "inexistent" architecture was, in fact, dependent on more conventional "existent" architecture and that it is the interdependence of the two that defines nightclub space. Furthermore, this essay will explore how this assemblage existed in relation to other entertainment architectures, or "stagings", such as theaters, television studios, cinemas, carnivals, and multi-media performances. If not spaces of the night, these were at least spaces of intense interiority, largely separate from conventional diurnal and nocturnal rhythms.

Stagings and rhythms are two key words for the approach adopted here. The former draws on what the philosopher Gernot Böhme called "the art of staging" in the 20th century when scenography expanded from the theater stage to festivals and discotheques, both of which are examples he gives. (297) With his interest in architectural atmospheres and his understanding of how these are produced by "constellations" of people and things, Böhme is a crucial voice underpinning this research. (298)

Also key is the temporal dimension of nightclub space, drawing on Henri Lefebvre's 1992 *Rhythmanalysis*. (299) Rhythm is embedded in nightclub architecture: in its music most obviously, but also in lighting effects of different durations and intensities, in interiors designed to be experienced for delineated periods of time, at spaced intervals, and different tempos, with demarcated spaces for dancing, relaxing or observing, as well as more licentious activities.

This attempt to contextualize nightclubs within other entertainment architectures is motivated by a desire to assert the value of club culture by showing its interrelationship with other creative industries. It is encouraged by sources such as *Lighting & Sound International*, a British trade magazine set up in 1985 and devoted to industries such as theaters and discos that it declared to be 'of the same genus'. (300) The magazine contained adverts marketed equally to the film, television, theater, and disco industries, and its articles juxtaposed and compared the latest international innovations in the design of auditoria, TV sets, theaters, scenography, and discotheques.

The rest of this essay is divided into broadly two parts to tell two different but related stories of nightclub architecture. The first half will focus on Space Electronic. The second shorter section looks at Studio 54, selected for being what *Lighting & Sound* described as the disco that 'first focussed the industry's attention on the relevance of theatre'. (301) This deliberately split story asserts the heterogeneity of club culture while showing the thread of inexistent and existent architecture and intercultural connectivity that runs through nightclubs more broadly.

---

295 Aaron Betsky, *Queer Space: Architecture and Same-Sex Desire* (New York: William Morrow & Co., 1997), 5. 296 Ivan López Munera, "Discotecture: The Bodily Regime of Archi-Social Exploration" in *Night Fever: Designing Club Culture 1960 to Today*, eds. Jochen Eisenbrand, Mateo Kries, and Catharine Rossi (Weil am Rhein: Vitra Design Museum, 2018), 127. 297 Gernot Böhme, "The Art of the Stage Set as a Paradigm for an Aesthetics of Atmospheres," *Ambiances: The International Journal of Sensory Environment, Architecture and Urban Space*, February (2013), 5, https://doi.org/10.4000/ambiances.315, accessed November 8, 2023. 298 Böhme, *Atmospheric Architectures: The Aesthetics of Built Space,* edited and trans. A.-Chr. Engels-Schwarzpaul, (London; New York: Bloomsbury, 2017), orig. published 2013, 3. 299 Henri Lefebvre, *Rhythmanalysis: Space, Time and Everyday Life*, trans. Stuart Elden and Gerald Moore, (London; New York: Continuum, 2004), orig. published 1992. 300 John Offord, "The First Edition", *Lighting + Sound International*, 1:1 (1985), 6. 301 Tony Gotellier, "All the World's a Stage," *Lighting + Sound International,* 1:1 (1985), 35.

"Stagings" at Space Electronic: Carnival, The "Architecture of Involvement" and "Allatonceness"

This section examines three co-joined spatial and temporal stagings that Space Electronic arguably drew on from within and outside of architecture as part of its continuous interior design. This is not a finite list but rather a first attempt to consider the club as part of a broader cultural context and international avant-garde in the 1960s and 1970s.

The first staging is the carnival. Existing outside of everyday rhythms and behaviours, Space Electronic exemplifies what Lefebvre called spatial and temporal phenomena, which 'punctuate everydayness', of which he gives festivals and carnivals as examples. (302) Writing earlier in the 20th century, Mikhail Bakhtin proposed the carnival as a temporary extraterritoriality that permitted freedom and an inversion of the social order. This required the creation of 'ever changing, playful, undefined forms' and participatory spectacles in which there was no separation between actor and audience. (303)

In Space Electronic, 9999 exploited the carnivalesque literally and conceptually through immersive interior stagings of different rhythms and degrees. In 1976, as part of one of its semi-regular refurbishments, the ground floor was furnished with fairground teacups and a huge papier-mâché clown head made in Viareggio, a nearby town with a strong carnival tradition that had also furnished UFO's Bamba Issa beach club. 9999 also regularly organized festivals in the venue, dressing the 'existent' architecture with temporary décor. The most notable of these was in 1971, when, for an architecture festival co-organized with Superstudio, 9999 installed a 20cm-deep lake in the club's basement, potted with shrubs and a stepping-stone path so that guests would not get their feet wet. Upstairs was another nature-inspired installation—a vegetable garden packed inside refrigerator casings temporarily installed on the dancefloor.

The carnivalesque desire for a participatory architecture leads to the second staging that can be seen to have informed Space Electronic in what the Italian architecture professor Leonardo Savioli termed the 'the architecture of involvement'. In 1966–67, Savioli led a course at Florence University called "Piper, furnishings for leisure". His teaching assistants included 9999 member Mario Preti. Writing about the course in *Casabella* magazine in 1968, Savioli described how one of the architect's "fundamental tasks" was to undo "the fixity, the schematicism, the authoritativeness of current urban architectural space" as it forced users into a submissive relationship with their surroundings. (304) Savioli advocated for a more participatory architecture, one that would require architectonic elements of different durations, the formation of less definitive spaces, and a new understanding of the architectural interior as a space that generates behaviours and experiences.

Savioli identified the "architecture of involvement" in the Piper. Originally the name of the first discotheque in Italy, which opened in 1965 in Rome, the Piper was so successful that it became the eponym for Italian discos more generally, used even as the name for the Radical Design-associated Piper in Turin, designed by Giorgio Ceretti and Pietro Derossi, who was listed as a 'collaborator' on the

302   Lefebvre, *Rhythmanalysis*, 94.   303   Mikhail Bakhtin, *Rabelais and his World,* trans. Helene Iswolsky, (Bloomington: Indiana University Press, 1984), orig. published 1936, 11, 154.   304   Leonardo Savioli, "Spazio di Coinvolgimento," *Casabella,* 326 (1969).

Piper course. (305) The Turin Piper was a single-volume windowless cuboid environment furnished with pop-coloured fibreglass seating that could be moved around the space, a scaffolding mezzanine that was also movable, and a set of rails suspended from the ceiling equipped with lights, microphones, and speakers. This highly transformative space was fitting for the Piper's diverse programme—it hosted everything from music performances to fashion shows, yoga, meditation, political meetings, and happenings led by Arte Povera artists—with a space flexible enough to accommodate the different layout requirements of each. Arguably, Space Electronic sought to have a similar sense of participatory and flexible space through lighting that ignored the distinction between stage and non-stage, through the use of the dancefloor as a theater-in-the-round, and through its movable furniture.

The third staging of interest is the media theorist Marshall McLuhan's 'allatonceness', a concept derived from the venue that inspired Space Electronic, namely the Electric Circus, which opened in a former ballroom in New York's East Village in 1967. (306) A long mirrored corridor took you into the club's main area, a large volume with a stage at one end. Above was a balcony with different rooms for sound and light projections. Occupying the space was a tensile structure designed by American architect Charles Forberg, onto which light and sound could be projected. (307)

9999 architects Caldini and Mario Preti visited Electric Circus, where they seemingly encountered the Andy-Warhol run Exploding Plastic Inevitable (EPI), a sensorially overwhelming multi-media performance which featured the Velvet Underground and Nico, film screenings and projections. Others who experienced the EPI included McLuhan, who understood it as the manifestation of 'allatonceness' for its immersive, participatory qualities that moved beyond a purely visual experience to a synaesthetic one. (308) It surely isn't a coincidence that after their visit, the architects brought back a parachute as a souvenir, and fellow 9999 architect Fiumi brought back projectors from his own trip to California, which they then installed in Space Electronic.

'Allatonceness' seems analogous to 'inexistent' architecture. Architectural historian and theorist Sylvia Lavin describes how the EPI's sensory overloading and overwriting of the existing architecture through multi-media projections meant that the physical building of the Electric Circus, "both its structure and its space became irrelevant, a mere prop". (309) While Lavin's argument makes sense, a question lingers. Surely the "existent" architecture of the former ballroom played its part in EPI? After all, it provided a high-ceilinged, column-free volume with a stage at one end. The same goes for Space Electronic: 9999 leveraged the existing space, from the narrative possibilities of the ramps that led into the basement and then up to the ground floor with its unbroken volume ripe for large gatherings, and the windowless walls that meant an easily controllable space. And while Lavin dismissively uses the word 'prop', it is potentially a productive word to describe how these architects conceived their design approach, particularly given that it is a theater term.

Ideas of the carnival, participation, allatonceness, props, and pre-existing entertainment buildings all resonate with the second club this essay will consider: Studio 54.

---

305 Leonardo Savioli, "Spazio di Coinvolgimento." 306 Marshall McLuhan and Quentin Fiore, *The Medium is the Massage* (London: Penguin, 2008). 307 Anon, "Portfolio II: Beginning to See the Light" in *Night Fever* 75, eds. Eisenbrand, Kries and Rossi, 77. 308 Sylvia Lavin, "Architecture Animé or Medium Specificity in a Post-Medium World", *Wissenschaftliches Kolloquium vom 19. bis 22. April 2007 in Weimar an der Bauhaus-Universität zum Thema: Die Realität des Imaginären. Architektur und das digitale Bild* (2008), 137–138, https://www.academia.edu/74608996/Architecture_Anlm_e_or_Medium_Specificity_in_a_Post_Medium_World, accessed November 8, 2023. 309 Lavin, Andy. "Architect™ — Or, a Funny Thing Happened on the way to the Disco", *Log*, 15 (2009): 100.

Opened in 1977, The club occupied a building that had started life in 1927 as the Gallo Opera House and became Studio 52 after it was bought by CBS. (310) When the TV network left New York, the building was taken over by Schrager and Rubell. To transform it into a club they hired Experience Space, a local firm that included architect Scott Bromley and interior designer Ron Doud, and worked with sound designer Richard Long and lighting designers including Jules Fisher and Paul Marantz. (311)

Writing in *Lighting and Sound International*, Tony Gottelier attributed Studio 54's theater-like quality to the venue's 'structural entity', but also due to the 'conscious effort…to achieve … theatrical flexibility.' (312) In terms of its 'structural entity', Studio 54 mobilized elements of the venue's "existing" architecture and earlier stagings as an opera house and TV studio, from the ornate foyer to the balcony with seating to watch the action below. (313) The club benefitted from the expansion of the stage and fly system dating from the venue's time as a TV studio and its rewiring for TV cameras and lighting, which enhanced its electrical capacity. (314) One of Bromley's most significant interventions was the removal of the orchestra pit and seating area, turning the whole venue into a stage. (315)

'Theatrical flexibility' informed the lighting arrangements. Broadway lighting designers Fisher and Marantz, who had previously worked on Electric Circus, created a brightly lit dancefloor with lighting of different colours, rhythms, and intensities. (316) It included moving chase poles suspended from the ceiling, lined with pulsating red and yellow lightbulbs and a red police beacon at each base, and a "flying ceiling" suspended from the rigging, which consisted of rotating and reconfigurable mirrored panels with pink neon tubes. (317)

'Theatrical flexibility' appeared elsewhere in Studio 54—at the beginning of the evening, a cut drop by set designers Aerographics (Richie Williamson and Dean Janoff) was lowered from the rigging to divide the 11,000 square ft dancefloor into smaller areas, a technique known as "divided staging." (318) As it filled up, the curtain was raised, releasing dancers across the dancefloor—a physical transformation that also altered the club's atmosphere. Aerographics were also responsible for a variety of scenery for the club, including the moon and the spoon, the latter infamously complete with cocaine to fuel the disco's partygoers.

Conclusion

This essay has sought to tell stories of two very different episodes in the architecture and design history of nightclubs. Using ideas such as atmosphere, rhythm, carnival, involvement, allatonceness, and scenography, it has sought to show nightclubs' embeddedness in architectures and stagings from other cultural realms and how they combined "existent" and "inexistent" elements in their scene setting for the nightly drama of dancing, socialising, intoxication, experimentation and more. There is a richer and bigger story to tell here, one that would weave in other clubs and other cultural architectures and stagings and tie together the threads laid out here more strongly. The architectural history of nightclubs may be largely "inexistent," but that makes it all the more ready to be brought into existence.

310 Bobby Ellerbee, "The History of CBS New York Television Studios: 1937–1965", 56, https://eyesofageneration.com/studios-page/cbs-studios-new-york/, accessed November 8, 2023. 311 Tim Rohan, "Bringing the Disco Home: Manhattan's Disco-Influenced Residences of the 1970s" in *Night Fever*, eds. Eisenbrand, Kries and Rossi, 108. 312 Gotellier, "All the World's a Stage," 36. 313 Ian Schrager, *Studio 54*, (New York: Rizzoli, 2017), 41. 314 Gotellier, "All the World's a Stage," 36; Rohan, "Bringing the Disco Home," in *Night Fever,* eds. Eisenbrand, Kries and Rossi, 108. 315 Rohan, "Bringing the Disco Home," in *Night Fever,* eds. Eisenbrand, Kries and Rossi, 108. 316 Schrager, *Studio 54*, 33, 388. 317 Rohan, "Bringing the Disco Home," in *Night Fever*, eds. Eisenbrand, Kries and Rossi, 111. 318 Matthew Yokobosky, *Studio 54 Night Magic* (New York: Brooklyn Museum, 2020), 6; Stephen Benedetto, *The Provocation of the Senses in Contemporary Theatre* (Hoboken: Taylor & Francis, 2010).

THE SPACE OF MTV
From Inner-City Clubbing to Basement Suburbia
Léa-Catherine Szacka

In 2013, art critic Jonathan Crary published the essay *24/7: Late Capitalism and the Ends of Sleep*, a book in which he explores some of the damaging consequences of the expanding non-stop processes of twenty-first-century capitalism. A specialist in the study of vision and modernity, Crary focuses on the ongoing management of individual attentiveness and the impairment of acuity within the compulsory routines of contemporary technological culture to show how the marketplace now operates through every hour of the clock, ignoring any forms of distinction between day and night.
In an epoch in which "any persisting notions of sleep as somehow natural are rendered unacceptable", (319) late capitalism is dominated by global infrastructures for continuous work and consumption. As shown on the cover of Crary's book—the façade of a generic skyscraper glowing at night-time—this condition of sleeplessness is undoubtedly linked to perpetual illumination, itself a prerequisite condition of modernity. Multi-story buildings also saw their windows lit by the glow of television sets. Indeed, as argued by Crary, "the cathode ray tube was a decisive and vivid instance of how the glare and gossip of a public transactional world penetrated the most private of spaces." (320)
From the 1950s onward, "television was the site of a destabilization of relations between exposure and protectedness, agency and passivity, sleep and awakening, and publicness and privacy." (321) A stable system, with a small number of channels—often public monopolies—it offered a durable programming format. Therefore, viewing was synchronized and television networks were providing content at hours of the day that conformed with traditional sleeping patterns. (322) But by the early 1980s however,

319 Jonathan Crary, *24/7: Late Capitalism and the Ends of Sleep* (New York/London: Verso books, 2013), 13.   320 Jonathan Crary, *24/7*, 79.
321 Jonathan Crary, *24/7*, 80.   322 Jonathan Crary, *24/7*, 82.

the post-war era of television was clearly over when a myriad of new privately owned and often specialized channels embarked on a quest for content to fill viewing hours that often expanded into the night. (323) Commercialized cable television significantly altered the positions and capabilities of television as it had existed up to then, (324) colonizing important areas of lived time and of our houses.

In this paper, I argue that, with the advent of the American subscription television channel MTV in 1981, the typical modern idea of the media house was pushed and transformed into a space of domestic performativity, dominated by night vision, and organized around continuous streams of omnipresent images. By transposing certain functions of inner-city nightclubs into the typically suburban houses, MTV shifted the relationship between center and periphery. How did MTV come about and what were the *modi operandi* and politics of distribution of this new television channel? What were the new forms of domestic performativity and interactivity that emerged around the late 1970s and early 1980s? Which architectural projects represented new forms of domestic performativity that expanded into the night and involved the interaction with television sets?

The Invention of MTV

On 1 August 1981, Music Television (or MTV)'s very first transmission opened with the famous: "Ladies and Gentlemen, rock and roll!" over footage of the 1969 NASA moon landing. Combining rock music with holy images—of what was still seen as both the most famous moment in the history of television and the most technologically advanced moment of mankind—the MTV theme turned into the emblem of an entire generation. The network, initially focusing primarily on rock music, had been launched by two of America's largest conglomerates: In 1979, American Express bought half of the Warner Cable corporation, (325) as they envisioned cable TV as a sales tool, to deliver goods and services directly into the home. (326)

If the idea of showing music videos around the clock first sounded like a foolish idea to most specialists and businessmen, visionary minds such as MTV's co-founder Robert W. Pittman, succeeded in creating a need that did not previously exist. Directed at teens, a demographically defined group of people, located primarily in the suburbs and rural regions of America, the new TV channel had to construct its own audience by cultivating the demand for a particular audio-visual format: the music video. As explained by Rob Tannenbaum and Craig Marks, "teenagers were 'the demographic group least interested in TV', because TV wasn't interested in teens. Children had cartoons, adults had evening news and most of the shows that followed it. Teens were an untapped audience, an invisible power. MTV gave them what they wanted, and got them not only interested in, but obsessed by MTV, making it their clubhouse." (327)

In the United States particularly, the cable market was, in the early 1980s, suddenly in search of new and original content, to fill the long programming hours, and MTV appeared as the easiest and cheapest solution—using promotional music videos as its

323 According to broadcasting studies specialist Andrew Crisell, "We can identify 19 January 1972, the day when all restrictions on broadcasting hours were lifted, as the beginning of the era of modern television." Andrew Crisell, *An Introductory History of British Broadcasting* (London: Routledge, 2002), 152. In the early 1980s specialized 24h channels such as Cable News Network (CNN) and Music Television (MTV) started to appear because of the considerable expansion of broadcast hours in television. Introducing the continuum of the 24/7 cycle, these channels inaugurated a new sense of immediacy, as well as the end of programming and of an organized flow of content. By offering specialized and targeted content (be it real-time journalism, or video clip) they heavily contributed to the shattering of the sense of dispersed belonging engendered by the synchronization that use to characterize television.   324 Jonathan Crary, *24/7*, 83.   325 Together they formed Warner-Amex Satellite Entertainment Company (WASEC), which created and developed several successful cable networks (MTV but also The Movie Channel and the children's entertainment and educational channel Nickelodeon).   326 Rob Tannenbaum and Craig Marks, *I Want my MTV: The Uncensored Story of the Music Video Revolution* (London: Plume Book, 2012), xii.   327 Tannenbaum and Marks, *I Want my MTV*, xxxviii.

main input, MTV was thus able to produce an entirely new form of cultural production that came to dominate the music industry for most of the 1980s and 1990s. The music video, a perfect alliance between music and picture, did indeed "kill the radio star". (328) Although music videos existed way before the arrival of MTV, it was the new cable network that really created an industry for them by foreseeing that the target audience for the channel, "young people who had money and the inclination to buy things like records, candy bars, video games, beer and pimple cream" (329) had an increased economic power. In the early 1980s, record companies started to frenetically produce music videos, thus providing MTV with free content that could fill the programming hours. And it was this format—"extremely short (four minutes or less) texts that maintain us in an excited state of expectation" (330) which contributed to the hypnotic effect and constant sense of expectation that made the success of MTV.

The new TV channel was also conditioned by the politics of broadcasting. Unlike clubs and other inner-urban phenomena, MTV reached out to suburban and small-town areas. The distribution logic of cable television and early experiments in narrowcasting meant that MTV "first appeared in suburban and rural areas, where the cost-per-mile for digging and installing cable was cheaper than in cities." (331) Therefore, parallel to the institutionalizations of new forms of domestic entertainments, MTV also operated a territorial shift, introducing young American suburb dwellers to the culture of urban city centers. American teenagers could suddenly take part in a whole tranche of cultural activity from the family living room, or, via the second television set, from their own bedrooms. This domestication of youth entertainment ushered in a wider cultural shift of focus, from public and collective spaces to the private space of the household. MTV did not only contribute to selling records and advertising, it also ushered in a profound and pervasive transformation of the home that was now also becoming a stage from which people could perform and "talk back to their television". It colonized the space of the home and family time, day and night.

Between Domestic Performativity and Early Technological Interactivity

In 1956, artist Richard Hamilton produced the collage *Just what is it that makes today's home's so different, so appealing?*, for the *This is Tomorrow* exhibition at the Whitechapel Art Gallery in London. The image, which is seen as an icon of pop art and ranks among the most famous in British post-war art, came to define the rise of consumer society in the mid to late 1950s. (332) Made of images sourced from popular media, in particular a stash of American magazines, it also points to the increasing importance and centrality of the television in 1950s British domestic life. Often seen as "a window into the world", the television set then became "an integral part of family life and homes were transformed into theatres." (333) Therefore, one could read, in Hamilton's collage, a comment on the relation between inside and outside the home, suggesting that the space of entertainment, the new form of spectacle was gradually shifting from the urban space to the domestic space.

328   This is in reference to "Video Killed the Radio Star", the 1979 Music video by The Buggles and the first video to be aired on MTV.   329   Steven Levy, "Visions of MTV," *Rolling Stones*, n. 410, December 8, 1983.   330   E. Ann Kaplan, *Rocking Around the Clock: Music Television, Postmodernism and Consumer Culture* (London/New York: Routledge, 1987).   331   Tannenbaum and Marks, *I Want my MTV*, xii.   332   Tate Modern, "Just what was it that made yesterday's homes so different, so appealing? (upgrade) 2004," https://www.tate.org.uk/art/artworks/hamilton-just-what-was-it-that-made-yesterdays-homes-so-different-so-appealing-upgrade-p20271, accessed November 8, 2023.   333   Lynn Spigel, *Make Room for TV: Television and the Family Ideal in Postwar America* (Chicago: University of Chicago Press, 1992), 15.

If we come back to MTV and the music video, we can trace a genealogy for the format in the very public space of the discotheques, in early 1980s New York. Indeed, the music video was arguably invented by Merrill Aldighieri, the first-ever Video Jockey (or VJ, a term invented by Aldhighieri herself). Aldighieri started to make a video installation as a prominently featured component of the club's design with multiple monitors hanging over the bar and dance floor. When New York City nightclub Hurrah invited Aldighieri to show her experimental film, she asked if she could develop a video to complement the DJ music so that then her film would become part of a club ambience. From 1980 to 1981 Aldighieri was a full-time VJ, creating a new alliance between music and picture. Unlike rave parties and other inner-city phenomena proliferating in the 1980s, MTV brought music and club culture directly into the suburban home, colonizing domestic spaces such as basement living rooms and teenage bedrooms. With a set mimicking the '15-years-old's ideal basement hideaway', MTV intended to offer viewers a room of their own that also echoed an alternative world. (334)

MTV appeared suddenly. American musician Dave Grohl (Nirvana, Foo Fighters) remembers "It seemed like a transmission from some magical place. Me and all my friends were dirty little rocker kids in suburban Virginia, so we spent a lot of our time at the record store or staring at album covers. With music videos, there was a deeper dimension to everything. On Friday night, you'd go to a friend's house to get fucked up before going out to a party, and you'd have MTV on." (335)

Before the advent of MTV, music television programmes were bringing the family together in front of the television, often before a night out. *Top of the Pops* (TOTP), a British music chart television program, was broadcasted weekly, every Thursday evening on BBC One, since 1964 with 15 million viewers every night in its heyday of the 1970s. Each weekly show consisted of performances from some of that week's best-selling popular music records that would bring the whole family together in front of the television: "I remember it was a ritual, the whole family gathered around the TV to watch *Top of The Pops*. Even if your dad used to slag off the acts that were on, it was still a family thing. It was a mixed bag in those days in the charts…something for all the family" commented Noddy Holder, a former Musician from the British rock band The Slade. In the 1980s, the set of TOTP had been redesigned to place the crowd in the studio around and behind the bands, so they were in full view. The audience had always been part of the program, but now they were completely staged, with professional dancers that would encourage an unnatural 'party' atmosphere.

But beyond performativity, early-days MTV also embraced the idea of television as an interactive medium. MTV was born from an early experiment in interactive television. A few years before the creation of MTV, Warner Cable, a division of Warner Communication, had come up with QUBE, the first two-way interactive cable television system and an early form of narrowcasting. From 1977 onwards, QUBE computer terminals were being test-marketed as part of a highly sophisticated cable communication system in Columbus, Ohio. QUBE had the particularity of offering a plethora of specialized

---

334 Pat Aufderheide, "Music Videos: The Look of the Sounds," *Journal of Communication* 36, no. 1, (March 1986): 64.   335 Tannenbaum and Marks, *I Want my MTV*, 1.

channels, one of which was *Sight on Sound,* a channel dedicated to concert videos and other music programming. Following a logic of participatory programming, Warner Cable had commercialized a two-way multi-programmed cable television interactive system that allowed spectators to "answer back to [their] television". Offering a new type of interaction with technology, QUBE was branded as "the TV of the people, by the people and for the people."

QUBE marked the beginning of the era of participatory as opposed to passive television. As explained in a 1978 special report on QUBE, the system held the potential of revolutionizing the entertainment, audio-visual instruction and educational industries, amongst others. (336) By greatly expanding the programming choice and by allowing the viewer to become an active participant, QUBE operated a radical shift and advancement over what television or cable television had heretofore offered, bringing the potential of opening up the cities of America to cable television service on a profitable basis.

The same report predicted that "QUBE could be the first market skirmish in programming, marketing and technological revolution that could profoundly affect the economy, the gross national product, the entertainment habits and the lifestyles of America." (337) And, indeed, it's the commercial potential of QUBE-like systems that had an enormous impact on the music recording and publishing industries.

What MTV brought into the house was the performative atmosphere of the nightclub. It transposed the idea of nocturnal entertainment from centers to peripheries: from inner-city nightclubs to basement suburbia. Moreover, it conveyed a sense of interactivity with the television set. This idea that watching television was no longer merely a passive activity but that one's living room could become a dancefloor for the night, to experience on one's own or in the company of a small, restricted group of friends.

Transforming the Media House

Towards the end of the twentieth century, Beatriz Colomina historicized and theorized the Media House, stating, in her eponymic 1995 article *Assemblage*, that "at one level, the architecture is transformed by the media in which it is exhibited. On another level, the design of the house concerns the media itself." (338) In each moment of the twentieth century, she writes, "the house has been made to stand for different things and in each case this polemical use of the home depends on a particular use of the media." (339) Yet, in the early 1980s, the media house changes and starts to reflect conditions of postmodernity, all of which can be found in the ethos and format of MTV. Fragmentary in nature, it portrays a new relation to space and technology, but also to time and identity. In response to the advent of neoliberalism and the growing importance of the 24/7 condition described by Crary, it starts to function more actively at night, and to open to the possibility of multiple, changing identities.

In April 1982, radical architect and researcher in the visual arts, Ugo La Pietra, proposed his project for "La Casa Telematica" (The Telematic House) at the 61st Fiera Internazionale di Milano. The displayed project explored the implications of electronic memory and the potential impact of engineering and technology on domestic spaces. Beyond its

336 *The Videocassette & CATV Newsletter, special report*, Warner Cable's QUBE, qube-tv, last accessed February 16, 2020, http://www.qube-tv.com/qube-tv/QUBE-REPORT.pdf. 337 *The Videocassette & CATV Newsletter,* qube-tv. 338 Beatriz Colomina, "The Media House," *Assemblage* no. 27 (August 1995): 47. 339 Colomina, "The Media House," 64.

techno-utopian rhetoric, La Pietra's house characterized the shift between the radical ethos of the 1970s and the hedonistic aesthetics of the 1980s: a total embracing of unbridled consumerism resulting in a house full of screens and cameras dominated by abstracted columns, neon lights and pastel colours. (Fig. 4) The house started to emulate the domestic quality of the urban space and vice versa. La Pietra writes:

> "The television-centric family seems to have abandoned all festive traditions (going to the cinema on Sundays, Saturday night parties, trips to the countryside) in exchange for a routine of watching television, in other words for the continuous use of the television set. [...] From a physical point of view, there has not been much change in the spatial and distributive evolution of the home. However, if we carefully examine behaviours, it is noticeable how being together and talking (a functional characteristic that shaped the space and the distribution of objects) were in fact habits that gradually fell into oblivion. These were habits that were associated with a certain rituality and that still existed during the 1950s, even with the presence of the television, when there was only one channel, one film a week (on Mondays), the rerun on Saturday night and the comedy on Friday!" (340)

With the arrival of television, however, the layout of this type of setting (living-dining room) has been transforming from when the divide first appeared, often either hidden or placed inside a bookcase, to having an increasing presence in the setting to the point of changing the arrangement and orientation of armchairs, shifting the focal point from the center (coffee table) to a corner of the room (television). From 1954 to the 1970s this was a slow process, and it is only in these last few years that we can see an acceleration in the transformation of the domestic space due to factors such as an increase in the number of channels, colour TV and nonstop programmes extended to 12, 16, 18 hours a day. In this way, television also appeared in the bedroom, changing our evenings and habits within this space too." (341)

La Pietra's exhibition house suggested a new sensory sphere in which the information and spectacle prevails, the home transformed into a theater where everyone was at once actor, spectator and set designer. The house itself looked like a television set in which different domestic spaces were adapted to the presence of the screens: While the dining table mutates into a triangular shape focusing on the television set, the living room presented a multiplicity of richly decorated armchairs, each equipped with its own screen at the back. The more intimate space of the bedroom included a vanity table equipped with surveillance cameras and a control station formed of three miniaturized screens, and a double bed split in two, each half having its separate screen. La Pietra's project constitutes a key example of the media house in which screens multiply, while media content invades the domestic space, increasingly blurring the boundaries between the simulacra of the set and the reality of the house while letting the outside world in. The project had an earlier iteration, the telematic house as a living cell presented at the 1972 MoMA exhibition *Italy: New Domestic Landscape* curated by Emilio Ambasz. With this project, La Pietra anticipated the use of telematics and information technology within the home suggesting a constant exchange of information between a single person in his home and people in the public space. Yet, we see that, ten years later,

340 Gianfranco Bettetini, Aldo Grassi and Ugo La Pietra, eds., *La Casa Telematica* (Societa editrice Kata: Milan, 1983), 32. 341 Ugo La Pietra, *Domestic City/Citta Domestica* (Salerno: Plectica, 2021), 93–94.

La Pietra's aesthetics has changed. The house is not only lit by the multiplicity of television screens, but also by an abundance of brightly glowing multicolour neon lights, suggesting an atmosphere of nightlife and postmodernity.

A few years later (in 1986), in the context of the 17th Milan Triennale (The Domestic Project), OMA presented the project Casa Palestra (house gymnasium)—a fundamental but overlooked project in OMA's career. Starting from the premise that "modern architecture was always presented as lifeless, puritanical, empty and uninhabited," OMA's proposed "modern architecture is in itself a hedonistic movement, that its severity, abstraction and rigor are in fact plots to create the most provocative settings for the experiment that is modern life." In this project, OMA bent the Barcelona Pavilion to form a curve and produce a "programmatic intensity" and systematically develop a project of its all-human occupancy related to physical culture in the widest possible sense of the word. The house was both desecrated and inaugurated and showed its perfect appropriateness for even the most suggestive aspects of contemporary culture. Action suggested by projection and light effects and an abstract soundtrack of the human voice—somewhere in the ambiguous zone between exercise and sexual pleasure—completed this spectacle, whose aim was to shock people into an awareness of the possible 'hidden' dimensions of modern architecture."

Like a nightclub, the house contained exercise elements, mirrors, sound boxes and horn speakers, reflection panels, lasers, light spots, light boxes, neons and a television set. It also included a smoke machine, blowers and projections.

Conclusion

In 1974, Korean artist Nam Junk Pai produced *TV-Garden*, a piece which, while revealing the artistic potential lurking behind television screens, suggested an uncanny merging of nature and technology. Today, our domestic space is undergoing dramatic changes and, at the center of this revolution is the presence of a multiplicity of screens which are no longer windows into the world, but rather propel our private interiors into the public sphere. The forms of uninterrupted infrastructure pioneered by MTV marked the end of programming and the synchronization of continuous flows of content, paving the way for narrowcasting, in itself a technological form of fragmentation. The new television channel and its related format of the music video were an important component of this late twentieth-century media environment: through the screen, they achieved a new type of spatial and temporal construction. They emerged at a precise moment in time and through the convergence of three different factors: technological, social and economic. And while they became, for a time, central to the music industry they also shaped the space around us: both at the macro scale of the territory—it modified the relation between centers and periphery—and the micro-scale of the home. A perfect embodiment of the 24/7 theorized by Jonathan Crary, MTV blurs the distinctions between day and night and transforms the house into an uninterrupted nightlife media environment dominated by interactivity and performativity.

Now outdated, MTV and music videos have been replaced by other transient regimes of visions whose impact on domesticity and territoriality is yet to be fully appraised.

This research was supported by the Graham Foundation

TOPOGRAPHY, LIGHT DESIGN, AND INDUSTRIAL HERITAGE IN THE RUHR REGION
The Night Vision of IBA Emscher Park
Hilary Orange

Once the center of Germany's coal, steel, and iron industries, around 5.3 million people live in the fifty-three towns and cities that make up the Ruhr region, one of the most densely populated areas in Europe. This Metropolis or "city of cities" is bounded to the west by the Rhine river and to the north and south by tributaries of the Rhine—the Lippe and Ruhr. The south is slightly hilly, but further north a third canalized tributary, the Emscher, flows through the center of the region. Here the land is relatively flat except for a range of slag heaps that mark the former coal mining territories. In Germany, the era of coal ended in 2018 as part of the nation's energy transition to low-carbon, renewable sources, but heavy industry went into decline much earlier, starting with the coal and steel crises of the 1960s and 1970s. Since then around half a million jobs have been lost. (342) Steel continues; most significantly ThyssenKrupp operate steel plants on the banks of the Rhine in Duisburg and the chemical and mechanical engineering industries have sizeable footprints in the region, but industrial landmarks are now more likely to be associated with heritage than with extraction, production and manufacturing.

342 Gert-Jan Hospers, "Restructuring Europe's rustbelt: The case of the German Ruhrgebiet," *Intereconomics* 39, no. 3 (2004): 149.

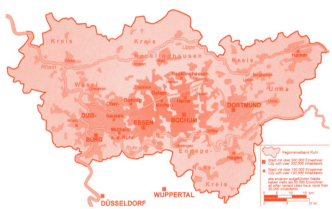

This essay considers the light designs commissioned by the *Internationale Bauausstellung Emscher Park* programme (henceforth IBA Emscher Park), an urban development programme that ran from 1989-1999 in the Ruhr, and explores the relationship between topography, light art and industrial heritage. Light designs were installed on redundant industrial sites to create new landmarks and, in so doing, industrial sites became subject to new processes of culturalization linked to the development of industrial heritage tourism. Torgeir Bangstad has reflected that these "staged ruins" were both "ciphers of the industrial past and as signs of something new as well." (343) They represented a bold, new vision for the Ruhr, one that embraced artistic expression while, nonetheless, holding the industrial past close. Several decades have passed since IBA Emscher Park took place and the light designs are of the same era as 1980s fashion—shoulder pads, drainpipe jeans and mullets—and the decade's greatest hits on the radio. They need to be understood in the context of their own time.

The origins of IBA Emscher Park's night vision for the park will be outlined by drawing on material held in the Archiv für soziale Bewegungen im Haus der Geschichte des Ruhrgebiets, Bochum. A key observation is that the light designs are topographic agents that shape bodily movement. They connect to landscape, as shaped by industry, to movement through the climbing and accessing of high points and through well-established mountaineering and Alpine metaphors. Height and light characterize industrial heritage tourism in the Ruhr despite

343 Torgeir Rinke Bangstad, "*Defamiliarization, Conflict and Authenticity: Industrial Heritage and the Problem of Representation*" (PhD diss., Norwegian University of Science and Technology, 2014), 7. LaBelle has also commented that the light designs connect the past to the future, "Emscher Park", 226.

the relative flatness of the region's underlying geology. The light designs also have various other functional, aesthetic, and emotional dimensions including orientation – wayfinding – security – visual appeal – comfort – atmosphere – place-making. (344)

IBA Emscher Park was a direct response to economic decline during a pervasive period of deindustrialization. By the 1980s, the federal government of North Rhine-Westphalia recognized that the region's economic problems were structural e.g. long-lasting or permanent, rather than cyclical. (345) In 1988, the government initiated IBA Emscher Park based on previous International Building Exhibitions (*Internationale Bauaustellungen*) held in Germany. (346) Dubbed a 'Workshop for the Future of Old Industrial Regions', the Ruhr programme focused on the most heavily industrialized part of the region, a corridor of some 70km that followed the Emscher river. By concentrating on the significant problems that existed in this area, such as high unemployment, a shrinking population and environmental pollution, (347) the government sought to manage regional economic transition, a process known in Germany as 'structural change' or 'structural transformation'. (348) With emphases on new forms of business, science, technology, and culture, a total of 117 individual projects were instigated in the ten-year period from 1989 to 1999. Most of the individual projects were run through a decentralized approach whereby single project proposals were made by city authorities and civic groups in response to five guideline areas:

344 "Spoil heaps in the Ruhr Valley," Ruhr Tourismus, https://www.ruhr-tourismus.de/en/ruhrindustrialculture/industrial-heritage-trail/spoil-tips-in-the-ruhr-valley.html, accessed January 16, 2022. 345 Hans-Werner Wehling, *Zollverein and the industrial cultural landscape Ruhr. Report on its theoretical/conceptional foundation and its spatial operationalization* (Dortmund: Stiftung Industriedenkmalpflege und Geschichtskultur, 2015), 25. 346 Robert Shaw, "The International Building Exhibition (IBA) Emscher Park, Germany: A model for sustainable restructuring?," *European Planning Studies* 10, no. 1 (2002): 84; the previous International Building Exhibition had been held in Berlin in 1987. 347 Sarah Hemmings and Martin Kagel, "Memory Gardens: Aesthetic Education and Political Emancipation in the Landschaftspark Duisburg-Nord," *German Studies Review* 33, no. 2 (2010): 247; Heiderose Kilper and Gerald Wood, "Restructuring policies: the Emscher Park International Building Exhibition," in *The Rise of the Rustbelt: Revitalizing Older Industrial Regions*, ed. Philip Cooke (London: UCL Press, 1995), 208–9. 348 Stefan Moitra and Katarzyna Nogueira, "(Post-)Industrial Memories: Oral History and Structural Change," *BIOS—Zeitschrift*

1) ecological regeneration of the Emscher river system;
2) housing and integrated urban development;
3) working in the park;
4) new uses for industrial buildings and monuments;
5) social initiatives, employment and training. (349)

From 1994-95 onwards, IBA Emscher Park's priorities shifted toward art and tourism and it was within this phase of programming that light designs were commissioned from leading international light designers and architects through competition-like procedures. Buildings and other industrial features were seen as carriers of culture and key to the ongoing memoryscape and identity of the region, however, industrial relics were primarily instrumentalized through the development of leisure and tourism opportunities. (350)

Schurenbachhalde is a relatively low (approximately 50 meters high), but large (50 hectares) slag heap located on the southern bank of the Emscher that had been worked by Zollverein coal mine and other mines in the area. The flanks of the heap have, over time, revegetated, but the summit remains a stark expanse of grey and black rock and dirt with only a few shrubs. In the center of the heap is a 14.5 m high rolled steel slab, graffitied to within an arm's reach. The sculpture entitled *Bramme für das Ruhrgebiet* (trans. Slab for the Ruhr) is the work of the

für Biographieforschung, Oral History und Lebensverlaufsanalysen 31, no. 2 (2018). 349 Shaw, "The International Building," 85–87. 350 Hemmings and Kagel, "Memory Gardens," 257; Anne Browley Raines points out that IBA Emscher Park recognized that "the entire landscape was steeped in industrial heritage, and that other traces should be called out and treated in some way" beyond buildings and machinery. Anne Brownley Raines, "Wandel durch (Industrie) Kultur [Change through (industrial) culture]: Conservation and renewal in the Ruhrgebiet," *Planning Perspectives* 26, no. 2 (2011): 195.

American artist Richard Serra who is known for his large-scale minimalist creations. Installed in 1998, the sculpture was commissioned by IBA Emscher Park. (351) It is unlit, but nevertheless has significance in the story of the lighting of IBA Emscher Park.

The Director of IBA Emscher Park, Karl Ganser, had a background in human geography and town planning and had previously been working as the head of the North Rhine-Westphalia's Department for Urban Planning. In 1993, Ganser wrote a memo to colleagues, referring to a visit to Schurenbachhalde on a "quiet and stormy evening" where he had the opportunity to further consider his idea to create a "spatially connected system" of landmarks encompassing a large interior. The landmarks were to be utilized as "vantage points" where the "external limitation as well as the visibility of the landmarks in the interior" could be perceived. [my translation]

In considering the spatial and aesthetic qualities of the urban landscape by night, Ganser was thinking about the use of temporary lighting e.g. fireworks, "there must be constant playful movement of balls [of light] in the sky, which is at the same time a symbol of the process of IBA Emscher Park, a system of decentralized, varied project ideas". (352) The lighting of landmarks, he wrote, would provide a means to make the regionality of IBA more visible [at night] then during the day." [my translation] (353) In due course, Ganser's landmark idea moved from using temporary lighting to the commission of permanent light installations.

351   Roy Kift, *Über alle Berge* (Essen: Klartext, 2016), 109–112; "Schurenbachhalde," Wikipedia, https://de.wikipedia.org/wiki/Schurenbachhalde, accessed November 8, 2023.   352   Archiv für soziale Bewegungen, IBA, Signatur 1347A.   353   Archiv für soziale Bewegungen, IBA, Signatur 1347B.

An undated sketch in the archive, titled in English "Seven Ups", shows the *Slab for the Ruhr* at the center of a group of landmarks. Accompanying documentation, unauthored and undated, refers to the "Seven Ups" and a series of weekend tours of landmarks. The meeting point was Schurenbachhalde which, the documentation reads, offers very impressive views of the six other excursion points. The *Slab* is referred to as the geographic center of Emscher Park (354) (a point picked up by the art historian Ira Mazzoni who referred to the *Slab* as a "compass point" at the center of the Park in a 1999 news article. (355)) Times written next to the landmarks show estimated arrival and departure times. One of the proposed stops is the Zollverein coal mine in Essen. There are sketches of the double-headed tower frame over Shaft XII at Zollverein as well as the gasometer at Oberhausen. There is a sketch of a triangle and the word "Tetraeder" written top right.

The Prosper Haniel colliery in Bottrop created several mine heaps in the city including two heaps situated opposite each other, Haldenereignis Emscherblick (heap event Emscher view) and Halde Prosper, which are both linked to adventure tourism. Halde Prosper has an alpine center with a snow dome and ski run built into its slopes while the summit of Haldenereignis Emscherblick can be accessed via a 400-step steel staircase that ascends 78 m to the summit, marketed for sports enthusiasts as the "Tetraeder stair run." There is a gentler serpentine path. (356) On the summit of Haldenereignis Emscherblick is the *Tetraeder*, an IBA Emscher Park light art project. A steel and

354   Archiv für soziale Bewegungen, IBA, Signatur 1347A.   355   Ira Mazzoni, "Viel Terz um eine Stele," [Much ado about a slab] *Süddeutsche Zeitung*, December 13, 1999, 17.   356   "Tetraeder Bottop," Ruhr Tourismus, https://www.ruhr-tourismus.de/en/ruhrindustrialculture/industrial-heritage-trail/spoil-tips-in-the-ruhr-valley/tetraeder-bottrop.html; Kift, *Über alle Berge*, 121–129, accessed January 14, 2022.

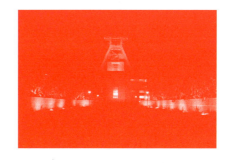

concrete pyramidal structure, around 60 meters high, it was designed by the German architect Wolfgang Christ and installed in 1995. The structure can be climbed via a series of steel staircases that lead to three viewing platforms. At the top, a light design—*Fraktal*—by Jürgen LIT Fischer traces the uppermost sections of the pyramid in yellow light. At night those who climb the pyramid are encased within both the structure and the source of the light. From this vantage point, there are sightlines to other illuminated landmarks such as the headframe at the German Mining Museum in Bochum, the Gasometer (the summits of both are accessible to visitors), and the headframe at Zollverein. From below, in the city streets, the effect of the *Tetraeder* light design is slightly uncanny, a yellow pyramid free-floating in dark space. The structure is also visible from the Ruhr's main arterial roads, the A2 Bundesautobahn and the A42 Emscherschnellweg. Like other light art projects, the *Tetreader* operates as a lighthouse or beacon, but instead of warning of impending danger, it draws attention to fixed points in the landscape and provides orientation at night. A letter from Karl Ganser, dated 1998, refers to Emscher Park as a "confusing sea, with reefs and islands." He wrote that those who travel around needed both day and night orientation. (357) The largest 'lighthouse' in the Ruhr is IBA Emscher Park's flagship project in the Meiderich district of Duisburg. Landschaftspark Duisburg-Nord is a 230-hectare industrial park designed by landscape architect Peter Latz around the decommissioned Thyssen iron and steelworks. (358) In 1996, a light show, designed by Jonathan Park, was installed on the furnace complex at

357 Archiv für soziale Bewegungen, IBA, Signatur IBA 1347B.
358 Peter Latz, "Landscape Park Duisburg-Nord: The metamorphosis of an industrial site," in *Manufactured Sites: Rethinking the Post-Industrial Landscape,* ed. Niall Kirkwood (London: Taylor and Francis, 2001), 150–61. Opening in 1994, the park has been rewilded and has sports facilities including a flooded gasometer for diving.

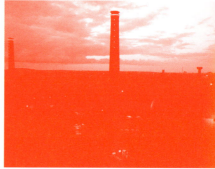

the heart of the park. The tops of three chimneys are the first features to light up, followed in succession by other features, a gasometer, blast furnaces, and bunker complexes, all timed on a loop. (359) Landschaftspark Duisburg-Nord signalled IBA Emscher Park's brand as much as its vision, for the colours of the light show—red, blue, green—are the same colours as IBA Emscher Park's logo.

The architecture of the industrial complex at Landschaftspark Duisburg-Nord has also been reutilized for climbing and the creation of look-out towers and vantage points. Visitors can climb up and around the furnace and bunker complexes via elevated metal walkways and staircases. The German Alpine Club has a branch in the Park, and its members climb in the former bunker complex. Sarah Hemmings and Martin Kagel have noted the feeling of the industrial or technological sublime that is evoked in encounters with the size and complexity of the industrial structures in the park, made all the more disorientating at night when the light show abstracts forms and surfaces. They quote Der Spiegel reporter, Ullrich Fichtner's, description of the view from the 70 m high vantage point of Blast Furnace Five, "The horizon is blocked up in its entire breadth with smokestacks and furnaces and powder metal facilities [...]. It is a view as if one was looking onto a mountain range, a monumental panorama of German industrial history" [their translation]. (360) Fichnter goes on to note that the industrial facilities are like mountains—quiet and dead [author translation] (361) Their monumentality is a mirror to the 'mountainality' of the mine heaps,

359 The scale of the light show is illustrated by a *Westdeutsche Allgemeine Zeitung* newspaper report from 6 November 1996, on the 400 lamps, 126 circuits and 40 km of cables that create a light show at the center of the Park. Archiv für soziale Bewegungen, IBA, Signatur 869B. 360 Hemmings and Kagel, "Memory Gardens," 257, quoting Ullrich Fichtner, "Die Rűckkehr des Proletariats," *Der Spiegel,* May 29, 2005, 105. 361 Fichtner, "Die Rűckkehr des Proletariats," 105.

both with accentuated access and lights at the summit. Industry as mountains and the climbing of industrial features are interrelated themes that are repeatedly applied to industrial heritage in the Ruhr area, creating a form of *Industrieklettern* (industrial climbing) that is less about the rope-work required by technicians at work, and more about sport, tourism, and leisure.

The popularity of the light designs, particularly Landschaftspark Duisburg-Nord, led to an inflation in light art projects across the wider Ruhr region in the years following IBA Emscher Park. The Ruhr was awarded the title of European Capital of Culture in 2010 and Ruhr2010, as the resulting year-long programme was called, invested in further light art projects. At the beginning of that year, 135 permanent light installations were counted in 25 Ruhr district municipalities, (362) a significant increase on the 13 that were installed by IBA Emscher Park. Light art features across the 400 km *Route der Industriekultur* (Route of Industrial Culture), another project instigated under the auspices of IBA Emscher Park, but led by the regional planning association Kommunalverband Ruhrgebiet, and across the overlapping *Route der Landmarken-Kunst* (Route of Landmark Art) which opened two years earlier in 1997. (363) Aside from programmes such as Ruhr2010, the spread of light design was also caused by inter-city rivalry. Gert-Jan Hospers has noted that a "climate of rivalry" in the Ruhr region is often symbolized by the city football club (364) and, as Andrea Kath has argued, despite regional marketeers' attempts to portray the region as a Metropolis,

362 Stefan Hochstadt, Dennis Köhler and Manfred Walz, eds., "Künstliches Licht im Ruhrgebiet: Ein Indikator kultureller Identiatät?," in *Lichtregion: Positionen und Perspektiven im Ruhrgebiet* (Essem: Klartext, 2010), 13. 363 Torgeir Rinke Bangstad, "Routes of industrial heritage: On the animation of sedentary objects," *Culture Unbound: Journal of Current Cultural Research,* no. 3 (2011): 288–93. 364 Hospers, "Restructuring Europe's rustbelt," 149.

neighbouring cities are rivals in more than just football. Indeed, there is a common past in the Ruhr, but no common identity (365), and the cities wanted landmarks of their own. The 'organic' growth of light art throughout the region was, to some extent, a continuation of IBA Emscher Park's decentralized approach, albeit one instigated and governed by city and municipal interests. Stefan Hochstadt and colleagues have pointed out that artificial light affects many levels of the ecological, economic, social, and cultural characteristics of life in the Ruhr region, and an integrated lighting strategy, which they believe is lacking, would better support sustainable urban development. Since IBA Emscher Park there has been perhaps less emphasis on how the lights may relate to each other (366) and Ganser's original concept has become lost in the mix.

One 'progeny' of IBA Emscher Park is the Henrichshütte Ironworks in Hattingen where the furnace complex was lit by staff, initially in a DIY fashion in 1999. (367) Hattingen lies on the banks of the Ruhr river and the ironworks museum is one of the eight industrial museums managed by the regional association Landschaftsverband Westfalen-Lippe (LWL). Like other industrial heritage sites, Henrichshütte offers evening events programmes such as torchlit tours, outdoor cinema, and concerts. Once a year, the highly popular Night of Industrial Culture in the Ruhr region (*Extraschicht*) sees heritage venues staying open till the early hours of the morning. Alongside any permanent illuminations, there may be fireworks as well as food and beer stalls. The sense of conviviality fostered at outdoor events

365 Andrea Kath, "Rätsel Ruhrgebiet," in *Mysterious Zone: Geheiminisvolles Ruhrgebiet,* ed. Frank Schultze (Essen: Rainruhr, 2010), 8–9. 366 Hochstadt, "Künstliches Licht im Ruhrgebiet," 18. 367 Interview with Olaf Schmidt-Rutsch, September 7, 2017.

means that visiting industrial heritage at night is a popular activity in the Ruhr. The night also attracts hobby and professional photographers who share images on social media and, in so doing, strengthen the nocturnal industrial aesthetic that already features strongly within city/regional branding and marketing. (368)

Not everyone is in favour of the aestheticization of industrial monuments in the Ruhr region. In 1995, the *Westdeutsche Allgemeine Zeitung* newspaper reported on a protest at the opening of the *Tetraeder*. Representatives of the local green party Bündnis 90/Die Grünen complained that the installation was a waste of money and energy. (369) More recently, Kerstin Barndt has commented that the "postmodern play and fun" at Landschaftspark Duisburg-Nord "tends to pacify history, rather than mining it for critical reflection." The viewing platforms and walkways, Barndt goes on to say, enable "visitors to rise above local history. The elevated artworks create the conditions of possibility for 'setting the subject free' of systemic structures and long-lived traditions..." (370) An image that comes to mind is that of Casper David Friedrichson's painting the *Wanderer above the Sea of Fog* add painted in 1818, of a figure surveying a landscape that they are above, but not necessarily a part of. In a similar vein, Stefan Berger and colleagues have recently challenged both the aestheticization of industrial relics and "histotainment" in the Ruhr region, for them exemplified by the Bottrop Alpine Center. Such places do nothing, they say, "to invite people to critically rethink the industrial past." (371)

368   See photography by Thomas Pflaum, *Fotografieren im Ruhrgebiet* (Bonn: Rheinwerk Fotografie, 2015); Rolf Arno Specht, *Kathedralen im Revier: Zechenlandschaft Ruhrgebiet* (Essen: Klartext Verlag, 2017).   369   *Westdeutsche Allgemeine Zeitung*, October 5, 1995, Facsimile Archiv für soziale Bewegungen, IBA, Signatur 869B.1777B.   370   Kerstin Barndt, "'Memory traces of an abandoned set of futures': Industrial ruins in the postindustrial landscapes of Germany," in *Ruins of Modernity*, ed. Julia Hell and Andreas Schönle (Durham: Duke University Press, 2010), 278–79.   371   Stefan Berger, Jana Golombeck and Christian Wicke, eds., "A post-industrial mindscape? The mainstreaming and touristification of industrial heritage in the Ruhr," in *Industrial Heritage and Regional Identities* (London: Routledge, 2018), 85. Following Jörn Rüsen, "Industriedenkmale und Geschichtskultur im Ruhrgebiet," *Forum Geschichtskultur an Ruhr und Emscher: Industriedenkmalpflege und Geschichtskultur,* 2 (1998): 4.

These are valid viewpoints. The light designs in themselves do little to convey *in-depth* historic cues regarding regional history. Neither do they challenge visitors and climbers to contribute directly to social and economic debates. That was not their purpose, as objects primarily of pleasure and leisure. The Ruhr was described as Germany's "problem area number 1" in a 2019 poverty report. That year, 21.1% of the region's population was estimated to be living in poverty. The lights are seen by some as 'art-washing' ongoing and deeply set social problems. (372)

In defense of art, the technical skills and employment opportunities of designers, architects, engineers, electricians, museum, and heritage site staff etc. could be acknowledged and while the creative and leisure sectors have, thus far, filled spaces like the *Tetraeder* with new post-industrial purpose and meaning, public history is presented elsewhere in Ruhr area through industrial museums, oral history and guided tours. I do not see it as a competing scenario. Rather, the question as I see it is in better understanding how visitors to sites, whether the Alpine Center, the *Tetraeder* or LandschaftsPark Duisburg-Nord, access different experiences and make historical meanings from those experiences. Is their experience transformative and, if so, in what directions? A set of questions arises. What are the relative strengths and weaknesses of various on-site approaches to interpreting and re-utilising industrial relicts, whether those approaches are historical, artistic, sporting, or other? What are the relationships between different on-site emotive, affective, bodily engagements and forms of historical knowledge and meaning-making?

372   "Germany: Poverty gap widens between rich and poor regions," *Deutsche Welle*, December 12, 2019, https://www.dw.com/en/germany-poverty-gap-widens-between-rich-and-poor-regions/a-51637957, accessed November 8, 2023.

And, fundamentally, what else could be done with slag heaps (presuming something needs to be done) beyond the kinds of initiatives that have been undertaken in the Ruhr region? In terms of 'doing'—interventions do not necessarily need to be solid and 'permanent', they can be transitory and leave few material traces.

The aestheticization of industrial monuments in the Ruhr area has been substantively broadcast through the medium of digital technology, a point that is as glaringly obvious as it is overlooked. In his 1994 book *American Technological Sublime,* David Nye writes on the admiration that writers and artists have had for "aesthetically pleasing" factory areas, (373) an interest that runs back through the 20th century to earlier traditions of the sublime and picturesque in the fine art of the 19th century and beyond. (374) The difference, from then to now, is that electricity, and more recently LED lighting have largely replaced fire light, and digital photography has largely replaced analog photography. The industrial aesthetic in the Ruhr region has become increasingly visible due to the growth in consumer digital technology, something that IBA Emscher Park did not predict. Indeed, photography is barely mentioned in the archive. The year 1995, the same of the installation of the *Tetraeder* (and protest against it) was also, coincidentally, around the same time that Casio and Kodak both introduced consumer digital cameras. (375) It is, therefore, not surprising that the increasing aestheticization of the industrial landscape in the Ruhr region has led to concerns regarding the pacification or sanitization of complex industrial histories. But the genie is out of the

373 David E. Nye, *American Technological Sublime* (Cambridge, MS: MIT Press, 1994), 126–127. 374 Francis D. Klingender, *Art and the Industrial Revolution* (London: Paladin, 1972), [originally pulbished in 1947].

digital bottle. As communication theorist Marshall McLuhan famously wrote in 1964, "the medium is the message." The way that content is transmitted plays an important role in shaping perception.

Where the light designs do intersect with history, aside from their own place in history, is by acting as proxies for the 'lost' lights of working industry. They filled in the dark gaps in cities after industries closed down. As Hochstadt and colleagues have pointed out, the Ruhr region has its own "light past" (376), one that is particularly associated with the firelight of steelworks. A moniker for the region is *Das Land der Tausend Feuer* (land of a thousand fires). The term appears in a 1924 book of poetry and short stories within which a poem by Adolph Potthoff also entitled "Das Land der Tausend Feuer" romantically links senses of belonging and homeland to the familiarity of the blazing steelworks at night. (377) The cover features three stylized fire-breathing dragons sat in a landscape of flames, while the frontispiece has an illustration of steelworkers stoking a furnace. The phrase *Das Land …* is likely to be older.

To conclude, artificial light is used widely across the Ruhr to present and promote industrial heritage. IBA Emscher Park is an example of how culture and art were incorporated into old industrial sites and lent impetus toward the creation of a new regional identity. The light designs were influenced by, and part of, the topography of the Ruhr and were utilized as a means to shape nocturnal space. The lighting has historical roots, the 'lost' firelight of steel as well as the traditions of the industrial and technological sublime in fine art. However, on aesthetics, the light

375 Hunter Skipworth, "World Photography Day 2014: The history of digital cameras," Digital Sky, 2014, https://www.digitalspy.com/tech/cameras/a591251/world-photography-day-2014-the-history-of-digital-cameras/, accessed November 8, 2023. 376 Hochstadt, "Künstliches Licht im Ruhrgebiet," 13. 377 Bernhard Zytur, ed., *Das Land der Tausend Feuer: Dichtungen aus Bergbau und Industrie* (Frankfurt: Diesterweg, 1924).

designs can be envisaged not just as 'things' to see, but also as 'things' to engage with bodily—climbing, orientating oneself at night, driving past, touching, waiting at for twilight. The affect/effect is linked to the relative position of the viewer to the source of light, as well as their position in relation to historical memory.

With the advent of consumer digital cameras, digital photography has become an increasingly popular way for people to engage with the light designs at night and, in turn, with online representations thereof. However, the context of the topography of the Ruhr region, as experienced and felt by the body, is best gained by being in situ. In particular, climbing the industrial structures that host the light art reveals their forms as topographic agents in the landscape at night. Such experiences align more closely with IBA Emscher Park's original intent and vision for lighting the park.

Acknowledgements

I thank the Alexander von Humboldt Foundation for the funding that supported my research. My gratitude also extends to my host, Professor Stefan Berger, at the Institut für soziale Bewegungen as well as the team in the Archiv für soziale Bewegungen im Haus der Geschichte des Ruhrgebiets, Bochum. I would also like to thank the Historisches Archiv Krupp for access to their archives. Lastly, I thank Dr Olaf Schmidt-Rutsch (LWL Henrichshütte Museum) for consenting to be interviewed.

NOCTURNAL SPACES
Rediscovering an Architecture of Darkness
Nick Dunn

Introduction

The interplay between light and dark shapes our relationship with place. At night, artificial illumination can profoundly affect our experience of architecture, both as interior space and urban realm. This essay examines the city of Manchester in the United Kingdom, its pioneering industrialization and subsequent legacy of an 'architecture of darkness'. It then explores recent developments in urban illumination to ask how we might develop nocturnal spaces that are convivial, inclusive, and ecologically sustainable. In doing so, it aims to demonstrate how such an understanding can enable us to rediscover an architecture of darkness as integral to shaping the future of urban nights.

Our relationship with light and darkness is fundamental to how most of us physically make sense of the world, especially spatially and materially. Crucially, it also shapes our perceptions, meanings, values, and cultural associations. In relation to architecture, there is a long history of how shadow has been employed in the design of buildings to articulate a variety of cosmological and philosophical ideas about its relationship with light (378). Following the birth of artificial illumination, we have used to it create light and, as a result, sought to reduce if not entirely eliminate darkness. Across the history of different lighting technologies, the widespread growth in illumination has had a significant impact upon darkness, often to the latter's detriment. Schivelbusch, (379) in specific reference to nighttime artificial lighting, observes that perceptions of it throughout history have consistently merged the literal with the symbolic, while Schlör (380) points directly to the dominance of light over darkness in considering the urban night. Perhaps unsurprisingly, the nighttime economy and issues of labour, safety, security, entertainment etc., remain the dominant area of inquiry for night studies. Yet I suggest that the nocturnal city remains an enigma, poorly understood and standing in need of new inquiries to examine the tension and coexistent nature of light and darkness. Recent inquiries across the humanities and social sciences have identified the rich potential for positive engagements with darkness in places after dark. (381) As designers, I think we can go beyond this and ask what might a future nocturnal urbanism look like and what role might interior architecture perform in this endeavour?

Through the Past, Darkly

As the crucible for the Industrial Revolution, Manchester has been widely recognized as the world's first industrial city growing as it did from a market town with a population of less than 10,000 at the beginning of the 18th century to a population of 89,000 by the end of that century. Perhaps unsurprisingly, such population growth brought with it extremely poor and dense living conditions for many of the city's inhabitants. In 1798, George and Adam Murray completed the first phase of their steam-powered urban cotton mill in Ancoats, the first suburb to

378 Stephen Kite, *Shadow-Makers: A Cultural History of Shadows in Architecture* (London: Bloomsbury, 2017). 379 Wolfgang Schivelbusch, *Disenchanted Night: The Industrialization of Light in the Nineteenth Century* (Berkeley, CA: University of California Press, 1988). 380 Joachim Schlör, *Nights in the Big City*, trans. Pierre Gottfried Imhof and Dafydd Rees Roberts (London: Reaktion Books, 1998). 381 Nick Dunn, *Dark Matters: A Manifesto for the Nocturnal City* (New York: Zero Books, 2016); Tim Edensor, *From Light to Dark: Daylight, Illumination, and Gloom* (Minneapolis, MN: University of Minnesota Press, 2017); Robert Shaw, *The Nocturnal City*. (London: Routledge, 2018).

integrate housing and industry. (382) When completed in 1806, the complex housed two separate cotton spinning mills, two warehouses, preparation and office ranges, all arranged around a central quadrangle. The importance of the Murrays' Mills development was evident with visitors travelling from the rest of the UK, Europe and the US to witness the huge complex, housing powered machinery and illuminated by gas lamps. Parallel to this development in the adjacent town of Salford, the first gas street lighting in the world illuminated part of Chapel Street and the Philips and Lee Factory. This deployment of lighting technology was to transform the world as it was then known since it transferred and reframed the 'working day' to a non-stop, continually functioning place where the previous relationship between labour and time was shattered. Through his discussion of *Arkwright's Cotton Mills by Night* painted by Joseph Wright of Derby circa 1782, Jonathan Crary (383) makes clear that it is not simply the unusual sight of a large brick building within a countryside setting that makes the image so strange. In addition, he notes: "most unsettling, however, is the elaboration of a nocturnal scene in which the light of a full moon illuminating a cloud-filled sky coexists with the pin-points of windows lit by gas lamps in cotton mills" (384) For it is here that the artificial lighting of the factories announces its victory over the long-held light-dark cycle and circadian rhythms that had previously connected time and work.

Pivotal to this endless labour was of course the need for constant energy production to power its machinery. The use of coal was essential to this process with all the attendant environmental and health hazards that contributed to significant commentators of the period such as the historian Thomas Carlyle (385) decrying the condition of England and using "Sooty Manchester" which was "every whit as wonderful, as fearful, unimaginable, as the oldest Salem or Prophetic City" as evidence. There is an interesting point to be made here about the impact of energy production upon the light and darkness of its surrounding context. The soot produced by the coal-burning furnaces to power the machinery around them was airborne and quickly built up on the surfaces of the buildings across the city. As Alexis de Tocqueville reported when visiting Manchester in 1835, "A sort of black smoke covers the city. The sun seen through it is a disc without rays. Under this half-daylight 300,000 human beings are ceaselessly at work. A thousand noises disturb this dark, damp labyrinth, but they are not at all the ordinary sounds one hears in great cities". (386) Within his account of his seven-day trip to the city, de Tocqueville relates the extremes of the Manchester experience and the paradox that lay at the heart of its industrial success.

Architecture of Darkness

The nascent industrialization accelerated an energy production and artificially lit landscape that was subsequently much replicated and expanded around the world. Whilst the conditions for working-class people reached a nadir in Manchester for the time, its role as a blueprint for the modern city proved more the dominant pattern of development than an exception as the drivers of industrial capitalism swept around the world during the remainder

382 Mike Williams, "The Mills of Ancoats," *Manchester Region History Review*, no. 7 (1993).   383 Jonathan Crary, *24/7: Late Capitalism and the Ends of Sleep* (London: Verso, 2013).   384 Crary, *24/7*, 61–62.   385 Thomas Carlyle, *Past and Present* (London: n.d, 1843), 247.   386 Alexis de Tocqueville, *Journeys to England and Ireland*, ed. Peter Mayer, trans. George Lawrence and K. P. Mayer (London: Faber and Faber, 1958), [Reprint], 108.

of the 19th and early 20th century. (387) The edifices of Manchester would remain blackened for many years, material deposits that serve to recall the city's dark history as its grandest buildings were coated with soot. Although furnished with some spectacular Victorian architecture, the coal fires and smoke from the nearby industry obscured many of the city's landmarks under a blackened shroud. Having laid claim to being the first industrial city in the world, in the first half of the 20th century Manchester could arguably also have been the dirtiest as its buildings and streets were filthy and drab. The blanket of soot produced a city of light and darkness that was dramatic, unified, and uncanny. This highly affective landscape was further enhanced by the significant amount of smog present in the city during this period.

The implementation of the Clean Air Act of 1956 quickly removed the smog in the city but it took a number of years, in some cases several decades before the city's architecture was returned to its original state. This was achieved either by cleaning or the soot being gradually washed off by the rain, although two examples of Manchester's 'architecture of darkness' endure to the present day. With this term 'architecture of darkness', I am referring to a two-fold aspect of the city's architectural landscape. Firstly, the literal transformation of the built environment due to this layer of material deposit. Only two blackened buildings from the industrial era stand as architectural testaments to Manchester's atmospherically darkened past, namely the interior courtyards of Alfred Waterhouse's Town Hall (1867–1877) and 22 Lever Street by Smith Woodhouse & Willoughby (1875). Secondly, and perhaps less obviously, the darkened built environment also provided a specific context for Manchester's subsequent architecture to be designed for. The most notable example of this approach is the District Bank Headquarters (1969) by Casson and Condor. Casson compared the building to a lump of coal, its unusual form the result of rights of light studies, and its dark Swedish granite cladding being hand-tooled, vertically ribbed and specifically chosen to absorb the soot in the city's air. (388) It was also believed that this dark material brought an appropriate seriousness and symbolic power to the bank's northern headquarters.

Designing the Nocturnal City

Let us now fast forward a few decades to the 21st century. Cities themselves are understood as dynamic entities of material and immaterial flows, processes and systems. Architecture is typically understood as the material, sometimes literally concrete, facts of the built environment. Its presence and function reflect the values of the society that produced it. However, no matter how stable our buildings may appear, they are constantly changing, inside and outside, through the effects of weather, occupation, ageing, and, of course, lighting and darkness. Manchester, like many places around the globe, is also a city of disappearances certainly in terms of its nightscapes and nocturnal ambiences. The view shown in the image no longer exists. This is because since early 2014, Manchester City Council announced its intention to roll out replacement of 56,000 lamps with LEDs and has slowly been replacing

387 Harold L. Platt, *Shock Cities: The Environmental Transformation and Reform of Manchester and Chicago* (Chicago, IL: The University of Chicago Press), 2005. 388 Richard Brook, *Manchester Modern* (Manchester: The Modernist Society, 2017).

389 Manchester City Council, *Street Lighting LED Retrofit Programme*, Executive Report, February 12, 2014, https://democracy.manchester.gov.uk/Data/Executive/20140212/Agenda/17_Street_Lighting_LED_Retrofit.pdf, accessed November 8, 2023. 390 Chris Otter, *The Victorian Eye: A Political History of Light and Vision in Britain, 1800–1910* (Chicago, IL: University of Chicago Press, 2008), 10. 391 Nick Dunn, Dark Futures: The Loss of Night in the Contemporary City?," *Journal of Energy History/Revue D'histoire De L'énergie* Special Issue: Light(s) and darkness(es)/Lumière(s) et obscurité(s) 1, no. 2 (2019): pp. 1–27 392 Tim Edensor, "The Gloomy City: Rethinking the Relationship between Light and Dark," *Urban Studies* 52, no. 3 (2015): 15.

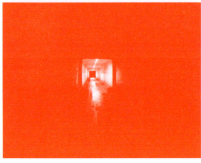

their sodium streetlights ever since. (389) Such implementation serves to further flatten the diversity of experiences available in the nocturnal city, a process that was already underway with the expansion of standardized light design. The latter, as Chris Otter (390) has observed shifted the aesthetic experience of the city at night away from "multiple, overlapping perceptual patterns and practices."

It is important to state that this loss is not absolute but a direct experience of the current variety of different types of darkness is likely to be obstructed, or at least hindered, by the profusion of LED street lighting. This extensive replacement of sodium-vapour lights has profoundly changed the ambience of numerous places after dark. It is largely changing the exterior spaces of the urban environment but, inevitably, these are entangled with the interiors of the city at night. For the last eight years, I have been documenting how these places have been changing across the city and the wider borough. (391) To capture some of the different ambiences of urban places after dark in Manchester and how they are changing, this endeavour has led to many hundreds of hours nightwalking through nightscapes and the production of an archive of photographs, maps, and autoethnographic notes.

Writing about gloom and the urban landscape, Tim Edensor (392) provides an elegant argument for embracing it, "[r]ather than being lamented, the re-emergence of urban darkness, although not akin to the medieval and early-modern gloom that pervaded city space, might be conceived as an enriching and a re-enchantment of the temporal and spatial experience of the city at night." This relational understanding between light and dark is crucial to how we might conceive of better ways to design for and engage with our cities at night. As our cities, not least Manchester, seek to evolve into 24-hour places, reducing further the different interplays of light and dark appears contrary to the increased diversity of their populations, cultures, social meanings, and values. It is perhaps hard to know what is lost if you have never experienced it. So, since 2016 I have been leading groups of people on collective nightwalks around the Greater Manchester city region to share with them different nocturnal ambiences that they may have first-hand encounters of how the quality and quantity of lighting in these places mediate experiences of the built environment. We have sometimes done drawings, written short texts, or used our bodies in different arrangements to explore our entanglements with darkness.

Since March 2020 and during the ongoing pandemic, I have been learning how other people make sense of and use the nocturnal city in ways that support what they are doing, whether during labour, respite or other activities. This image, taken during the second national lockdown, shows a security guard, one of only five people I encountered during six hours in the city center that night, the others were a street cleaner and three young women returning home from work. The question, however, of how we design with darkness also requires us to reconsider fundamental practices since, "if night means the ephemeral, the fragile, the spontaneous, how does one construct this element without distorting it? To observe the cityscape by night means to ask oneself about nocturnal design values". (393) To respond to this question, I have previously proposed the concept of 'Dark Design', defined here as those principles and practices that aim to design with darkness rather than against it. (394) Richard Kelly, one of the pioneers of architectural lighting design, drew on his background in stage lighting to introduce a scenographic perspective for architectural lighting. (395) Challenging the engineering mindset that dominated lighting design in the mid-twentieth century, he introduced three principles: focal glow, ambient luminescence, and play of brilliants. Revisiting these principles from the contemporary position of working with rather than against darkness, the diversity and subtleties of lighting promoted by Kelly can be understood to have been quickly lost as urban centers in particular drove artificial illumination into a competing arena where brightness and power became prized over other lighting characteristics. This has not gone undetected by lighting professionals as Edward Bartholomew (396) succinctly observed, "as I gaze upon over-lit lobbies and malls. I sense that what is being lit is not the space but merely a fear—legal or otherwise—of the consequence of darkness."

But is this all a city at night can be? Critical to understanding nocturnal ambiences is the acknowledgement of the dynamic qualities of those elements that form and shape them in material, spatial, and temporal terms. The potentialities and capacities of nocturnal ambiences to provide a wider array of sensations and interactions than are often present in urban landscapes require methods through which to rediscover and reimagine our relationships with darkness. This is where design can play a valuable role. By developing new visions and interventions for nocturnal ambiences, shared atmospheres that promote positive behaviour for human and non-human sensitivities can be designed with darkness rather than against it. This also presents fertile ground for interior architecture to connect with the wider urban realm at night by providing a spectrum of different coexistences between light and dark. The boundaries between interior and exterior can certainly become blurred at night and I think this represents a significant opportunity for designers.

Walking through Manchester in the dark, the city slowly but perceptibly shifts in its composition of different combinations of light and darkness, reflecting the history of its lighting energy landscape. Perhaps unsurprisingly, historical accounts of lighting have focused on the routine circumstances of the urban night. Though more recent studies have redressed this by providing investigations into unique, temporary, and performative illuminations, there may be an important overlap between these two areas of inquiry. That we can go and enjoy our nocturnal urban landscape in an improvised way, without recourse to consumerism, suggests that by engaging with the 'every night', we might find ourselves open to new forms of experience and place. Although there is an increasing amount of research across various disciplines related to the notion of the reciprocity and nuances between light and darkness being essential to each, there are also historical clues to how we might learn to embrace this. In his seminal 1933 meditation on his country's culture, *In Praise of Shadows*, the Japanese novelist Tanizaki Jun'ichirō highlighted the importance of this coexistence when he observed, "[i]f light is scarce then light is scarce; we will immerse ourselves in the darkness and there discover its

393 Marc Armengaud, Matthias Armengaud and Alessandra Cianchetta, *Nightscapes: Paisajes Nocturnos/Nocturnal Landscapes* (Barcelona: Editorial Gustavo Gili, 2009), 12.   394 Nick Dunn, "Dark Design: A New Framework for Advocacy and Creativity for the Nocturnal Commons," *International Journal of Design in Society* 14, no. 4 (2020): 9–23.   395 Dietrich Neumann, "Theater, Lights, and Architecture," in *The Structure of Light: Richard Kelly and the Illumination of Modern Architecture*, ed. Dietrich Neumann, 11–42 (New Haven, CT: Yale School of Architecture, 2010).   396 Edward Bartholomew, "A Place for Darkness," *Professional Lighting Design* (Sept/Oct 2004): 39.

own particular beauty". (397) Over the last six months, I have been documenting those places across the city at night that have the quality of a 'nocturnal room'. By this term 'nocturnal room', I am referring to their common characteristics of enclosure on most sides and, due to the combination of light, materiality, sound, and smell, they offer temporal sanctuary and different sensitizations of place. Recent shifts in understanding about darkness offer an important opportunity for designers to shape the nocturnal world anew. As Claire Downey (398) writes, by "understanding how articulations of architecture—envelopment, permeability, scale, edge, recess—influence nocturnal spatial practice, alternatives in building and lighting can be imagined."

Conclusion

When we think about the future of cities, it is difficult to ignore the many visions produced for urban places which communicate clean, green and daylit environments. (399) Where darkness is present in such visions, it is usually employed to shape the depiction of a foreboding future that is dystopic, dirty and dangerous. However, I contend that it is in the city at night where we can find fertile opportunities for imagining how places might change and for whom. If day is the rehearsal, night is the performance. It is the dark twin of the city in the most positive sense. It is both psychological and physical. The nocturnal city awaits our wanderings and wonderings. It is the temporary city where identity can be reinvented, and this includes places. For at night, amidst the urban shadowlands, the ghosts of the past leak out of the city's cracks and pores while the future appears in fleeting glimpses, sneak peeks of what the city might become. To experience the city at night is to be immersed in a landscape of greater possibility than in the daytime, where the characteristics of place can appear more open and provisional than during the day. As light pollution now presents a global challenge, recognising the diversity of interplay between light and dark is critical in moving towards an overall goal where its impacts on human and non-human bodies can be tackled in a local and situated way through creativity, commitment and action. This is the collective responsibility of designers, to create and share alternatives. Now more than ever we all need to engage with reimagining the nocturnal city and its interior architecture beyond the narrow frame of the nighttime economy and move towards a nocturnal urbanism that is convivial, ethical, and quiet as much as it is safe and supportive of biodiversity. Rediscovering the value of an architecture of darkness will be vital to this positive transformation for the benefit of society, other species, and the planet.

397 Jun'ichirō Tanizaki, *In Praise of Shadows*, trans. Thomas J. Harper and Edwards G. Seidensticker (London: Vintage, 2001[1933]), 48. 398 Claire Downey, "Shape Shifting: Architecture in a Wakeful City," in *ICNS Proceedings*, ed. Manuel Garcia-Ruiz and Jordi Nofre, (Lisbon: ISCTE, 2020), 16. 399 Nick Dunn and Paul Cureton, *Future Cities: A Visual Guide* (London: Bloomsbury, 2020).

POST-SCRIPTUM: THE NIGHT, ON THE MARGINS
On the Nocturnal Studios at HEAD – Genève
Youri Kravtchenko

It began as a feeling, a small tune that wouldn't go away. When we started thinking about teaching a practice of interior architecture, we realized that what distinguished it from architecture is something that seems to exist "on the margins." (400) On the margins of the rules and teaching habits of architecture, which mainly follows a result-oriented objective, but also on the margins of a predominantly diurnal vision, where the clarity of ideals, necessarily illuminated by the sun, posed as conditions for the construction of the world.

The margin—as opposed to the limit—is not a line but rather a space of play with deliberately vague contours, pretending to be "on the other side" in dissent and moving. It's a field of research where night, and in our case, interior architecture, can unfold without limitation. A genius loci where we willingly accept to lose ourselves in the meandering of uncertainty, jumping from one form or domain to another.

Studying and advancing in the night, as magical as it may be, often resembles the representation we have of a mysterious and secret ocean floor exploration. In a submerged vehicle equipped with devices to mutate this reality into ours (headlights, radar, sonar), blindness and silence (401) prevail until the possible encounter with ancestral oceanic species, unknown life forms, like so many silent witnesses of an ancient prehistoric history. Just as we would follow these submerged creatures at a reasonable distance, we study the night through poetic portions, trying to extract objective data and deduce or feel (once again) a phenomenology of perception. (402)

Teaching at night would be an opportunity for infinite research and a pretext for exploring an alternative architecture: with blurry or even invisible contours, where the maps are redistributed in other codes of creation on the one hand and representation on the other. This is how the original beginnings and corollary projects of the research on the night were born, which we were able to develop with our students for five years.

Of course, an oceanic vision would reduce the night to a primary poetic form, obscure and silent. Our studied species take on mutant faces: rain on a sidewalk, a gas station

---

400 Baldine Saint Girons, *Les Marges de la nuit : pour une autre histoire de la peinture* (Paris: L'Amateur, 2006). 401 "When silence allies with the night, we discover that the purity of silence paradoxically decomposes into a multitude of light cracklings; these cracklings do not break the silence, but on the contrary make it even more silent." Vladimir Jankélévitch and Béatrice Berlowitz, *Quelque part dans l'inachevé* (Paris: Gallimard, 1978). 402 Maurice Merleau-Ponty, *Phenomenology of Perception*, trans. Donald Landes (London: Routledge, 2012).

in Texas, a corner shop open all the time, Adolf Loos's American bar, a hospital waiting room, a parking lot in a non-place between city and countryside, a nightclub, etc.
We envisage these trivial fragments of ordinary nightlife as so many "scenes". This word derives from the Arabic sakan, which means habitat, and the fragments are nothing less than places and times of action. To stage them is, in essence, to learn to look at them as we learn to look through an aquarium. So, the question arises: How to study these scenes, and with what tools?

In 2018, as part of a first studio entitled *Scènes de Nuit* –Night Scenes–, student Lolita Gomez imagined the staging (literally the boxing) of the moment when rain falls on a Viennese facade and sidewalk for one night. To achieve this, she drew and built a box of black-smoked glass mounted on a tubular structure, just as supportive as it was hydrant. It was created in the form of a perfect three-dimensional trompe-l'oeil of the facade and sidewalk of Adolf Loos's American Bar. The rain was then collected in a basin and returned to the circuit via a pump. The viewer, through the famous "fourth wall," dear to the theater (403), could observe the scene as one observes a diorama through a subjective framing that isolates this world from ours, intensifying the visual and auditory resonances of our relationship to this benign moment.
This project was the starting point for an research method using common acts of observation, study, drawing, fabrication, and finally, restitution.

As the geneticist François Jacob said, "Complexity is often the result of a combination of very simple elements." By starting with simple stolen moments (in photography, painting, architecture, poetry, or film), borrowing from the Greek Demiurge the fabrication of a mini-cosmos established with great or small technical efforts, it is possible to fathom the complexity of the world built or to be built. These reconstructions of spaces were carried out according to three modes of display that we call "Walking in," "Looking at," and "Catching in," as described in Milica Topalovic's essay "Models and Other Spaces" (404), which was appropriated, edited, and iterated upon by our students multiple times:

Walking in
As fragile as theater sets, dioramas, and artistic installations, 1:1 scale models, also known as life-size models, make it possible to create three-dimensional, experimental, and studiable freeze-frames in circumstances that simulate nighttime reality through the artifice of construction.

Looking at
Models at other scales, when placed at a distance, are by definition uninhabitable and can only be perceived by the eye and imagination. When the life-size model allows an area to be constituted and reconstituted from an image or a memory, reduced-scale models make it possible to produce a new image from a miniaturized space.

---

403 "I can take any empty space and call it a bare stage. A man walks across this empty space whilst someone else is watching him, and this is all that is needed for an act of theatre to be engaged." Peter Brook, *L'Espace vide: Écrits sur le théâtre*, trans. Christine Etienne and Frank Fayolle (Paris: Seuil, 1977).   404   Milica Topalovic, "Models and Other Spaces," OASE, no. 84 (2011): 37–44

Catching up
Fragmental models explore how collective memory influences recollections, emotions, and perceptions of the built environment and nocturnal space. Like the archaeologist's method, these fragments result from in-depth spatial analysis, forming a catalog of elements—relics, images, photos, and documents—that collectively define the essence of the night.

In continuation of the rain Box proposal and sharing the same reference, the #LOOSLAB project, realized in 2018 for Designers' Saturday Langenthal, embodies the first protocol put in place ("Walking in"). Students at HEAD – Genève (405) explored the role of image culture in the construction of contemporary interior spaces and their associated media. The project was an illusion: originally modeled after Adolf Loos' American Bar and its successive iterations, the proposal sought to document and reflect upon the re-samplings and manipulations of the original scheme. #LOOSLAB imposed its own representation of reality, no longer a copy or a simulacrum but rather a ubiquitous instance of its original image, like an experimental framework for critical research on the construction and perception of a visual experience. The project became foundational for the research that absorbed us during these years, also establishing a work protocol for several subsequent projects (406): 1. Search for images online. 2. Blur differences between originals and copies. 3. Collage/sample 3D fragments. 4. Iterate the samples to create new spaces. 5. Create a physical structure out of the model. 6. Fake all materials (in the case of #LOOSLAB, they were all stickers). 7. Perform the space. 8. Visitors create their images. 9. Share it online. 10. Remove the decor, iterate it elsewhere. By modifying the articulation between image, space, and materiality according to an established protocol, the project in Langenthal became both contextual (it accepted the conditions of the context as a backdrop for the digital and physical environment), shareable (it functioned as both space and image), and iconic (through historical references and their contemporary manipulations)

After the obsession with Loosian references, and in another modality, namely that of "Looking at" mentioned before, a completely mundane nocturnal image that is now framed and displayed on the Department wall has continued to be the field of experimentation in recent years. By typing "Corner+shop+night" into a Google Image search and preselecting high-resolution images, I came across a captivating image that summarized a socio-economic nocturnal design, an picture that has unfortunately lost its power to surprise, due to the banalization of nocturnal and precarious work scenes in our daily lives: We see a corner shop that we could qualify as vernacular. It seems to be placed in a precarious situation, somewhere in a region that appears to be a remote location on the one hand, and the corner of a long, timeless night, serving consumers accustomed to 24/7 (407) policies on the other hand. Too quick a glance

405 Students: Estelle Béroujon, Camille Berra, Lolita Gomez, Lucien Muchutti, Jérôme Nager, Xavier Plantevin, Joëlle Progin, Alexandre Simian, Sergio Streun, Pascaline Vuilloud, Marie Widmer Assistants: Alice Proux, Bertrand Van Dorp; Under the direction of de Youri Kravtchenko and Javier F. Contreras; assistant Florine Wescher, Alice Proux.   406 Javier F. Contreras, Youri Kravtchenko. "#LOOSLAB. Instructions". In: Javier F. Contreras, Youri Kravtchenko, *Herbarium of Interiors.* Insert to Volume #57, *Bye Default* (Amsterdam: Archis-Volume, 2020): 7.   407 Jonathan Crary, *24/7 Late Capitalism and the Ends of Sleep* (New York: Verso, 2013).

at the disorderly pile of international products lit by a harsh light from the ceiling and too hasty a visual sweep over the silhouette of a dark-skinned person would question our preconceived assumptions: this image by photographer George Voronov (408) was actually taken in Dún Laoghaire to the south of Dublin and shows "Dun Leary's Last Corner Shop" at the corner of George Street West and Clarinda Park Upper which was a local landmark and recently closed down when its owner, John Hyland, retired. In 2019, students Alizé Fassier, Clémence Lablancherie, Gaïane Legendre, Raphaëlle Marzolf, and Rui-Filipe Bernardes Da Silva decided to undertake a simple and radical act of observation of this particular image, drawing inspiration from the "as found" approach dear to Alison and Peter Smithson (409). Fragment by fragment, object by object, they drew by hand and then on CAD software all the objects in the space, creating an "arbitrarily precise" survey, which was then reproduced in an highly detailed 1:10 scale model for the sole purpose of being photographed again to verify its fidelity with the original image. In an act of mediatization, a film of the model was projected alongside the model itself. These seminal operations were incorporated into exhibitions in Lausanne (410) and Toulon (411) a few months later through the creation of full-scale facade projects designed to re-enact the original

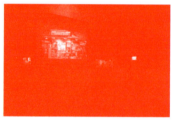

photograph and prove, incidentally, that the corner shop could be copy-pasted from one country to another without any qualms.

The last of the three modalities mentioned above, "Catching up," presented a cathartic moment in the exhibition *Scènes de Nuit*, held in 2019 at the forum d'architectures (f'ar) in Lausanne. This exhibition served as the playground and experimentation field that confirmed our research in many ways. Merging five nights and five themes (shop, film, club, city, food) spread over the month of May, the students were not only able to elaborate on the exhibition scenography but also to create performances that would take place there, alongside lectures by guest speakers, for an audience that was either initiated or neophyte. After plunging the exhibition space into darkness, the students imagined and manufactured fragments of architectural objects at various scales, drawing on various nocturnal universes. Among other things, we saw a bus shelter, a moon, a popcorn stand, a window in the night, the lights of a gas station, a dance floor, a banquet table, a lamppost, and a corner shop. This time, in addition to exploring and constructing objects or reference spaces to be observed, the students, the public, and ourselves were able to test and experience specific nocturnal episodes. The "Shop" night was an opportunity to reflect on the place of consumption and night work in our society. In "Film", Matthieu Bareyre's documentary *L'Époque* was

408 "Visual Diary," George Voronov, http://www.georgevoronov.com/dailies. 409 "Through their observation of Nigel Henderson's post-war photographs of London's streets, the English architect duo declare to have found an interest in the raw material of existence, consisting of things as they are, in their immediacy and availability. This perspective implies a discovery of the essence of daily life, of the ordinary as a study material and basis for projects, but also a respect for history and its traces on the existing city." (See the excellent dissertation by Michele Franzoi, "As Found: Theory and Procedures" (Master's thesis, École d'architecture de la ville & des territoires Paris-Est, 2019). 410 *Scènes de Nuit*. Nocturnal Exhibition at f'ar Lausanne. Curated by Javier F. Contreras and Youri Kravtchenko, with the contribution of students from HEAD – Genève. See: *Scènes de Nuit. Night and Architecture,* ed. Javier F. Contreras, Youri Kravtchenko and Manon Portera (Geneva: HEAD—Publishing / Madrid: Ediciones Asimétricas, 2021). 411 "SHOP by night," HEAD — Genève at Design Parade Toulon, 2019, https://www.hesge.ch/head/evenement/2019/shop-night, accessed November 8, 2023.

screened in the presence of the director. "City" allowed the exploration or situationist wandering of the town with the complicity of the Stalker collective (412). "Club" was a successful attempt to create a real ephemeral disco. Finally, "Food" involved the dinner excursion around a Russian-style banquet with the Domingo artist collective (413).

If the nocturnal wandering of my teaching at HEAD – Genève during these years of research on the night resembles an underwater observation mission dedicated to the study of ordinary or extinct species, the *Herbarium of Interiors* studio, and in particular, the Milk Bar project curated by the interior architect India Mahdavi (414), approaches the creation of new, unpublished species of space. Capitalizing on the polysemy of the word "herbarium" (an object that becomes its own image), the students (415) were invited to develop a project through three stages: Load, Reload, Unload. The first stage consisted of collecting textual, drawn, or photographed fragments from about thirty famous public indoor entertainment spaces throughout history. Like hip-hop producers, researchers were later invited to sample the captured fragments in order to create spatiotemporal remixes. Finally, the result could take the form of a performance or installation in the context of upcoming exhibitions.

Through this process, the Korova Milkbar from Stanley Kubrick's 1971 film *A Clockwork Orange* became the pretext for inventing a new ritual for the "Salone del Mobile" in Milan in 2021. Here, visitors were invited to sit on floating stools around an almost phosphorescent milk fountain and listen to the dramatic music of the Funeral March of

Queen Mary performed on a synthesizer. They were given a cup resembling a breast inspired by the porcelain cups of Sèvres originally designed by Marie-Antoinette for her dairy servings. Milk was served from a tap attached to a hydraulic network that was connected to heavy tanks visible in the cowsheds and hanging in the installation above the visitors' heads.

During this Milan performance-installation, I watched the magic unfold. A little music that didn't want to leave. We had aligned ourselves with an unparalleled nocturnal realm, one that spanned different media yet lingered on its margins. This, once more, underscored the significance of a prominent place for the night within our architectural endeavors. Having observed it carefully and silently, we were able to manufacture it.

412 "Stalker, expédition dans la périphérie romaine," le Temps, November 26, 2020, https://blogs.letemps.ch/istituto-svizzero/2020/11/26/stalker-expedition-dans-la-peripherie-romaine/, accessed November 8, 2023.   413 "Night food," Scènes de Nuit, May 2019, https://scenesdenuit.ch/scenes/nightfood, accessed November 8, 2023.   414 *Herbarium of Interiors*, MAIA studio led by Youri Kravtchenko with the curatorial support of India Mahdavi. HEAD – Genève, 2019-2021. The studio was finally presented at the Milan Design Week 2021. See: *Scènes de Nuit*, September 2021, https://scenesdenuit.ch/scenes/herbarium-of-interiors, accessed November 8, 2023.   415 *Herbarium of Interiors*, students: Blanca Algarra, Kishan Asensio, Sarah Bentivigna, Dany-Sarah Champion, Robin Delerce, Nina D'Elia, Azadeh Djavanrouh, Marina Ezerskaia, Lolita Gomez, Camila González, Elizaveta Krikun, Nourbonou Missident, Filza Parmar, Patrycja Pawlik, Karen Pisoni, Louise Plassard, Léa Rime, Patris Sallaku, Camila G. Tapia, Marion Vergne, Nobuyoshi Yokota; Milk Bar (winning proposal): original design by Blanca Algarra, Lolita Gomez; Project curated by India Mahdavi, under the direction of Youri Kravtchenko and Javier F. Contreras; Assistant: Manon Portera; Exhibition assistant: Alice Proux